MAKING A DIFFERENCE FOR STUDENTS AT RISK

MAKING A DIFFERENCE FOR STUDENTS AT RISK

Trends and Alternatives

Edited by

Margaret C. Wang
Maynard C. Reynolds

CORWIN PRESS, INC.
A Sage Publications Company
Thousand Oaks, California

For information address:

 Corwin Press, Inc.
A Sage Publications Company
2455 Teller Road
Thousand Oaks, California 91320

SAGE Publications Ltd.
6 Bonhill Street
London EC2A 4PU
United Kingdom

SAGE Publications India Pvt. Ltd.
M-32 Market
Greater Kailash I
New Delhi 110 048 India

Printed in the United States of America

Library of Congress Cataloging-in-Publication Data

Main entry under title:

Making a difference for students at risk: trends and alternatives /
    edited by Margaret C. Wang, Maynard C. Reynolds.
        p.   cm.
    Papers from a conference held in October 1993.
    Includes bibliographical references and indexes.
        ISBN 0-8039-6188-X (cl: alk. paper).—ISBN 0-8039-6189-8 (pb:
    alk. paper)
        1. Socially handicapped children—Education—United States—
    Congresses. 2. Education, Urban—United States—Congresses.
    3. Educational change—United States—Congresses. I. Wang,
    Margaret C. II. Reynolds, Maynard Clinton.
    LC4091.M257 1995
    371.96′7′0973—dc20   94-32842

This book is printed on acid-free paper.

95 96 97 98 99 10 9 8 7 6 5 4 3 2 1

Corwin Press Production Editor: Diana E. Axelsen

Contents

Preface

P roblems of great severity exist for many children and youth in this nation's major cities, particularly the inner-city communities. Their families, their neighborhoods, and the community agencies that serve them, including schools, are desperately depleted of resources and spirit. Problems abound, including lack of employment opportunities, stressful life experiences, poor health care, and highly fragmented patterns of services. The problem of inadequate learning and competence, the widespread academic failure in the schools that could cripple the next generation, is sometimes overshadowed by this litany of troubles. Solutions to these problems are certain to require insights drawn from many disciplines and professions, collaboration among a wide range of public and private institutions, and a broad-based commitment to ensure a high standard of educational outcomes of all children, including, especially, those placed in at-risk circumstances.

Although major pronouncements have been made in recent years about the crucial role education must play in improving the life chances of children and youth at risk of educational failure, and although significant actions have been taken by multiple stakeholder groups, including government agencies, educational institutions, community-based civic groups, and the business community, efforts tend to be disjointed, superficial, and unsuccessful. There is no mechanism currently in place for structuring knowledge and expertise for dealing with the problems of human development and education in a deeply penetrating and coherent manner. Within this context, in an attempt to address the fundamental question, "What do we know from research and practical wisdom that can be systematically applied to significantly improve our capacity to achieve a high standard of educational outcomes for all, including those with poor prognoses for schooling success?", an invitational conference was held with leading researchers and field-based professionals and policy makers.

The conference, entitled "Making a Difference for Students at Risk," was sponsored by the National Center on Education in the Inner Cities (CEIC) in October 1993, in collaboration with the National Center on Cultural Diversity and Second Language Learning. The chapters included in this volume were commissioned specially for the conference, serving as a springboard for discussion. The discussions and recommendations from the conferees were incorporated into the final revisions of the chapters included in this volume.

The authors whose work makes up this book are researchers, practitioners, and policy makers, and are representative of a variety of disciplines and perspectives, including anthropology, economics, education, psychology, sociology, urban studies, and other social-sciences-related fields. Although each author concentrates on a specific aspect related to the education of at-risk students, one common goal shared by all is the emergence of alternatives for those students for whom the present system is inadequate. Authors were asked to be entirely candid in examination of "special" programs, mainly through a review of research and of practices, with a particular emphasis on examining ideas for improvements. The intent for this publication is to bring critical attention to the educational and related service needs of students and programs and critical reexaminations of policies and research activities in the field.

Two topics dominated the discussion at the conference: the basic forces that affect development and schooling of children and youth placed in at-risk circumstances, particularly those whose achievement falls at the margins; and innovative initiatives that apply research and practical knowledge to foster far-reaching changes in institutional policies and practices.

Finding ways to harness all the major resources and expertise to improve our capacity for education and to achieve equity in educational outcomes of children and youth placed at risk of educational failure was identified by the conferees as one of the most pressing challenges to educators of our time. The term *at risk* as used here refers to the circumstances that adversely affect those students who are struggling in their academic programs and in their social behavior in the schools, as well as those who are highly talented and are not challenged and nurtured to their fullest potential.

The conferees also stressed the need to overcome the disturbing and persistent problem of significant racial disproportionalities among students placed at risk of school failure. The discussion at the conference and the papers included in this volume reflect candid, critical, and forward-thinking dialogues. It is assumed that better approaches to the restructuring and improvement in programs for students placed at risk would cause a general improvement for every student—through more coherence in management of all programs, more efficient use of resources, and more sharing or teamwork among educators.

We believe the interdisciplinary perspective of this work will be of much interest to educators, researchers, practitioners, and policy leaders from a variety of disciplines and professions, particularly those operating in inner-city settings. The chapters in this monograph are organized thematically by programs and research designed, in part, as a response to current concerns surrounding labeling and the process of categorization. Each chapter is followed by summarized commentaries from researchers, representative urban school administrators and teachers, and policy leaders.

The introductory chapter coauthored by Wang, Reynolds, and Walberg provides a general orientation to definitions of "at-risk" students as used throughout this volume. This chapter includes such areas as the history behind school programs for students at risk and the social and economic conditions currently making the topic critically important; a summary of legislative, administrative, and organizational arrangements in programs for at-risk students; a general review of provisions for and outcomes of evaluative studies; a review of major trends and policies; critiques on key topics such as school suspensions and expulsions, school dropout rates, special funding systems, and parental involvement; and proposals for some of the key topics on which policies and practices must be revised.

Marleen Pugach outlines in Chapter 2 the challenges faced in educating children in urban schools in conjunction with the reform of special education and Chapter 1, and discusses historical contextualization and trends; reviews of research reflecting programmatic outcomes; validity of classification and placement systems; and coordination across programs (e.g., across special education, Chapter 1, other categorical programs, and regular education); the report of the Commission on Chapter 1; and other salient issues.

In Chapter 3, Joseph Renzulli, Sally Reis, Thomas Hébert, and Eva Diaz tackle the problem of addressing the needs of high-ability students in inner-city settings. Methods to create optimal environments are delineated, in which the focus is on data, programmatic and other types of trends, funding, evaluative studies, racial and gender proportionalities, and needs in inner-city schools.

Chapters 4 and 5 center on alternative programs such as street academies that operate for students who have dropped out of or have been expelled from regular schools. Often such programs are provided by private agencies. Antoine Garibaldi describes programs and participants, identifies major issues concerning their operations, outlines relationships with other programs, and generally indicates potentialities for programs operated outside of ordinary school arrangements. The focus of Mary Anne Raywid's research is on descriptions of alternative school programs and enrollees, results of evaluative and research programs, the case for smaller schools, and the relationship to ideas about "choice." Considerations also include home teaching, "charter schools," schools within schools, and ability grouping.

In the last chapter, Eugene Garcia presents a review of the present status of special programs for students whose primary language is not English and who live in minority cultural communities. His research also includes a discussion of trends, issues, and relationships with other categorical programs.

Many of our colleagues put in much effort to make this volume possible. We would like to especially acknowledge our deep appreciation to the administrative and editorial staff at the Temple University Center for Research in Human Development and Education for providing crucial support throughout the preparation of the conference and this volume. We especially wish to thank Julia St. George and Sherrie Madia for a well-managed and productive conference. Sherrie Madia and Don Gordon also provided invaluable editorial support to ensure the timely completion of this publication.

We owe a special thanks to Oliver Moles and Jackie Jenkins, from the Office of Educational Research and Improvement (OERI) of the U.S. Department of Education, for their guidance and encouragement in our work on improving our capacity to effectively respond to the educational needs of children and youth placed at risk of educational failure. Finally, we would like to acknowledge the funding support from OERI. The opinions expressed in this volume, however, do not necessarily reflect the position of OERI, and no official endorsement should be inferred.

Margaret C. Wang
Maynard C. Reynolds

About the Authors

Harriet Arvey is Assistant Superintendent, Student Services, for the Houston Independent School District, the fifth largest public school district in the country. Her responsibilities in the district encompass supervision of the Child Study Bureau, Guidance Counseling, Drug Free Schools and Communities, Health and Medical Services, Psychological Services, and programs for at-risk students. She received an M.A. in Counseling and a Ph.D. in Educational Counseling Psychology from the University of Tennessee. She is a licensed psychologist, and serves on numerous local boards dealing with children's mental health, community psychology, and public education. She chairs the Hogg Foundation "School of the Future" Board in Houston, and sits on the National Advisory Committee for the National Center on Education in the Inner Cities, Temple University.

Pauline Brooks is Senior Research Associate at the Center for the Study of Evaluation at the University of California at Los Angeles, and at the UCLA Center for Research on Evaluation, Standards, and Student Testing. She conducts longitudinal evaluation research on the effects of after-school education and enrichment on lower-income, inner-city, culturally and linguistically diverse elementary school children, and directs a Centers for Disease Control and Prevention (CDC) ethnographic evaluation of an anthropological study of pregnancy within African American communitites in Los Angeles. She has conducted evaluations of a Latino parent training program in San Antonio, TX, and of a model technology program for inner-city, predominantly Latino youth. She directed a test-development project for training case workers for the Los Angeles County Department of Children's Service and has developed instruments for a multiple-state pilot survey of services provided by the Center for Family and Child Protection (Washington, DC) to culturally diverse families. She has made state, national, and international presentations on evaluation of child abuse and neglect prevention programs, design and evaluation of substance abuse prevention trainings, and issues in eduation related to cultural diversity. She has taught at UCLA and in the California State University system.

Eva I. Diaz is an instructor of bilingual education in the Department of Curriculum and Instruction at the University of Connecticut in Storrs. Born in Bayamon, Puerto Rico, she carried out her doctoral research in Connecticut on the underachievement of high-ability Puerto Rican students and obtained her Ph.D. from Pennsylvania State University in 1994. Her current research interests include identification of bilingual gifted students, personal and academic development of bilingual gifted students, and the effects of teaching learning strategies to bilingual gifted underachievers.

Eugene E. Garcia is Director of the Office of Bilingual Education and Minority Languages Affairs of the U.S. Department of Education in Washington, DC. He is former Dean of the Division of Social Sciences and Professor of Education and Psychology at the University of California, Santa Cruz (on leave). He earned his Ph.D. in human development from the University of Kansas, was a postdoctoral fellow in human development at Harvard University and a National Research Council fellow, and he received a three-year National Kellogg Fellowship. He has published extensively in the area of language teaching and bilingual development, authoring or coauthoring some

100 journal articles and book chapters along with 7 book-length volumes. He serves regularly as a proposal panel reviewer for federal, state, and foundation agencies. He was Codirector of the National Center for Research in Cultural Diversity and Second Language Learning funded by the U.S. Department of Education from 1990 to 1993. His most recent research is in the areas of language and education as they relate to linguistically and culturally diverse children and families.

Antoine M. Garibaldi is Vice President for Academic Affairs and Professor of Education at Xavier University, where he previously served as Dean of the College of Arts and Sciences and Chair of the Department of Education. He was also a research administrator at the U.S. Department of Education's National Institute of Education from 1977 to 1982 where he also served as a staff member of the National Commission on Excellence in Education. He is the author of 10 books and monographs, and more than 60 chapters and scholarly articles on historically Black colleges and universities, African-American males, minority teacher recruitment and retention, and urban education issues. His recent books include *The Education of African Americans* (1991, coedited with Charles V. Willie and Wornie L. Reed), *Teacher Recruitment and Retention* (1989), *The Revitalization of Teacher Education Programs at Historically Black Colleges* (1989), *Educating Black Male Youth: A Moral and Civic Imperative* (1988), and *Black Colleges and Universities: Challenges for the Future* (1984). He received his Ph.D. in educational and social psychology from the University of Minnesota.

Edmund W. Gordon is the John M. Musser Professor of Psychology, Emeritus, at Yale University, and Professor of Psychology at the City College of New York, where he served for one year as interim chair of the Department of Black Studies and Professor of Educational Psychology at the CUNY Graduate Center. He was formerly the Richard March Hoe Professor of Education at Teacher's College, Columbia University. For five years he was editor of the *American Journal of Orthopsychiatry*, and for three years was editor of the *Review of Research in Education*. His research interests include human diversity and pedagogy, human diversity and assessment, the modifiability of cognitive functions, the education of low-status populations, and life course analysis of persons who defy negative predictions for success. He has written extensively on professional and technical topics in education and psychology. He was one of the founders of the Head Start program, was its first national director of research, and has been associated with the conceptualization and evaluation of several other important experiments in U.S. educational reform.

Kris D. Guiterrez is Assistant Professor in the Graduate School of Education at the University of California, Los Angeles. Her research focuses on the social contexts of literacy learning for linguistically and culturally diverse students and on curriculum as sociocultural practice. Her ethnographic studies, conducted in urban schools in Los Angeles during the past six years, include *Studies of the Effects of Writing Process on Latino Children, Studies of the Construction of Classroom Culture, Communities of Effective Practice,* and *Novice Teacher Studies.*

Thomas P. Hébert is Assistant Professor of Teacher Education at the University of Alabama in Tuscaloosa, and has served as a research associate for the National Research Center on the Gifted and Talented. He was a public school teacher for 13 years, 10 of which were spent working with high-ability students at the elementary, junior high, and high school levels. He has taught in Maine, Georgia, Massachusetts, Connecticut, and West Germany with the Department of Defense Dependents Schools. His research interests include underachievement, high-ability students in inner-city schools, and the social and emotional needs of high-ability youngsters. He serves as an executive board member of the Association for Education of Gifted Underachieving Students (AEGUS) and as a contributing editor to *Roeper Review.*

Ann Masten, Ph.D., L.P., is Associate Professor of Child Psychology and Associate Director of the Institute of Child Development at the University of Minnesota. She is a Licensed Psychologist in Minnesota and coordinates an interdepartmental program of training in child clinical psychology. Her research explores resilence processes in development, particularly in the context of high cumulative risk and adversity. She has examined the effects of both normative and extreme rearing conditions on the adaptation and development of children and adolescents, with a focus on the processes by which academic and social competence and mental health are fostered or undermined by risks, vulnerabilities, assets, and protective factors. She has published empirical, theoretical and review papers on risk and resilience, competence, and developmental psychopathology. In 1994, she was awarded a Presidential Fellowship to attend the International Salzburg Seminar in Austria, which will focus on enhancing the well-being of children into the 21st century.

Barbara L. McCombs is Senior Director for the Motivation and Human Development Group at the Mid-Continent Regional Educational Laboratory in Colorado. She holds a Ph.D. in Educational Psychology from Florida State University. She has more than 20 years experience in directing research and development efforts in a wide range of basic and applied areas, including large-scale projects for the U.S. Department of Education on learning and motivational strategies for students and teachers, and social skills training curricula for enhancing job success. Her particular expertise is in motivational and self-development training programs for empowering youth and adults. She is coauthor of the *McREL Middle School Advisement Program* for enhancing student self-development in critical non-academic areas, and primary author of *Learner-Centered Psychological Principles: Guidelines for School Redesign and Reform*. She directed the development of a program based on these principles: *For Our Students, for Ourselves: Putting Learner-Centered Principles Into Practice*. In addition, she is directing a project to help school administrators, teachers, parents, and school boards utilize telecommunications technologies, and she is involved with efforts to develop community involvement programs for schools with a high percentage of students at risk of school failure.

Martin E. Orland is Associate Director for Analysis and Reporting at the National Education Goals Panel, an intergovernmental body composed of eight Governors, two senior members of the executive branch, four members of Congress, and four state legislators which annually monitors national and state progress in achieving the National Education Goals. The Panel also has congressionally mandated respon-

xviii Making a Difference for Students at Risk

sibilities in the areas of national standards setting, identifying promising and effective practices for achieving the Goals, and building the bipartisan consensus necessary for Goal attainment. He has been responsible for the production of the Panel's annual *National Education Goals Report*, and he managed the development of a *Community Action Tool Kit* designed to assist education reform leaders in using the National Education Goals and the emerging national standards movement as a framework for local educational renewal. He has been a senior analyst with the National Center for Education Statistics and at the U.S. Department of Education's Office of Research. He received his Ph.D. in social science from Syracuse University's Maxwell School in 1978, and has published widely in the areas of education policy reform, school finance, educating disadvantaged children, and intergovernmental relations in education.

Marleen C. Pugach is Associate Professor in the School of Education at the University of Wisconsin-Milwaukee, where she has been a member of the faculty since 1986. She received her Ph.D. from the University of Illinois at Urbana-Champaign. Her work focuses on fostering collaboration between general and special education in the schools, in teacher education programs at institutions of higher education, and in the realm of educational policy. Her work in urban educational settings concerns how educational practice can be conducted collaboratively so that labels of disability, race, ethnicity, gender, or language do not interfere with a teacher's commitment to educate all students. Her articles on these topics have appeared in *Exceptional Children, Journal of Teacher Education, Teacher Education and Special Education,* and *Journal of Special Education.* She is coeditor, with Renee Clift and Robert Houston, of the book *Encouraging Reflective Practice in Education: An Examination of Issues and Programs;* coauthor, with Lawrence J. Johnson, of *Collaborative Practitioners, Collaborative Schools;* and coeditor, with Cynthia Warger, of a forthcoming book on the relationship between the inclusion movement in special education and the reform of the academic curriculum in the schools.

Mary Anne Raywid is Professor of Administration and Policy Studies at Hofstra University in Hempstead, New York, where she is also the founder-director of the Center for the Study of Educational

Alternatives. Since 1990, she has also been an Adjunct Fellow of the Center for Educational Innovation of the Manhattan Institute for Policy Research. She has served as a researcher, evaluator, policy analyst, and staff developer, and has been active in a number of educational organizations, having served as president of the Philoso·phy of Education Society, the John Dewey Society, and the Society of Professors of Education. She has also been a member of the editorial boards of more than a dozen professional journals. Most of her current work is in the areas of school organization and the politics of education. For the last 20 years she has focused on school reform and restructuring, and she has written extensively on alternative schools and choice. She is a graduate of the University of North Carolina and the University of Illinois.

Sally M. Reis is Associate Professor of Educational Psychology at the University of Connecticut, where she also serves as Principal Investigator of the National Research Center on the Gifted and Talented. She was a teacher for 15 years, 11 of which involved working with gifted students at the elementary, junior high, and high school levels. She has authored more than 40 articles, 5 books, 7 book chapters, and numerous monographs and technical reports. She conducts workshops and provides in-service for school districts throughout the United States, using programs based on the Enrichment Triad and the Revolving Door Identification Models. She is coauthor of *The Revolving Door Identification Model, The Schoolwide Enrichment Model, The Secondary Triad Model,* and *The Triad Reader.* She serves on the editorial boards of the *Journal for Education of the Gifted* and *Gifted Child Quarterly,* and is on the Board of the National Association for Gifted Children.

Joseph S. Renzulli is Professor of Educational Psychology and Director of Teaching the Talented Program at the University of Connecticut. In 1990, he was appointed Director of the National Research Center on the Gifted and Talented. He is a fellow of the American Psychological Association and serves on the editorial boards of several professional journals. He has been a consultant to the Office of Gifted and Talented Education at the U.S. Department of Education and the White House Task Force on Education of the Gifted and served as an expert witness before the National Commission on Excellence in Education and on the Advisory Board of the National Science Foundation. He has authored more than 20 books and 150 articles and book chapters on exceptional children. His most recent book is titled *Schools for Talent Development* (1994).

Maynard C. Reynolds is Senior Research Associate at the National Center on Education in the Inner Cities at the Temple University Center for Research in Human Development and Education and serves as the DeForest Strunk Endowed Chair in the Department of Education at the University of San Diego. He is also Professor Emeritus of Educational Psychology, University of Minnesota. From 1950 to 1957, he directed the Psychoeducational Clinic, which served children and families who were experiencing school-related problems. In 1957, he assumed the chairmanship of a department concerned with preparation of specialized teachers and research relating to handicapped and gifted students.

He served in an endowed chair at the California State University in Los Angeles in 1990-1991. He is a past President of the International Council for Exceptional Children and received that organization's highest award, the Wallin Award. He played a major leadership role in the development of the All Handicapped Children's Act. He has been instrumental in forging an inclusive approach to serving students with special needs. He has published 28 books and more than 100 articles in the areas of special education and school psychology. He is the author of a basic textbook for teachers and school principals on human "exceptionality." One of his widely cited seminal works is *Knowledge Base for Beginning Teachers*.

Richard Ruiz is Associate Professor and Head of the Department of Language, Reading, and Culture in the College of Education at the University of Arizona. He was previously Instructor and Assistant Professor of Educational Policy Studies at the University of Wisconsin—Madison. He is recognized internationally for his research and scholarship in language planning and policy development, and has been a consultant to the governments of Mexico, Australia, the Northern Marianas, the Federated States of Micronesia, the Netherlands Antilles, and Native communities in the United States and Canada. He is on the editorial boards of *Urban Education* and *Teaching Educa-*

tion, and served on the Clinton-Gore Education Transition Team. He is Chair-Elect of the Committee on the Status of Minorities in Educational Research and Development of the American Educational Research Association, and a member of the English as a New Language Standards Committee of the National Board of Professional Teaching Standards. He holds a degree in French literature from Harvard University and in anthropology and philosophy of education from Stanford University.

Herbert J. Walberg, Research Professor of Education at the University of Illinois at Chicago, serves as Chairman of the Technical Committee on International Education Indicators for the Paris-based Organization for Economic Co-operation and Development—an organization of 24 member countries. He recently completed a term as founding member of the National Assessment Governing Board, which sets subject matter standards for American students. Formerly Assistant Professor at Harvard University, he has written and edited more than 50 books and contributed more than 380 articles to educational and psychological research journals on such topics as educational effectiveness and productivity, school reform, and exceptional human accomplishments. He frequently writes for widely circulated practitioner journals and national newspapers, serves as advisor on educational research and improvement to public and private agencies in the United States and other countries, and testifies before state and federal courts and U.S. congressional committees. A fellow of four academic organizations, he has won a number of awards and prizes for his scholarship and is one of three U.S. members of the International Academy of Education.

Margaret C. Wang is Professor of Educational Psychology and the founder and current director of the Temple University Center for Research in Human Development and Education (CRHDE), a broad-based interdisciplinary research and development center focusing on the human development and education-related fields. She also serves as the Director of the National Center on Education in the Inner Cities (CEIC), one of the national research and development centers established by the Office of Educational Research and Improvement of the U.S. Department of Education.

She is recognized nationally and internationally for her research on learner differences and classroom learning, student motivation, and implementation and evaluation of innovative school programs that are responsive to student diversity, particularly students with special needs. A major thrust of her research on student differences is analysis of the role of the learner in school learning contexts and of its implications for instructional practices and curriculum development. She is active in several professional organizations and serves on the editorial boards of several major research- and practitioner-oriented journals. She is the senior editor of the four-volume *Handbook of Special Education: Research and Practice,* and has authored and/or edited 12 books and more than 100 articles and book chapters. She has developed two widely implemented school programs: the Primary Education Program, an early learning curriculum, and the Adaptive Learning Environments Model, a comprehesive education program designed to support implementation of classroom instruction that provides for the individual differences among students.

Brenda Lilienthal Welburn is Executive Director and Chief Operating Officer of the National Association of State Boards of Education, where she was previously Director of Governmental Affairs. She is an association manager and legislative professional with more than 20 years experience in policy development and analysis in education and human service issues. She has served as a Research Analyst with the U.S. House of Representatives Select Committee on Assassinations, and as a Legislative Assistant to Senator Paul Tsongas of Massachusetts, with legislative responsibility for several issues including education, health and human services, child welfare services, and civil rights. She earned a bachelor's degree from Howard University, and has done graduate work at the University of Pennsylvania. She is the author of the report *The American Tapestry: Educating a Nation,* a guide to infusing multiculturalism in education, and has given workshops and presentations around the country on multicultural education. Active in her community, she is on the Human Relations Commission of Prince George's County in Maryland.

Kenneth K. Wong is Associate Professor in the Department of Education at the University of Chicago. A political scientist by training, he has conducted research in urban school reform, state and local politics, intergovernmental relations, federal social policy, education finance, and job training programs. He is the author of *City Choices: Education and Housing* and coauthor of *When Federalism Works.* He edits *Politics of Policy Innovation in Chicago* and coedits *Politics of Urban Education in the United States.* He is series editor of *Advances in Educational Policy,* a member of the editorial board in the Section on Social and Institutional Analysis for the *American Educational Research Journal,* and a member of the editorial board for *Educational Administration Quarterly.* During 1989-1990, he was awarded the Spencer Fellowship from the National Academy of Education. He is principal investigator of a research project "Systemwide Governance in the Chicago Public Schools: A Study Toward Institutional Redesign," funded by the Joyce Foundation. He is also a Senior Research Associate of the National Center on Education in the Inner Cities.

• • • • • •

1

• • • • • •

Introduction

Inner-City Students at the Margins

MARGARET C. WANG

MAYNARD C. REYNOLDS

HERBERT J. WALBERG

The menace to America today is in the emphasis on what separates us rather than on what brings us together. —Daniel J. Boorstin (1993)

The way to get a story together is not to head first and directly to the center of it, but to start somewhere at the edges or the margins.

AUTHORS' NOTE: The research reported here is supported in part by the Office of Educational Research and Improvement (OERI) of the U.S. Department of Education through a grant to the National Center on Education in the Inner Cities (CEIC) at the Temple University Center for Research in Human Development and Education (CRHDE). The opinions expressed do not necessarily reflect the position of the supporting agencies, and no official endorsement should be inferred.

So says the journalist James Reston (1991) in his memoirs. That may be the way to understand schools, too. In this book, as with the conference for which it was prepared, we look to the margins: that is, to students who have unusual needs and who challenge teachers to the far limits of their commitments, insights, and skills. In doing this, we express our concerns about students who are marginalized in the schools, but we also choose this course as a way of understanding all students and their schools, and of assessing what can be done to achieve schooling success for all the diverse students today, particularly those in the inner cities.

In the context of our discussion, we refer to a diverse set of students, including those whose primary language is not English and others who, for whatever reason, are struggling in their academic programs or in their social behavior in the schools; they are at risk in their private lives and at the center of growing concern about community order and growth.[1] They require instruction that is adapted to their individual needs. We refer also to students who show potential for outstanding performance in valuable ways and to high-achieving students who, despite adverse life conditions in the inner city, are learning and adjusting to school life especially well. Such resilient students receive far too little help in most inner-city schools even though, just like other students, they need instruction that is adapted to their strengths.

Disturbingly, there are disproportionate numbers of racial and ethnic minority children at the margins. These disproportions extend to the arrangements made for their schooling, so much so that it seems doubtful that progress has been made since the War on Poverty of the 1960s or even since the Brown decision of 1954. African American students, for example, are labeled retarded or behaviorally disturbed and set aside from regular classes at rates two or three times higher than those for white students. Similarly, African American students are suspended or expelled from school much more frequently than other students. No analysis of schooling situations is complete if it does not attend to this calamitous situation for minority students (Heller, Holtzman, & Messick, 1982).

Although inner-city schools have many problems, the biggest crisis is at the margins. In this chapter, our discussion is intended to be candid, critical, and forward looking, taking a look at the margins but with a commitment to try for improvements in the lives and learning of all children and youth in the inner cities.

Two basic assumptions undergird all that follows here. First, we understand and fully accept the obligation to offer education that is beneficial to every child. It is a great moral victory for our society that in wave after wave of legislative action, it has been declared that all children, even those who are most difficult to teach, have a right to education and that it should be appropriate for each individual. The universal right to education is now more than a rhetorical tradition— it is becoming a legal reality—but the struggle to make it meaningful continues, especially at the margins.

Second, we accept the moral imperative that the schools should be as fully integrated as possible. This means that separation, in whatever form, whether by race, gender, language background, abilities, or whatever, should be minimal and requires a compelling rationale. The aim is for totally inclusive schools. The burden of proof lies with those who advocate separation of students from such schools.

Taking a Closer Look

So let's go to the margins of the schools and look around at both students and programs. What do we see?

Special Education

We see special education in eight or nine varieties, with children labeled for the kind of special intervention they receive: learning disabled, mentally retarded, emotionally disturbed, blind, deaf, and so on. The state has awarded special certificates to "teachers of [categorical term]" following preparation in special programs in colleges for them.

Special subsidies by state and federal offices amount to about $20 billion per year for special education. Adding other state and local funds, some urban school districts find a total of 25% of school expenditures going to special education. Rules and regulations put these programs largely out of local control. Some cities still maintain whole schools for special education programs and pay high costs to transport pupils to "categorically correct" stations.

Two of the largest categories of special education are for children who are learning disabled (LD) or mentally retarded (MR). The latter category is for students who score low on IQ tests and are thus neither predicted nor expected to learn well in school. We are already experiencing deep difficulties due to carrying low expectations for many such children.

The LD category is for students who are the surprises, those who have slightly higher IQs and who are expected to do well but are not actually achieving in basic subjects such as reading. This is the middle-class category. Almost two decades ago, Featherstone (1975) predicted with remarkable vision that "[s]chools that carelessly mislabel poor children are very likely going to mislabel middle-class children as dyslexic or hyperkinetic" (p. 14). In the 1990s, we can read the last few words of this quotation as "learning disabled or attention deficit disordered."

LD was a relatively new label in 1975, but it is now carried by more than half of the disabled students in the nation's categorical special education programs. Classification as LD depends on calculation of a discrepancy between the rate of learning that could be expected of a child and what the child actually demonstrates in matters such as reading. It is often necessary to wait through the primary grades for the discrepancy to grow to acceptable magnitude for classification and placement, breeding failure, helplessness, and worse in the interim. The lack of early efforts to serve students who show slow starts in school learning is inexcusable.

There is no separate knowledge base for teaching children classified as mildly MR and LD. Yet we have in many places continued using psychologists only to give tests, calculate discrepancies, issue their expectations, and send children off to separate places with demeaning labels—all at high expense.

Distinctive instructional practices have been designed for special needs students who are blind or deaf, and much of what is offered by speech pathologists has distinctive credibility and utility. Emerging programs for severely and profoundly disabled students also have distinctive qualities and qualify for special arrangements. But for the remainder, there is often need for intensive and individualized education rather than a different kind of education. There is even less need for state and federal authorities to send in monitoring teams to ascertain that programs are separate, all labels in place, and all paperwork in order.

We believe we are justified in describing today's special education programs as contributors to the severe disjointedness of schools, as a bad case of "proceduralism" (in which norms for procedures have surpassed norms for true substance or credibility in operations), and as a cause of mutilation of the role of psychologists in the schools. The wildly accelerated development of the LD category is, or should be, an embarrassment to everyone involved. What is the excuse?

Chapter 1

Chapter 1 programs were started in the mid-1960s to assist disadvantaged children. At a cost of about $6 billion per year, this program serves about 5 million students, operating mainly by pull-out procedures. It provides little incentive for administrators to "pay attention to conditions and activities falling outside it" (Orland, 1993, p. 11). This isolation exists despite evidence that students served in Chapter 1 programs completely overlap, in terms of characteristics, with students in LD programs (Jenkins, Pious, & Peterson, 1988).

The Chapter 1 program is increasingly criticized as a fragmented and uncoordinated program that adds to the disjointedness of schools, especially those with large numbers of poor students. A proper remedy will require a broad approach to curriculum rather than narrowly focused skills training, and a renegotiated and more integral relationship with general education (Commission on Chapter 1, 1992).

The independent Commission on Chapter 1 is calling for a major change in the program, one that would remake entire schools that serve many poor children. We favor the commission's ideas for change, but not its strategy, which neglects the involvement of other categorical programs. Chapter 1 is large among federal programs, but at the school level it is relatively small and perhaps not in a position to lead a major transformation of the schools. Why not proceed in a broader fashion in concert with other categorical programs and general education (Wang, Reynolds, & Walberg, 1993)? We especially note the need to coordinate Chapter 1 programs with those for educable retarded and LD children. (See Chapter 2 of this book for a more extended discussion of special education and Chapter 1 programs.)

Language-Related Programs for Minority Students

In absolute numbers, the decade of the 1980s saw more immigrants (9 million) arrive in the United States than in any other decade of U.S. history.[2] More than 2 million immigrant children and youth entered the public schools of the nation in the 1980s, mainly in large cities such as Chicago, Los Angeles, Miami, and New York (McDonnell & Hill, 1993).

The evidence on outcomes of programs for immigrant children is limited and controversial. Some bilingual instruction that takes into account specific cultural differences and language differences appears to be successful (Moll & Diaz, 1987). Others believe that "bilingual education retards rather than expedites the movement of Hispanic children into the English-speaking world and that it promotes segregation more than it does integration" (Schlesinger, 1992, p. 108). The recent Rand report (McDonnell & Hill, 1993) makes a strong case for attending to the unique needs of newcomers to America's schools, but within the regular education framework. (See Chapter 6 of this book for extended treatment of this topic.)

High Achievers

A challenge of great significance concerns students in inner-city schools who somehow manage to achieve at high levels despite their adverse life situations. The rates of identification of inner-city students as high achievers or as gifted or talented are low. Expectations for their development tend to be low, and there are relatively few special streams of support for these students compared with those who fall to the bottom in school achievement and behavior. Able learners are, perhaps, no less burdened by poor identification and labeling systems than low-achieving students. One constantly hears echoes of old debates about general abilities versus more specific abilities and which are primary in cognitive structures. But few ideas have been carried to fruition in the form of well-confirmed ideas and valid tools to proceed with the education of those who show they are highly educable. The advanced placement program and kindred procedures for accelerating the curriculum for able learners are helpful in secondary schools and in facilitating the transition to college. Numerous possibilities for advancing programs at earlier levels can be offered, but they require leadership, which is not always present except in the limited areas of athletics and, often, music. (See Chapter 3 of this book for an extended treatment of this topic.)

A Large, Silent Category: School Demissions

A very large category, but one dealt with in relative silence, is made up of students suspended and expelled from schools. We should quickly note the overlap in categories. As Frankel (1988) stated, "After all, it's often the same kids . . . who've enrolled in less challenging classes or the 'soft areas' of special education; who don't come to school regularly and who—to no one's surprise—drag down the group averages on the standardized achievement test results" (p. 2).

Data are not plentiful on the subject of school demissions (excuses, exclusions, suspensions, and expulsions). There is no clear and powerful advocacy group for those demitted. They closely resemble those who attend school reluctantly and then drop out, but we have better data on these voluntary demissions. Perhaps there is some embarrassment about the data. The worry is that because there is little information one might conclude that there are few problems.

Data for the 1991-1992 school year in the city of Minneapolis, where 54% of students were minority and 46% were white, revealed the primary causes for suspensions: (a) fighting, (b) lack of cooperation, (c) pushing, shoving, and scuffling, and (d) disrespect. The following additional data were also compiled (Heistad & Reynolds, 1994):

- 20% of the students were suspended at least once, and, on average, 2.4 times
- 69% of those suspended were male
- 36% of African American students were suspended at least once
- 30% of special education students were suspended at least once

In the 1986-1987 school year in New Orleans, African American males accounted for 43% of the school population, but 58% of non-promotions, 65% of suspensions, 80% of expulsions, and 45% of the dropouts. Nonpromotion is clearly a factor associated with dropouts, attendance problems, and suspensions (Committee to Study the Status of Black Males in the New Orleans Public Schools, 1988). Disruption is the frequent precipitating behavior for suspensions, and rates for such behavior increase as one moves up the grades. There are promising practices to reduce suspension rates (Wager, 1992-1993).

Some General Observations About Categorical Programs

There are other categorical programs, but rather than describe each of them, we offer a few observations as we look across them all:

1. In the main, they are not working nearly as well as intended. Categorical programs tend to be organized around factors thought to be predispositional to poor school learning. Thus, for example, several programs serve children from economically poor families and migratory families or children described as MR or LD. (Many specialists see the LD label as proxy for underlying perceptual or neurological problems—often with little or no evidence.) The classifications are remote from what teachers can perceive and influence. The schools have organized programs separately, in accordance with categories specified in legislative action, even if there is no evidence that programs organized in separate ways work. Governmental bureaucracies, special funding streams, and monitoring systems have tended to force separation and to rigidify highly categorized and disorderly school systems. Broad accord is emerging in the view that there have been too few benefits from narrowly framed categorical programs and that there is need to recreate them in broader fashion in unity with regular education. Schools should instead organize programs around more directly assessed instructional needs (Reynolds & Zetlin, 1992).

2. Most programs operate, and are funded, on the basis of input variables, with little attention to outcomes. That is, students are qualified for special programs on the basis of their characteristics at

time of entry. Their school districts immediately qualify for special subsidies as students enter the special programs. For funding purposes, it does not seem to matter whether the programs do any good. Evaluations have been difficult, but few show positive results, and many show negative results. The programs generally do not work.

3. Categorical programs often settle for a limited curriculum and for a simple problem-minimizing instructional mode (Scardamalia & Bereiter, 1989). Maintaining good order, simplifying and reducing the curriculum, decreasing referrals to the principal's office, fixating on management, getting through the book, and teaching simple skills have sometimes seemed enough. But the world of today requires aggressive teaching for problem solving and complex thinking. Sadly, we think a problem-minimizing approach has also been observed among educational leaders. We note that at the time of this writing, a draft RFP (request for proposal) issued by the U.S. Department of Education for a research and development center focused on at-risk students is explicit in excluding disabled students from consideration. Similarly, a request being made by the U.S. Department of Education to the Congress for waiver authority apparently will exclude the entire field of special education. It is easier to set aside the categorical programs in these ways than to make inclusive arrangements in policies and procedures. No one needs the hornet's nest on their desk, so set it aside!

4. Many people are beginning to ask mainstream educators why so many students are set aside in categorical programs. Are there not ways to reform general education so that it will be more powerful in meeting the needs of all students, including those so often marginalized in today's schools?

5. Program administration and monitoring by federal authorities (and, to an extent, by state authorities) reflect a distrust that local educators will use the resources provided in service to the targets specified by legislators. The result has been a growing, heavy load of rules and regulations enforced by bureaucrats and a corresponding passive or hostile resistance by local educators. Lortie (1976) described teachers as feeling that they were left at the far tail end of a long chain of moral insight by policy makers and administrators inside the District of Columbia beltway. The assumption about superior moral

insight in Washington is doubted and resented by teachers who work long hours with children and are then required to produce massive paperwork for review by distant monitors. The same regulations set an essentially judicial model for meetings of parents and teachers in planning school programs for individual children. Mutual trust is an essential condition for teaching, and it has been diminished. The federal role in education programs has been to separate what should be integrated and to create distrust where trust is most needed. Reform is required.

6. We lack sufficient research and data on pupils and programs at the margins of the schools. Testing data and the large national databases often omit pupils in special programs (McGrew, Thurlow, & Spiegel, 1993), a practice that invites educators to inflate findings on average pupil achievements in their schools and districts. When there are no data, it is too easy to conclude that there are no problems or to leave them to vague approximations.

7. A serious estrangement has developed between universities and inner-city schools, resulting in a critical abandonment of such schools by the agency serving as prime custodian of research personnel.

Voices for Reform

A few years ago, when a number of educators launched what became known as the Regular Education Initiative (REI), a drive to unify categorical programs and regular education, a common criticism was that the only voices heard were those of specialists. Where, the critics asked, are the initiatives by regular educators? Now there is a virtual cascade of such initiatives by leaders in professional groups of regular educators and by some others as well.

Physicians and psychologists play key roles in some school programs, especially in the classification and diagnosis of students who exhibit special problems. Thus it is important to note the important changes now occurring in these related professions and fields. In 1989, a change in Title V of the Social Security Act established a new mandate described as "the only current foundation of a national health policy for children with special health care needs" (Ireys &

Nelson, 1992, p. 321). Children with special health care needs were defined as children "with disabilities and handicapping conditions, with chronic illness and conditions, with health-related educational or behavioral problems, and at risk for disabilities, chronic conditions, and health-related educational and behavioral problems" (p. 323). The definition is broad, and it is explicit about the relationship between health and education. Furthermore, new policies suggest that "development of separate service systems for each diagnostic group is not feasible"; instead, "all children with special health care needs should be considered as part of a single class" (p. 323). States are now required to spend 30% of their maternal and child health monies on children with special needs and on improvement of "the service system for these children and their families by promoting family-centered, community-based, coordinated care" (p. 321). These provisions dramatically alter the public work of the health professions in the direction of less categorizing of children and programs, more work on prevention of problems, and more coordination with schools and other child-serving agencies.

The National Association of School Psychologists (NASP), in association with the National Coalition of Advocates for Students (NCAS), recently issued a position statement on "appropriate educational services for all children" that, in part, proposed "the development and piloting of alternatives to the current categorical system" and advocated "policy and funding waivers needed for the piloting of alternative service delivery models" (NCAS & NASP, n.d., p. 2).

Other Voices Among Educators

> [F]or practical purposes, there is increasingly convergent belief that . . . subgroups of learning problems represent a continuum of cognitive and adaptive inefficiency and ineffectiveness in classroom learning situations, rather than discretely different disabilities. (Gerber, 1987, p. 171)

> Certain categories of students may have "special educational needs," but it is educationally dysfunctional to separate those students' curriculum, performance expectations, and

remediation strategies from those of other students. (Orland, 1993, p. 19)

[F]or . . . those identified as having learning disabilities . . . there are no agreed upon conceptual or operational criteria for classification. (Keogh, 1988, p. 229)

The most fundamental change may be the need to cease the current classification system, which focuses on within-child categories, and to begin funding programs based on the need for resources. (Epps & Tindal, 1987, p. 242)

Participation in support programs (e.g., Chapter 1 or special education resource rooms) often serves to replace core curriculum instruction. Students . . . actually ended up with less instructional time than students not served. (Allington & Johnston, 1986, p. 11)

The best way to help immigrant students is to strengthen the school systems that serve them, not to create new categorical programs that single out immigrants for special benefits. . . . Some way must be found for the federal government and states to move beyond their current emphasis on small categorical programs to help big cities improve their school systems across the board. (McDonnell & Hill, 1993, p. xiii)

Voices of Major Educational Organizations

- According to the Council of Chief State School Officers, "To ensure opportunity for all, states should be allowed to consolidate programs serving poor and ethnic or minority-language children—under a single administrative plan, [to] integrate services and commingle funds. . . . [F]ederal special education funds and Chapter 1 money could be merged to serve students in both programs" ("Chiefs Propose," 1992, pp. 1, 3).

- According to *Concerns* magazine, "The use of labels to determine a student's educational program is invalid" ("A Concern About—" 1992, p. 2).
- The National Association of State Directors of Special Education states that by the year 2000, "the needs of all children will be identified and met without reference to assigned labels or categories of severity of disability. . . . Schools will provide family-focused, one-stop support that includes multi-agency responsibility" ("The NASDSE's Commitment," 1993, p. 2).
- The "Reinventing Chapter 1" report of the staff of the U.S. Department of Education finds that the current program-improvement provisions of Chapter 1 "have not been a significant instrument for fundamental changes. . . . The authors recommend a series of changes designed to move Chapter 1 from a focus on remedial help for individual children to an emphasis on schoolwide improvement" (Miller, 1993, pp. 2-3).
- The National Association of State Boards of Education says that "state boards should encourage and foster collaborative partnerships and joint training programs between general educators and special educators . . . to work with the diverse student population found in fully inclusive schools. . . . Boards should sever the link between funding, placement, and handicapping labels" (National Association of State Boards of Education, 1992, p. 5).

Although the readiness to remove labels and separation and to try for integration and general effectiveness in school situations and conditions of life for marginal students seems at hand, there is reluctance in many quarters to engage with the problem. We see this as timidity at best and serious neglect at worst; it is, quite clearly, a case of the same kind of problem-minimizing behavior we decry in the schools. The problem has too often become one of keeping difficult problems off the principal's desk or off the agenda of reluctant leaders, and this must change. It may also be the case that some of the advocacy groups that moved aggressively in recent decades to secure special opportunities for children in the various categories succeeded too well, to the point of fault. They may now be inclined to retain their hard-won special categorical funds and policies and to resist full inclusion of children and funds in reformed general school programs.

Solutions

Many children, particularly those in the inner cities, live in unsafe, disorderly, and decaying environments. The schools, especially in their services to students at the margins, are also in disorder. They represent extreme cases of disjointedness, proceduralism, and ineffectiveness. Some of the disarray is forced by governmental policies concerning narrowly framed programs. Inner-city communities are unhealthy places, dampened by disinvestment in business and industry, high unemployment, lack of adequate health services, high rates of crime, and unstable and insecure family situations. The solution to this range and depth of problems is difficult to imagine.

Some observers doubt that there is a future for the inner cities and believe the goal should be to move people out as rapidly as possible. Hopefully, those leaving will have strong abilities so that they can cope with the challenges of an emerging global economy and the general complexity of modern life. Already such movement is apparent. However, this leaves the residual elements of the inner cities in a backwater status, lacking leadership and sinking ever further into decay. At least one prominent public figure has proposed something like a new Homestead Act that would cause massive movement out of inner-city environments, but with strong supports for people seeking to make their way in new environments (Kennan, 1993).

But our immediate task is to strengthen the schools of the inner city. To do that, priority must go to the schools themselves, focusing mainly on effective instruction. However, work is necessary in coordination with social, health, judicial, housing, and transportation agencies, among others, to help create coherent patterns of service and support to children and families. Some such efforts for coordination are emerging in many places. They are not always working well, but in time they may succeed. Here, as elsewhere, governmental rules and regulations are often less than helpful. For example, it is often difficult, even illegal, to share information across agencies because of limits imposed by federal laws.

Even the coalitions of community agencies now forming in many communities are limited in what they can do. So far, they are almost clinical in their orientation—for example, offering family therapy in conjunction with school-based remedial work with children. This leaves untouched broader problems such as unemployment and business disinvestment and shortfalls in housing, health services, and transportation. Somehow, we must find means to approach these broader problems in cohesive ways. They are basic for motivating students to be hopeful about the future and for demonstrating adults' deeply caring attitudes toward children.

Some things we can do. While we work for more coordinated services to children, we can also work for integration among professional organizations and bureaucracies and create expectations that they work together in coherent fashion. No doubt, there are seasons and reasons for separations in order to expeditiously move new ideas and practices in powerful ways. The separate formation of The Association for the Severely Handicapped (TASH) and its remarkable accomplishments over recent decades is one example. But now we have come to a season for integration, not only of students, but of bureaucratic and professional services. It will be difficult to achieve such broad integration if the schools are partitioned internally in ways reinforced by government agencies, professional associations, and advocacy groups.

Already it appears that local efforts to provide coherent programs for students are frustrated because of the separation of professional and bureaucratic agencies. Federal and state agencies send separate and narrowly oriented monitoring teams to schools to check separately on special education programs, Chapter 1 programs, and the like, even though research findings show there is much overlap in the characteristics of students served in several of the programs and that there is no separate knowledge base undergirding instruction in the several fields. The special panel created by the National Academy of Science reported, for example, that there is "no educational justification for the current categorization system that separates" mildly MR, LD, and Chapter 1 groups in the schools (Heller et al., 1982, p. 102). Yet the Office of Special Education asks school districts to report their operations in terms of categories that have no credibility as educational classifications.

Instructional Improvement

A first priority in seeking improvement in the learning of students, particularly those whose achievements are at the margins, is improvement of instruction. This need is most prevalent in inner-city schools. In data recently assembled for one urban school district, only 6 of 50 elementary schools showed average achievement (50th percentile) in reading comprehension at the national average. Of the students in elementary schools of that city, 20% scored below the 11th percentile of national norms for reading. Such data do not tell the whole story because some of the schools were in highly favorable situations. In the 10 lowest-scoring schools (in reading) of the city, the 20th percentiles on national norms were 1, 1, 2, 2, 3, 3, 4, 5, 5, and 6. Teachers in some schools report that students begin first grade not with a head start but with incredibly little background for learning at a primary level. Students at the margins, many of whom start with only poor readiness for academic learning, come to school for breakfast and stay for lunch, but learn little to nothing in the remainder of the school day. The academic achievement of many inner-city students is appallingly, disastrously low.

To make improvements, it appears that students need more instruction—in intensive, even aggressive, forms—not a different kind of instruction. They need it early and in continuing ways throughout the school years, and they need the most capable teachers.

In a recent study, a metareview of the research literature was combined with the judgments of researchers and practicing educators to identify the variables or practices that are well confirmed as a valid basis for instruction (Reynolds, Wang, & Walberg, 1992; Wang, Haertel, & Walberg, 1990). Figure 1.1 shows the 28 categories of variables in order of their influence on learning from highest to lowest. The figure reveals that direct psychological influences have, by far, the greatest effects. These direct influences include (a) students' cognitive abilities, motivation, and behavior; (b) classroom management, climate, and student/teacher interactions; (c) amount and quality of instruction; and (d) parental encouragement and

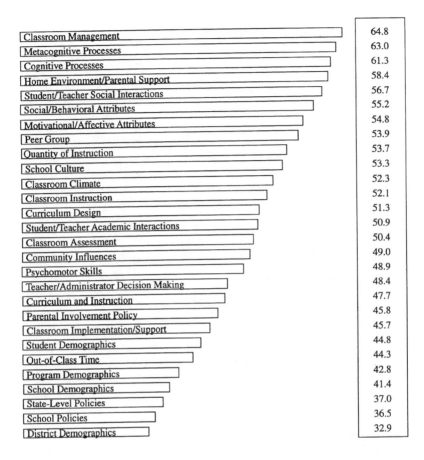

Classroom Management	64.8
Metacognitive Processes	63.0
Cognitive Processes	61.3
Home Environment/Parental Support	58.4
Student/Teacher Social Interactions	56.7
Social/Behavioral Attributes	55.2
Motivational/Affective Attributes	54.8
Peer Group	53.9
Quantity of Instruction	53.7
School Culture	53.3
Classroom Climate	52.3
Classroom Instruction	52.1
Curriculum Design	51.3
Student/Teacher Academic Interactions	50.9
Classroom Assessment	50.4
Community Influences	49.0
Psychomotor Skills	48.9
Teacher/Administrator Decision Making	48.4
Curriculum and Instruction	47.7
Parental Involvement Policy	45.8
Classroom Implementation/Support	45.7
Student Demographics	44.8
Out-of-Class Time	44.3
Program Demographics	42.8
School Demographics	41.4
State-Level Policies	37.0
School Policies	36.5
District Demographics	32.9

Figure 1.1. Relative Influences on Learning

SOURCE: M. C. Wang, G. D. Haertel, and H. J. Walberg, Synthesis of research: What helps students learn? *Educational Leadership*, December 1993/January 1994, pp. 74-79. Reprinted with permission of the Association for Supervision and Curriculum Development. Copyright 1993 by ASCD.

support of learning at home. Variables one step removed from learning have a relatively moderate influence. These include (a) school culture, (b) teacher/administrator decision making, (c) community influences, and (d) the peer group outside school. The variables that are far removed from the learning setting, which include school and district demographics, state-level policies, and school policies, have the least influence, even though many policy makers are currently preoccupied with educational restructuring at remote organizational levels.

The variables within these broad categories provide more specific illustrations of what directly and powerfully influences learning. Table 1.1 lists 20 of the variables most important for the learning of children (Reynolds et al., 1992). The first 11 items are principles of instruction, the next 3 reflect contextual considerations (all of them concerning parental involvement), and the final 6 represent characteristics of students that relate to learning.

Topping the list is time on task or student time engaged actively in learning. Time is the most ubiquitous factor observed in research on learning. To learn well, students must spend time actively seeking to learn. This means that parents and teachers must somehow cause children to commit time to learning. It helps enormously, of course, if other conditions favorable to learning are also applied consistently. We do not use time carefully now. Haynes and Jenkins (1986), for example, showed that students who go to Chapter 1 or special education resource rooms part-time for instruction often end up with no more total time on task in subjects in which they were intended to receive extra attention than if they had stayed full-time in their regular classes. Allington and McGill-Franzen (1989) reported a similar finding.

Imagine a situation in which psychologists measure the time that students spend actively in learning, rather than giving IQ tests, and in which they consult with parents and teachers on improved use of time by children. Imagine, too, that teachers have learned to manage classroom situations in partnerships with teacher specialists who have come out of their separate enclaves. The specialists offer intensive individualized or small-group instruction to pupils most needing direct instruction on basic skills.

Extending that scenario and moving down the list of principles shown in Table 1.1, we can envision teachers—working in small teams—who provide frequent individual and group feedback to students on their classroom performance, check each student for comprehension on elements of the curriculum, and explicitly promote metacognitive learning strategies.

TABLE 1.1 Variables Most Important for the Learning of Children, as Rated by a 12-Member Panel of Experts

Category	*Variables*
Instruction	Time on task (student time engaged actively in learning)
	Time spent in direct instruction on basic skills in reading
	Time spent in direct instruction on basic skills in mathematics
	Frequent feedback provided to students about their performance
	Comprehension monitoring by the teacher (planning; monitoring effectiveness of actions; testing, revising, and evaluating learning strategies)
	Explicit promotion of student self-responsibility and effective metacognitive learning strategies
	Use of clear, organized, and direct instruction
	Setting and maintenance of clear expectations of content mastery
	Appropriate reaction by teacher to correct and incorrect answers
	Appropriate task difficulty (students are challenged)
	Safe, orderly school climate
Out-of-School Contextual	Parental expression of affection to children
	Parental interest in student's schoolwork
	Parental expectation for academic success
Student Characteristics	Use of self-regulation and metacognitive strategies
	Level of reading comprehension ability
	Attitude toward school
	Attitude toward teachers
	Motivation for continued learning
	Level of general academic knowledge

SOURCE: Reynolds, M. C., Wand, M. C., and Walberg, H. J. (1992). The knowledge bases for special and general education. *Remedial and Special Education, 13*(5), pp. 6-10, 33. Copyright 1992 by PRO-ED, Inc. Reprinted by permission.

Surveys show that teachers of advantaged, disadvantaged, and special children agree that the principles listed in Table 1.1 are important in attempts to enhance learning. There is no different set of principles for instruction of Chapter 1 students, migrant children, or special education students. Undoubtedly, adherence to basic principles of education is especially important for students who have not learned well in the past. Yet they have not been followed well in inner-city schools.

We suggest that as we move toward integration of categorical programs, and as teachers and psychologists of all kinds are brought together for teamwork, these are the principles by which their activities should be prioritized. As we work with parents, these principles of learning can be reinforced for application at home. Schools with a high concentration of students living in high-risk circumstances need help of many kinds, but we think little will be gained in the learning of children unless and until there is rigorous application of the important principles of learning in the schools.

We believe that the diagnosis of learning problems could be much improved through close attention to the same variables stressed here for instructional improvement. Individual pupils, for example, might be studied in terms of how well they use time, how capable they are in self-management or in the use of metacognitive strategies, how orderly they are in classroom situations, how supportive their parents are in school-related affairs, and so on. All of these conditions can be influenced by teachers.

Policy-Level Changes in the Search for Improvement

We offer a number of suggestions for policy changes and for revised bureaucratic functioning in the form of scenarios for the future:

- The U.S. Department of Education (USDE) sends out only broadly consolidated monitoring teams to states and local schools and extends their mission to look for and encourage every form of collaboration among programs. Such teams represent all categorical programs, including special education, Chapter 1, migrant education, and bilingual and language-related programs. In the process of planning consolidated monitoring activities, an improved level of coherence in federally supported programs has been achieved.

- USDE has broad authority to grant waivers of rules and regulations to states and local school districts that wish to try for full integration of federally related programs and other programs for experimental periods. The conditions of waivers must include provisions such that no financial disincentives are created for schools undertaking experimental programs. In return for waivers, schools provide high-quality evidence on educational outcomes. No aspect of federal policy or programs has been excluded from waiver provisions.

- USDE establishes a priority of concern (for attention in all allocations of all discretionary funds) in areas of inner-city education. Attention is given to problems such as school attendance and dropouts, suspensions, and expulsions, as well as to special programs.

- A common sunset date has been set on legislation creating categorical school programs. Broad studies are commissioned on how such programs can be restructured as integral aspects of total school operations. New legislation reflects and encourages integration across formerly categorical programs.

- All federal agencies collecting and disseminating data on the schools are required to include data on *literally* all students.

- Data collected on special programs in the schools use classifications or categories only in cases that have scientific and professional credibility. For example, a moratorium is declared on the use of the categories of *learning disabled* and *mildly mentally retarded*.

- USDE seeks to combine its efforts with those of the Departments of Health and Human Services, Housing and Urban Development, Justice, and Transportation in experimental work of broad character in priority zones, defined mainly to include inner-city situations. New enterprise zone legislation defines areas in which multifaceted priority zones will operate.

- Changes are made in funding systems to emphasize, reward, and maintain programs in the schools that are noncategorical, oriented to prevention of educational problems, and evaluated in terms of outcome variables.

- The Council for Exceptional Children (CEC), The Association for the Severely Handicapped (TASH), possibly the National Association of School Psychologists (NASP), and other such groups have taken action to bring themselves together and to join the emerging movements for merger by the National Education Association (NEA) and the American Federation of Teachers (AFT) to create an integrated professional organization in education. From this unified base, there is strengthened work on integration of education within schools and with other human service professions and agencies outside of schools.

- Efforts are underway to encourage closer coordination of special and regular teacher preparation tracks in colleges and universities.

- Efforts are made to cause a merger among categorical parent and advocacy groups such that encouragement and support are offered to inclusive and integrated program structures in the schools.

We believe there is no more urgent issue in the nation than what we have touched upon here: improvement in the life and learning of *all* children in the inner cities. Disorder and neglect must be turned to hope and opportunity. Schools must be totally inclusive and powerful in their ability to serve children at the margins, those who present the greatest challenge to teachers. We emphasize that the policies of inclusion and integration should apply not only to children but also to bureaucratic and professional structures. Federal education policies in particular have fostered much separation of programs and students. The era of separation must come to an end.

Notes

1. The term *students at the margins* could about as well be *students at risk, exceptional students, disadvantaged and resilient students, margi-*

nalized students, and/or *gifted and talented students.* Each term lacks full clarity. Each has its critics. We use them all and somewhat interchangeably, trusting to the reader to understand and tolerate our roundabout approach to a construct with many names and nuances.

2. As a percentage of total population, immigration was greater in 1900-1910.

References

Allington, R. L., & Johnston, P. (1986). The coordination among regular classroom reading programs and targeted support programs. In B. I. Williams, P. A. Richmond, & B. J. Mason (Eds.), *Designs for compensatory education: Conference proceedings and papers* (Vol. 6, pp. 3-40). Washington, DC: Research and Evaluation Associates.

Allington, R. L., & McGill-Franzen, A. (1989). Children with reading problems: How we wrongfully classify them and fail to teach many to read. *Journal of School Research and Information, 8*(4), 3-7.

Chiefs propose elementary, secondary reauthorization bill. (1992, November 17). *Education Daily,* pp. 1, 3.

Commission on Chapter 1. (1992). *Making schools work for children in poverty.* Washington, DC: American Association for Higher Education.

Committee to Study the Status of Black Males in the New Orleans Public Schools. (1988). *Educating black male youth: A moral and civic imperative.* New Orleans: New Orleans Parish School Board.

A concern about—special education and school restructuring. (1992, March). *Concerns,* p. 2.

Epps, S., & Tindal, G. (1987). The effectiveness of differential programming in serving students with mild handicaps: Placement options and instructional programming. In M. C. Wang, M. C. Reynolds, & H. J. Walberg (Eds.), *Handbook of special education: Research and practice: Vol. 1. Learner characteristics and adaptive education* (pp. 213-248). Oxford, UK: Pergamon.

Featherstone, J. (1975, March 29). Children out of school: The expendables. *New Republic,* pp. 13-16.

Frankel, S. (1988, April). *Systems-oriented evaluation: A better approach to improving the achievement of minority students.* Paper presented at the annual meeting of the American Educational Research Association, New Orleans, LA.

Gerber, M. M. (1987). Application of cognitive-behavioral training methods to teaching basic skills to mildly handicapped elementary school students. In M. C. Wang, M. C. Reynolds, & H. J. Walberg (Eds.), *Handbook of special education: Research and practice: Vol. 1. Learner characteristics and adaptive education* (pp. 167-186). Oxford, UK: Pergamon.

Haynes, M. C., & Jenkins, J. R. (1986). Reading instruction in special education resource rooms. *American Educational Research Journal, 8,* 161-190.

Heistad, D., & Reynolds, M. C. (1994, February). *20/20: A closer look at students at the margins in Minneapolis public elementary schools.* Paper presented at the annual meetings of the American Association of School Administrators.

Heller, K., Holtzman, W., & Messick, S. (1982). *Placing children in special education: A strategy for equity.* Washington, DC: National Academy of Science Press.

Ireys, H. T., & Nelson, R. P. (1992). New federal policy for children with special health care needs: Implications for pediatricians. *Pediatrics, 80*(3), 321-327.

Jenkins, J. R., Pious, C. G., & Peterson, D. C. (1988). Categorical programs for remedial and handicapped students. *Exceptional Children, 55*(2), 147-158.

Kennan, G. F. (1993). *Around the cragged hill.* New York: Norton.

Keogh, B. K. (1988). Learning disability: Diversity in search of order. In M. C. Wang, M. C. Reynolds, & H. J. Walberg (Eds.), *Handbook of special education: Research and practice: Vol. 2. Mildly handicapped conditions* (pp. 225-251). Oxford, UK: Pergamon.

Lortie, D. (1976). Discussion. *Minnesota Education, 2*(2), 16-18.

McDonnell, L. M., & Hill, P. T. (1993). *Newcomers in American schools.* Santa Monica, CA: Rand.

McGrew, K. S., Thurlow, M. L., & Spiegel, A. N. (1993). An investigation of the exclusion of students with disabilities in the national data collection programs. *Educational Evaluation and Policy Analysis, 15,* 339-352.

Miller, J. A. (1993, February 2). E.D. study joins a chorus urging Chapter 1 reform. *Education Week,* pp. 2-3.

Moll, L. C., & Diaz, S. (1987). Changes are the goal of educational research. *Anthropology and Education Quarterly, 8,* 300-311.

The NASDSE's commitment for the 90's. (1993, Summer). *Counterpoint,* p. 2.

National Association of State Boards of Education. (1992). *Winners all: A call for inclusive schools.* Alexandria, VA: Author.

National Coalition of Advocates for Students and National Association of School Psychologists. (n.d.). *Position statement: Advocacy for appropriate educational services for all children.* Boston: National Coalition of Advocates for Students.

Orland, M. E. (1993). *From the picket to the chain link fence: National goals and federal aid to the disadvantaged.* Washington, DC: National Education Goals Panel.

Renzulli, J. (1993, October). *The plight of high-ability students in urban schools.* Paper presented at the "Making a Difference for Students At Risk" Invitational Conference of the National Center on Education in the Inner Cities, Princeton, NJ.

Reston, J. (1991). *Deadline.* New York: Random House.

Reynolds, M. C., Wang, M. C., & Walberg, H. J. (1992). The knowledge bases for special and general education. *Remedial and Special Education, 13*(5), 6-10.

Reynolds, M. C., & Zetlin, A. (1992). *20/20 analysis: A manual.* Philadelphia: Temple University Center for Research on Human Development and Education.

Scardamalia, M., & Bereiter, C. (1989). Conceptions of teaching and approaches to core problems. In M. C. Reynolds (Ed.), *Knowledge base for the beginning teacher* (pp. 37-46). Oxford, UK: Pergamon.

Schlesinger, A. M., Jr. (1992). *The disuniting of America.* New York: Norton.

Wager, B. R. (December 1992/January 1993). No more suspension: Creating a shared ethical culture. *Educational Leadership, 50*(4), 34-37.

Wang, M. C., Haertel, G. D., & Walberg, H. J. (1990). What influences learning? A context analysis of review literature. *Journal of Educational Research, 84*(1), 30-43.

Wang, M. C., Reynolds, M. C., & Walberg, H. J. (1993, March 24). Reform all categorical programs. *Education Week*, p. 6.

• • • • • •

2

• • • • • •

Twice Victims

The Struggle to Educate Children in Urban Schools and the Reform of Special Education and Chapter 1

MARLEEN C. PUGACH

The American educational system has elected to deal with children who are likely to have problems in school by designing special programs that place children apart from their peers. Although most children who attend these programs are not physically separated from their peers for the whole day, the academic, social, and psychological separation that results from even partial participation often permeates their entire school experience. In urban schools, where many students feel alienated from school already, participating in special education or Chapter 1, probably the most well known of the programs, is only likely to increase their sense of alienation—or at the least their sense of unconnectedness.[1]

It is an exceedingly serious state of affairs in education, because to be sure these forms of instructional support were not intended to make school even more problematic than it already is for urban children and youth. In fact, when teachers seek placement in one of these two programs they typically have the best interests of their students in mind. Teachers count on special education or Chapter 1 to provide for individualized attention tailored to their students' specific needs, and they rely on the special teachers' expertise as a means of giving students the unique remediation that seems to be required.

For teachers in the nation's inner cities, special education and Chapter 1 appear to provide answers to the individual problems of specific students in a context where many problems abound to begin with. These services provide a respite from the classic difficulties of urban schools: overcrowded classrooms, inflexible bureaucracies, test-driven curriculums, a lock-step, age-graded organizational structure, and children who need a great deal of every adult's attention. It is understandable that teachers readily turn to special education or Chapter 1 and put a great deal of energy into navigating the highly bureaucratic waters in order to get their students a place in these programs.

In reality, though, once designated as participants in such programs, students float between their special and general education classrooms and often have difficulty finding a real home in either place. The 1992 report of the National Association of State Boards of Education (NASBE) states it simply: Students who move back and forth from special to general education classes "are not part of the group or taken seriously as a member of the class" (p. 10). Although they may depend on their special education or Chapter 1 class teacher for an understanding ear, the instruction they receive, usually consisting of basic skills, is often neither challenging nor interesting (Means & Knapp, 1991). In the regular classroom, where the material might be more interesting, the instructional strategies used rarely offer them the opportunity to participate as full members of the class. Further, it is common to hear teachers refer to students as representatives of the particular categorical programs to which they are assigned—for example, "you mean my LD kid," or "he's Chapter 1"—and their individuality seems to be a lost resource in relationship to the educational process.

What we do not seem to know a lot about when teachers make the decision to refer a student for Chapter 1 or special education is the degree to which they think about how the institutional and curricular structure of the school in general may be contributing to the problems their students are encountering. In fact, the system we have institutionalized for identifying who needs special individual help is such that decisions regarding who is and is not in need are made almost wholly independent of the quality of schooling offered. In urban schools, where in many cases the majority of children are children of color, are disadvantaged economically, or cannot benefit from instruction in English alone, success in school often eludes the student population as a whole. In this context, where so many children bring so many different kinds of challenges to school, deciding when the challenge becomes great enough to warrant consideration of Chapter 1 or special education becomes tricky—especially if the outcome of participating is questionable.

In fact, many would say that the distinction between who does and does not get special education or Chapter 1 services is practically negligible given the high needs of so many students in urban schools. When children have clearly identifiable disabilities, such as a hearing or visual impairment, the distinction is more easily recognized and specific supportive services are usually needed, although not necessarily in a separate educational setting. But nearly 70% of the students in special education fall into the mild, and less objective, categories of learning disabilities, mental retardation, and emotional disturbance (U.S. Department of Education, 1992), categories for which programmatic structures and instructional practices most often resemble those used in Chapter 1.

It is not unreasonable to think of students in urban schools who are identified for Chapter 1 or special education as being victimized twice: first as a result of the difficult circumstances of their schools and school systems, and second as a result of the failure of Chapter 1 and special education to provide appropriate programs of support. New educational policies must be designed to overcome this double victimization if we are to help the current generation of urban students realize their potential and their ambitions.

From this perspective, several questions come to mind as we think about developing new educational policies for children who seem to be the most challenging to teach. How do we make distinctions between genuine problems that children bring to school and problems that the structure of school creates, seemingly leaving no choice but for special education/Chapter 1 to absorb those who are not resilient in the face of routine institutionalized practice? In other words, how do we invent general programs of education that take into account the wide range of student differences within each classroom and make sure that the overall program of education used is not making their problems worse? And once these programs are created, how do we still find a means of providing special assistance to individual students who will inevitably require it without jeopardizing them further for needing such attention in the first place? These framing questions should serve as a guide for thinking about the policy and practice implications of educating the most challenging students in urban schools—those for whom special education and Chapter 1 services were, with the best of intentions, originally designed.

Why Consider Special Education and Chapter 1 Together?

Because of their disparate origins, it is not altogether common for Chapter 1 and special education to be linked to the reform of urban education policy. Although Chapter 1 is a topic of much deliberation because of its roots in serving disadvantaged, low-income students, special education is conspicuous in its absence from most discussions of urban schools. For example, in an analysis of the complexities and confusions over the appropriateness of various programs for urban school reform appearing in the 1991 Yearbook of the Politics of Education Association on urban education, Cibulka (1992) does not mention special education as contributing to either the problem or the solution; this is particularly interesting because he recognizes that when considered in isolation, various program reform strategies have "too narrow a perspective on the scope of the knowledge dimensions of the problem" (p. 38). Likewise, Wehlage, Smith, and Lipman's (1992) research on restructuring urban schools, which bases much of its work on the need to eliminate tracking, does not see special education as a manifestation of this phenomenon. In her more general work on tracking, Oakes (1985) also fails to connect critical problematic dimensions of tracking to special education practice. In a recent interview, she aptly describes low-track classrooms as being "full of students who have a history of school difficulties, school failures, or misbehavior" (O'Neil, 1992, p. 20), which is precisely the case with many special education classes for students with behavior disorders, but the connection is never made.

Although the failure to make such connections is problematic, it is easy enough to understand why they are not made on a more consistent basis. Special education is theoretically designed to serve a well-defined population that requires a specialized set of instructional strategies. Funds are allocated to states depending upon how many children are counted as having disabilities, in an activity known as the "child count." In 1990-1991, special education served 4.3 million children; 2.1 million of those were classified as having learning disabilities (U.S. Department of Education, 1992). The fields of mental retardation and emotional disturbance account for nearly another million children, although students in each of these categories can range from having mild to severe difficulties.

In order to be identified as having a disability, a student is appraised with a variety of instruments, depending upon the problem described by the referring teacher or parent. Each identified student generates funds that flow through to the states and then to the individual districts; the greater the number of students who are identified, the greater the funding. If one thinks of the special education population as one that is defined objectively and scientifically and that requires lifelong adaptations of the standard curriculum in order for students to succeed, the relationship between special education and the more general problems of urban schooling is simply not salient. The failure to connect the two more readily and more consistently probably illustrates the degree to which educators have come to believe that this special population is correctly identified and exists independent of other problems in the education system and in society at large.

In practice, however, the objectivity associated with special education does not hold true, especially for the majority of students who receive special education services, those in the categories of mild disabilities. These categories, which include learning disabilities, school behavior/conduct problems (falling formally under the category of emotional disturbance), and mild mental retardation, are generally recognized by the high level of subjectivity that operates in the identification process (McLaughlin & Owings, 1992; Ysseldyke et al., 1983). With no objective guarantee regarding how students are identified, and with principal reliance on teacher referral to initiate the identification process, it should be clear that in urban schools these programs can too readily function to lighten the already impossible load most urban teachers carry. That is not to say that students in urban schools so referred are not having difficulties; instead, the question is whether they ought to be labeled as having a disability in order to receive assistance for their problems.

In contrast, Chapter 1 funds are specifically designated for disadvantaged children, and in urban schools this means minority children. School districts are identified according to the number of children whose families fall below the poverty level; districts with over 10 such children are eligible. Districts then disburse funds according to the needs of individual schools. Individual children are subsequently identified at their school sites depending upon scores on achievement tests (Rotberg, 1993). The Commission on Chapter 1 (1992) reports that approximately 5 million children were served by Chapter 1 in 1992; this translates into one out of every nine children in the nation's schools.

Together, then, Chapter 1 and special education serve at the least over 9 million children out of a total school population of over 40 million, or nearly 25% of the children who attend public school, an enormously high proportion. And although most general analyses of urban education policy do not tend to consider the two programs together, they have been regularly linked in the context of school reform by a small group of educational researchers (e.g., Allington & Johnston, 1989; Allington & McGill-Franzen, 1989; Slavin, Madden, Karweit, Livermon, & Dolan, 1990; Pogrow, 1993; Wang, Walberg, & Reynolds, 1992) who often focus on the specifics of classroom practice in urban schools. Their analyses have overtly compared the dynamics of special education and Chapter 1 pullout programming in terms of curricular and instructional practices or have developed alternatives that specifically include children in both programs.

Others who are also interested in curricular and instructional reform, and specifically the promise of cognitive psychology to transform education, tend to talk more generally of children who are "at risk" or "disadvantaged," and specify Chapter 1, and not special education, as the focal point for both criticism and reform (see, for example, Means, Chelemer, & Knapp, 1991). Although there seems to be an implicit understanding that the exemplary suggestions for reform in teaching and learning brought together, for example, by Means et al. (1991) are meant to apply broadly to disadvantaged students as well as students labeled as learning disabled, the specific parallels are only rarely alluded to in the various programs described (e.g., Bryson & Scardamalia, 1991; Palincsar & Klenk, 1991). It may be the case that the similarities are so apparent to researchers who offer such alternatives that explicit reference to Chapter 1 and special education as twin focal points of their reform proposals does not seem warranted. But in the absence of such explicit commentary, we cannot be certain of the importance that may be attached to this crucial link, especially when policy options are under consideration. Despite the general tendency to think of these programs as exclusive of one another, the similarity between special education for children with mild disabilities and Chapter 1 in terms of instruction, curriculum, and demographics is unmistakable.

Similarities in Curriculum and Instruction

In both programs, teachers and administrators generally expect special teachers to shore up students' basic skills so they can speedily return to their classrooms with greater success. Both Chapter 1 and special education are based on the practice of pulling students out in small groups that remain together for the entire year, students who have been identified in a variety of ways and who, for the most part, remain so identified throughout their school experience. Because individual students are usually pulled out for part of the day on an ongoing basis throughout the year, children in both programs regularly go through school as a disjointed social experience. They function as a sort of permanent underclass in school; everyone knows who they are because they are typically the only ones who see the special teachers, teachers who in general do not work with other students. The same dynamic may apply to students in bilingual education or English as a Second Language (ESL) programs depending on their structure. So although the criteria for program entry differ as described above, the mechanisms are similar in that once identified, students are rarely ever "unidentified" as no longer needing one or the other service. As a result, special education for children labeled as having mild disabilities and Chapter 1 both function as de facto forms of tracking.

Due to the difficulty of coordinating classroom schedules, students cannot always be pulled out of their regular school classes for the same subjects in which they are to receive instruction in their special classes. Therefore it is not uncommon for students to miss content area subjects like social studies or science to attend their special classes, or to stay in their regular classrooms for reading even though they cannot keep pace with their peers during those times.

To complicate matters further, the instructional approaches used in special education and Chapter 1 classes—even in the face of similar curriculum goals—are often different from those used in regular classrooms (Allington & Johnston, 1989). Although on the surface this seems reasonable because students are seen as requiring approaches that differ from the regular programs in which they have already failed, the reason for these disparities is not always clear to the students who are already having difficulty making sense of school.

In terms of curriculum, in special education classes for students with mild disabilities and Chapter 1 alike, the focus has traditionally been on instruction in basic, low-level skills in reading, language, and mathematics (Commission on Chapter 1, 1992; McGill-Franzen & Allington, 1991; Means et al., 1991; National Association of State Boards of Education, 1992). This approach is based on the philosophy that only when basic skills are firmly in place will children have the tools to deal with higher level content. Children may read controlled vocabulary books, they may work entirely on skills using worksheets for drill, they may learn only phonics and no other strategies for reading. Unfortunately, many urban schools follow a similar low-level curriculum for all of their students (Carlson, 1989; Commission on Chapter 1, 1992). In curricula such as these, basic skills are most often taught separately from naturally motivating content and from the background knowledge students bring to school, and many children are never exposed to higher level content at all.

The irony of taking such a narrow view of the curriculum is, of course, that students who have demonstrated that they are having difficulty with the standard curriculum and may lack motivation for the regular activities of schooling are expected to be motivated to learn what may be even less interesting material taught in a more repetitive and content-free fashion. In addition, they are expected to learn this low-level content separate from their regular education classroom peers. The irony is even more poignant in the face of special education requirements for developing an Individualized Education Program (IEP) for each child identified as having a disability. Despite the existence of the IEP requirement, which ostensibly guarantees curricular differentiation to meet individual needs, studies of these documents for students in mild categories of disability note the failure of special education to provide truly individualized instruction (Wesson & Deno, 1989). Observational studies also attest to the lack of instructional differentiation among categories and between special and general education (Ysseldyke, O'Sullivan, Thurlow, & Christenson, 1989). The IEP has become, in essence, a bureaucratic requirement, often completed using a computerized bank of goals and objectives and little real curriculum adaptation. In the Wehlage et al. (1992) study of urban school reform, the only aspect of special education mentioned was the adoption of an IEP-like document called an Individual Success Plan for each at-risk student in two of the middle schools included in the study. No such individual plan is required for students receiving Chapter 1 services. But whether the plan is required or not, curriculum and instructional practices do not seem to differ and cannot be defended as meeting individual needs in either program.

Current Chapter 1 policies now sanction experiments with moving away from the need to identify specific children in each school. In schools with a 75% incidence of poverty, it is now possible to create and implement schoolwide Chapter 1 projects that have the potential to contribute to the improvement of the entire educational program across the school. However, despite this loosening of regulations, most Chapter 1 programs still continue to operate on the small group remedial model of service delivery, in which students are identified individually and pulled out for instruction (Herrington & Orland, 1992), as in special education.

Demographic Similarities

In theory, Chapter 1 and special education are designed to serve different populations. Chapter 1 programs necessarily serve large numbers of urban minority students considered to be at risk for school failure; it is precisely these students that the program targets. On the other hand, the demographics of special education ought to reflect the real incidence of disability across all racial and ethnic groups. But despite these intended differences, a persistent awareness exists—however unwilling the field of special education may be to discuss it—that something is amiss with the demographics of disability that has resulted in the populations of Chapter 1 and special education being more alike than different.

The issue of minority representation—and overrepresentation—in the ranks of children identified as having disabilities is conspicuous in its absence from the reform literature in special education that has dominated the field for the past decade. Within these proposals for reform, the question of minority students in special education is simply not a popular topic. *The Fourteenth Annual Report to Congress on the Implementation of the Individuals With Disabilities Act* (U.S. Department of Education, 1992) states rather dispassionately that "the proportion of youth with disabilities who are black is higher than the general population of youth" (p. 48); one explanation offered by the authors is that "some observers believe that . . . school professionals may be more likely to refer children from racial minorities for special education placement, because of lower expectations regarding their skills and abilities" (p. 48). This same report offers no explanation for its observation that Hispanics are underrepresented nationally. In a highly unusual and little publicized survey, the Arkansas Department of Education (1991, April) documented that only seven states had any kind of procedure for "red-flagging" districts having an overrepresentation of minority students in special education; only one state had actually developed rules and regulations to address the disparity. It is interesting to observe that over a decade ago, a thorough and well-balanced analysis of the overrepresentation of minority students in classes for the educable mentally retarded (Heller, Holtzman, & Messick, 1982) identified nearly all of the now commonplace arguments regarding how this problem might best be addressed. Yet the report did not spur a great deal of activity in the field.

Although the overrepresentation of minorities in special education is only sporadically addressed in the professional literature (see for example, Chinn & Hughes, 1987; Harry, 1992; Hilliard, 1992), it is addressed with relative regularity in the popular press regarding urban and suburban schools alike. For example, a report of reform in a middle school in Philadelphia includes the following statement:

> Nearly one-fourth of Stetson's students today are classified as needing special education—well more than twice the national average but a number not unusual for Philadelphia middle and high schools. Every single one is in that amorphous, ill-defined category of "mildly handicapped," which in the inner city more often means handicapped by poverty than by a physiological learning disability. (Mezzacappa, 1993, p. 4)

The situation seems similar in New York City, where the *New York Times* ("Guiding Students to Failure," 1992) reports that 75% of all special education students in the New York City schools also fall into the "amorphous" categories of learning disabilities and emotional disturbance. Further, in New York City a disproportionate number of Hispanic students appear to be enrolled in classes for learning disabilities (in contrast to national statistics), and African American students in classes for emotional disturbance. In Chicago during the 1990-1991 school year, "Blacks made up 58 percent of total school enrollment but 77 percent of enrollment in classes for children who are educable mentally handicapped (EMH)" (Cattau, 1992, p. 4). In suburban schools the problem manifests itself when greater and greater student diversity begins to characterize formerly homogeneous schools; it is not uncommon to find high proportions of minority students funneled into special education classes in changing demographic situations (Schemo, 1992). Of the inconsistency regarding the special education placement of students with linguistic diversity, Cloud (1993) states that "in the end, over- and under-referral of CLD [culturally and linguistically diverse] students can be viewed as two sides of the same problem: a lack of responsiveness of the programs we offer to the needs of CLD youngsters both outside of and within special education" (p. 68).

One interpretation of the all too common phenomenon of over-representation, apparently the one to which special education as a field subscribes, is that it is probably better for minority students so identified to be in special education than not, because at least special education offers the advantage of personal attention, individually designed instruction, and small classes. However, the data on recurring problems with instructional organization and delivery and on the narrow focus of the curriculum would suggest that this argument is not defensible. Further, there is beginning to be evidence that when an intellectually challenging curriculum is offered, a decrease in behavior problems seems to occur (Collins, Hawkins, & Carver, 1991; Palincsar & Klenk, 1991), suggesting that difficulties attributed to the existence of emotional disturbance may be capable of being overcome through careful curricular and instructional reform. These observations have obvious implications for the demographics of classes for students with behavior problems.

It is difficult to understand why the field of special education, which prides itself on its commitment to the individual and on meeting individual needs, seems unwilling to pay more attention to the degree to which individual minority students, by their collective overrepresentation, are being inappropriately served. This omission is even more significant in the face of several recent reports that refer to the alarming shortage of special education teachers (Hales & Carlson, 1992; Task Force on a National Personnel Agenda for Special Education and Related Services, 1992; U.S. Department of Education, 1992). Although some viable reasons for this shortage are raised in the literature, for example, the general need for more teachers in all fields across the profession (Singer, 1992), or increased numbers of children with special medical needs (Task Force, 1992), the assumption upon which the overall personnel "crisis" is based is that all children labeled as having disabilities are in fact properly identified. The increased need for special education teachers in inner-city schools is cited as one important factor (Simpson, Whelan, & Zabel, 1993), usually because of the high proportion of teachers who are not properly certified in the categories of disability in which they are teaching. In many urban areas the majority of special education teachers with temporary, provisional licenses are working in the field of emotional disturbance, a category that enrolls a disproportionately high number of minority students, and particularly African American males. What is not raised in the context of these increasingly frequent references to the critical shortage of special education teachers is that one explanation for the shortage is the overrepresentation of minority students, especially in categories like emotional disturbance.

Special education has begun to acknowledge the problem in only the most indirect manner. This acknowledgment appears as special educators are called upon to consider serving both students labeled as having mild disabilities and those considered to be generally "at risk" for a school failure (see Will, 1986). In linking special education and the education of children at risk, however, there has still been no *explicit* discussion of the degree to which minority students are consistently overrepresented in categories of mild disability as one reason for making the linkage in the first place. Nor has there been enough recognition at the level of special education policy that the field has quietly acquiesced to becoming a place to house minority children in schools, and particularly in urban schools. The larger question, of course, is whether this is how the educational establishment—and, more important, the democracy—wishes to respond to the question of how to educate minority students in urban schools, students whose problems stem less from the existence of real disabilities than from a dysfunctional societal context, poverty, or the need for bilingual or ESL programming.

Where Do Chapter 1 and Special Education Diverge?

If the majority of special education programs in urban schools include primarily minority children of low socioeconomic status, and if programmatic structure, curriculum, and instructional practices parallel what occurs in Chapter 1, then do these two programs diverge at all? Should they universally be treated as one when the reform of urban education is considered? Despite the similarities that characterize the majority of students served by these programs, some differences do in fact exist, differences stemming from their unique origins.

The critical distinction that needs to be made is between the dominant group of students in special education whose school experiences closely parallel those of children in Chapter 1 programs and who fall into the large proportion of students labeled as having mild disabilities, and students in low-incidence categories whose disabilities are more enduring in character. The concept of enduring disabilities would include, for example, students with hearing, vision, or physical impairments, with severe and profound disabilities, with severe emotional disorders, with moderate to severe cognitive disabilities, or with multiple disabilities—students who may or may not require intensive academic instruction but who certainly will need some type of accommodation to be educated successfully with their nondisabled peers. Students with sensory or physical disabilities whose cognitive capacity is not impaired require some form of adaptation for purposes of communication and/or mobility. Barring new technologies, the need for such adaptations does not usually change over time. The needs of students with severe and profound disabilities clearly diverge from the intentions of the standard academic curriculum (Pugach & Warger, 1993). Additionally, students with severe emotional problems—as differentiated from students with milder school conduct problems, who are counted in the category "serious emotional disturbance" for funding purposes—may require intensive psychological interventions.

So no matter how ideal our general education programs may become, students in these low-incidence categories will almost always need some specialized assistance and special teacher expertise in school. It is these students for whom well-defined special education services are needed and will probably always be drawn upon in some form; their difficulties are not going to be "cured" (Forest & Pearpoint, 1992). It is also the case that students in these categories have probably benefited most from the passage of Public Law 94-142 in 1975 and its successor legislation, the Individuals with Disabilities Education Act, because it is they who, as a result of this legislation, have been able to leave segregated schools and institutions and begun to participate as peers in schools and in society. The ongoing need for these services to be available should not be confused with the question of where they are delivered; students do not always need to be educated in segregated classrooms or facilities to be educated successfully.

Noteworthy in regard to this discussion is the fact that the total number of students with low-incidence disabilities, namely, those in the categories of hearing, visual, orthopedic and other health impairments, deaf-blind, and multiple disabilities, together constitute only approximately 287,000 children, or approximately 7% of students served in special education (U.S. Department of Education, 1992). Although the percentage of those with enduring disabilities would be slightly higher because students in the categories of mental retardation and serious emotional disturbance span the range of mild to severe disabilities, and those with severe problems would continue to need services, nevertheless the percentage of students with clearly identifiable disabilities would be far smaller than the entire population of students now labeled as having disabilities.

We have a situation, then, in which there are marked similarities between populations of urban students who receive Chapter 1 and those who receive special education for students with mild disabilities. These services are generally recognized as being weak in their capacity to improve students' chances for school success and thus life success. At the same time, a smaller population also exists for whom special assistance is clearly justifiable in terms of what we traditionally think of as special education services, children for whom the challenge is to provide those services in the context of general education.

This distinction should not be interpreted to mean that the nearly 10 million children who now receive Chapter 1 and special education services in the mild categories do not need some form of special assistance to be successful in school. On the contrary, it is evident that in urban schools, the combination of school structure and traditional curricular and instructional policies and practices interacts with students' challenging life circumstances to create a situation where urban children often have a much harder time achieving success in school, making some form of individualized academic help critical. In fact, in Slavin et al.'s (1990) summary on the first year of the Success for All program in an inner-city school in Baltimore, it was reported that 22% of students from kindergarten through third grade required special assistance in the form of individual tutoring in reading; at the first-grade level alone, the figure jumped to 40%. That help is warranted is not at issue. The question is, what kind?

The Policy Challenge for Urban Schools

To date, the only institutionalized programs to provide special assistance that we have developed in American schools, of which Chapter 1 and special education collectively represent the largest and most well used, place students in what is effectively a lower academic track, with all its attendant characteristics (see Oakes, 1985). They represent a discontinuity with the general program of instruction. As such, students are penalized for requiring—and receiving—assistance purported to help them succeed in school. Moreover, by opting for policy options that institutionalize pullout programs characterized by narrow curricula, low levels of interest, and permanently lower student status, the educational establishment has bypassed the regular classroom as the locus of a child's life in school. This social phenomenon occurs even though children who receive Chapter 1 and special education services do in fact spend a fair amount of time in regular classrooms.

As a result, schools have institutionalized a low level of tolerance for difference by making it easy for even minor differences to be seen as major personal deficits, and no other real options exist in the traditional educational policy environment of schools for helping individual students. Because of this policy choice, our compensatory and special education practices not only have failed to meet students' individual academic and behavioral needs but also have lacked the capacity and power to preserve children's sense of belonging to a community of peers in school.

The special circumstances and pressures of urban schools lead to unmistakable conclusions about the role these programs play in the life of a school, and, as is typically the case, it is in urban schools that the problem exists in the extreme and we can see it most clearly. Because of the pressure that operates in practically all urban schools, special education programs in mild disabilities and Chapter 1 function as a safety valve for students and teachers alike, providing at the least a small class atmosphere.

Any reform proposal, no matter what its point of origin, must grapple with the appropriateness of the general curriculum and the degree to which the system itself is failing to meet students' needs. If, on the other hand, needing individual assistance has become the norm in our schools, then reform must also lead to designing and providing for such assistance *in the context of a healthy community of learners* and as a routine part of educational practice. But just as Chapter 1 and special education have distinct programmatic and philosophical origins, the proposals for reforming them that have appeared in the past few years emanate from different perspectives. These recommendations for policy reform have proceeded largely in isolation and as parallel activities. As we deliberate on the reform of urban education policy, the relationship between such proposals can inform the policy options we choose to implement.

Inclusion as Urban Reform Strategy?

Driving reform efforts across special education as a whole is a commitment to the concept of *inclusion.* Like its predecessor concept, mainstreaming, *inclusion* refers to a preference for locating the education of children with disabilities within the regular education environment. But unlike mainstreaming, which in practice has evolved such that children shuttle back and forth between special and general education, inclusion is principally focused on finding the means to support the majority of—if not all—students with disabilities in their home schools in regular classrooms with the appropriate curricular, instructional, social, and personal support to make such integration possible. Although special educators are not in agreement regarding whether all children with disabilities should be fully integrated into general education classes, and although some have called for a complete merger of special and general education (Gartner & Lipsky, 1987; Stainback & Stainback, 1984), there does seem to be agreement that inclusion represents a wise and ethical trend.

Urban school systems have shown varying degrees of commitment to the goal of inclusion. For example, at the district level the Milwaukee Public Schools provides leadership by supporting a group of consulting teachers who are responsible for providing technical expertise for inclusion efforts across the district and across categories of disability (Milwaukee Public Schools, 1991); they also link staff and schools at varying levels of development in their integration efforts. Conversely, in Chicago, despite efforts of individual schools, inclusion has been met with much caution (Cattau, 1992).

But inclusion is not a unitary concept and has a different meaning depending upon whether one is talking about students with mild disabilities or students with sensory, severe, or multiple disabilities. For students with severe disabilities, inclusion represents the opportunity to take part in the common community of schooling, with the overriding goal being social integration. For those with sensory disabilities, it means the opportunity to participate in school with the accommodations necessary to make such participation possible. Stemming from a philosophical and political commitment to these goals as a fundamental human right for students so identified, inclusion has been rather heartily embraced (Sailor, 1991). Not coincidentally, inclusion from this perspective does not place much pressure on educators to make fundamental changes in the academic curriculum. This is the case because, for students with severe disabilities, mastering the academic curriculum is not the goal; for students with sensory disabilities, accessing whatever the prevailing academic curriculum is constitutes the goal (Pugach & Warger, 1993). But the practice of inclusion does place great expectations upon special and general education teachers to work collaboratively to enable children with sensory or severe disabilities to be successful in the general classroom environment.

What does the concept of inclusion mean for students with mild disabilities who in urban schools are primarily disadvantaged minority students? The dominant policy shift is the degree to which special and general education teachers are encouraged to collaborate to deliver appropriate instruction within the regular classroom environment. Collaboration can take the form of periodic consultative interactions between special and general education teachers, team problem solving, or more permanent arrangements for team teaching. In this framework, the greater the degree of collaboration, the more likely it will be that special education teachers will be able to serve not only children labeled as having mild disabilities but also the larger population of children deemed to be at risk for school failure. In other words, inclusion for mildly disabled populations is based on the assumption that few, if any, definable differences exist in what teachers may provide for students with mild disabilities and those who are generally thought to be at risk. It is also based on the belief, emanating from the goal of inclusion for low-incidence disability categories, that the school as a whole ought to take responsibility for all of the students who attend, and especially for students with disabilities (Sailor, 1991).

What remains unclear in terms of the inclusion agenda for mild disabilities is identifying the best instructional approach to respond to the school problems of this expanded group, a group that is now squarely meant to include Chapter 1 students and others who are having difficulty in school. On the one hand, many special educators are calling for broad-based fundamental reform in curriculum and instruction that will improve the quality of schooling for all students, among them students with disabilities (Palincsar & Klenk, 1991; Pugach & Warger, 1993; Sailor, 1991). These reform proposals are often grounded in an appreciation for constructivism and its potential for shifting the focus of education from children's deficits to the capacities upon which teachers can build. Implicitly (and sometimes explicitly) they also tend to be grounded in the belief that significant improvements in the general quality of schooling are the best way to overcome the faulty distinctions between students that have been constructed in the name of special education.

For those who advocate a schoolwide reform approach, increased collaboration between special and general education teachers has the potential to provide the human resources teachers will need to support each other as they experiment with alternative approaches to curriculum and instruction (Pugach & Wesson, in press). But despite the trend toward greater teacher collaboration and the potential for schoolwide reform, the content of these collaborative professional interactions still remains focused largely on student, rather than curricular or systemic, deficits (Warger & Pugach, 1993), creating the possibility for continued reliance on traditional approaches to remediation.

That is, the near universal acceptance of collaboration as a new philosophy for the conduct of special education for mild disabilities does not necessarily mean that special educators will be interested in changing the content and process of their teaching; the investment in traditional skill-based and behavioral models of instruction and intervention is substantial and has dominated for decades. Further, at the same time that special education is trying to overcome the problems created by these mild disability categories through practices like collaboration, others are pressuring special education to increase traditional services for new categories of mild disability—for example, to develop programs for children with attention deficit disorders (Viadero, 1993). If inclusion is to be successful as a reform strategy for students now labeled as having mild disabilities in urban schools, what goes on in general education must change in a manner that both captures the interest and builds on the capacities of the children it serves. This will necessitate a major shift in how special educators think about curriculum, instruction, and service delivery; anything less will seriously diminish the promise of inclusion.

In addition to the broad-based changes required to develop a general model of schooling that includes the disproportionately large number of minority students now in special education, new policies must also take into account the ongoing needs of the smaller numbers of children with low-incidence disabilities, those for whom identifiable services need to be protected until such time as society, and the schools, fully accept them and provide for their needs as a routine responsibility. This represents a serious challenge for policy makers and needs to be accomplished in a manner that ensures that the system cannot be misused to segregate minority students in the name of disability.

Inclusion and Chapter 1 Reform as the Same Agenda?

To the extent that a real commitment to schoolwide and system-wide reform in curriculum and instruction is part of special education's goal of inclusion, that agenda can converge well with efforts to shift the structure of Chapter 1 services so that schoolwide programming can occur. Developing schoolwide plans for Chapter 1 provides the opportunity to overcome problems with instructional fragmentation as well as the unnecessary isolation of students (Herrington & Orland, 1992). To permit such changes in Chapter 1 and special education, it will be necessary to shift away from a child-by-child means of identification to one in which programs are supported. The practice of schoolwide programming in Chapter 1 supports this shift, but no such flexibility is currently permitted under special education legislation. As a result, the impact of local and school-specific efforts to reform special education practice is usually only felt within specific classrooms, and not schoolwide.

Rotberg (1993) reminds us that "permitting schoolwide projects is not the same as funding them adequately" (p. 13). From this perspective it makes sense for reforms to progress not as parallel activities, but rather in a completely integrated manner, drawing on the resources of special and compensatory education alike to accomplish fundamental change in the quality of teaching and learning, with a focus on the belief that children in urban schools are fully capable of learning and being challenged at a high intellectual level in school. Working from a unified framework has the potential to reduce the effect of having multiple categorical projects operating at odds with each other, a situation that is most commonly found in urban schools (Rotberg, 1993).

For urban schools, this pooling of resources means that a significant cadre of special education and Chapter 1 teachers would be freed up to work in a variety of alternative teaching capacities. How those teaching functions are conceptualized and implemented is the unknown factor in terms of how successful schoolwide reform might be. With regard to Chapter 1 schoolwide plans and inclusion alike, one prevailing assumption seems to be that individual assistance will rarely need to be provided to students now considered to be at risk/mildly disabled because the quality of the general education program will undergo such extensive improvements that all students will be successful (see Pogrow, 1993). A second assumption is that should individual assistance be needed, it is acceptable only when offered within the physical space of the regular classroom.

There is little disagreement that the best and most wide-reaching strategy for improving education for students in urban schools is to make the radical changes that are needed to create motivating and challenging programs of general education, based on projects that make sense to students and enable them to build on the natural skills and talents they bring to school (Collins et al., 1991). But to make the assumption that as a result of these changes no student will need individual or small group assistance, or worse, that such assistance may somehow be taboo, seems to be a simplistic reaction to problems with traditional pullout models of remedial education.

Rethinking Special Assistance as Inclusion in Restructured Urban Schools

The challenge for those who are committed to restructuring urban education such that all children receive the educational assistance they need is to create a school culture in which providing for the varying needs of individual students is not an appendage to general education but rather an integral part—and expectation—of the general education process. Within schools and classrooms, we need to build an understanding that getting special help is not so unusual, that all of us can probably benefit from special help at one time or another in our school careers, that there is great value to be placed on both giving and receiving such assistance, and, most important, that for any given academic situation, different children are likely to need help for different reasons. From this perspective, the psychological context for receiving help—whenever it is needed—can be squarely located within the community of the regular classroom, with the peer group as the reference point (Pugach & Wesson, in press).

A good example of a systemwide approach to meeting the needs of a challenging population comes from bilingual education in the Calexico, California, schools (Schmidt, 1993). To better serve its primarily Mexican American population, bilingual methods have been integrated throughout the district's curriculum; few distinctions now exist between bilingual education and the general curriculum. According to its administrators, the district is successful "because it does not rely on any one program to get the job done, but instead has focused the attention of its entire school system on the education of L.E.P. [Limited English Proficiency] students, bringing almost every teacher on board" (p. 6). In this situation, schools as a whole were committed to finding the most effective ways of working with all of their students, even if it meant a substantial shift in method or curriculum. In this way, a situation that seemed unusual became the norm.

This is precisely the lesson that the philosophy of inclusion in special education means to teach: that variation ought to be acceptable because it is natural, and that it is the responsibility of the school to develop the capacity to deal with this variation schoolwide among staff, students, and families alike. For students with severe and profound disabilities or sensory disabilities, the help required will extend throughout their school careers. With respect to children who have traditionally been served in Chapter 1 or special education for mild disabilities, what needs to be broken to make this philosophy work is the pernicious pattern in which a group of children are identified early in their school careers as needing academic assistance and form a permanently stigmatized pullout group distinct from their peers. Then we need to make sure that what goes on in the name of special assistance really does give children what they need— namely, a high quality of instruction that enables them to be successful in school. Only if both of these criteria are in place should we feel confident in providing individual and small group assistance in urban schools.

But the first line of responsibility for reshaping the educational lives of urban students who have formerly been in Chapter 1 or special education is to provide a schoolwide program of instruction that allows the general school population to (a) feel that school is an important place to spend time, (b) become motivated learners, and (c) succeed. Until opportunities have been made to see how children whom everyone has considered to be at risk or to have a disability fare when they are treated as competent learners capable of dealing with high-level material as a routine part of schooling, it is not possible to know with conviction who will need what kind of special assistance. Chapter 1 and special education students need the chance to shed their inappropriate labels and be included in the first place. Preliminary reports are cause for optimism; when students are permitted to participate in this type of challenging educational programming, their problems begin to dissipate (Collins et al., 1991; Palincsar & Klenk, 1991). Other evidence suggests that when learning-disabled students are teamed with their general education peers on a permanent basis, their teachers do not perceive the differences between them to be salient (Pugach & Wesson, in press). Finally, when general school reorganization occurs with a focus on prevention, as in the Success for All program, a high rate of reduction in referrals to special education can be expected (Slavin et al., 1990).

These trends are important because they provide urban teachers with examples of academic success for students who have been in Chapter 1 and special education. Changing curriculum and accompanying instructional practices will only be effective to the extent that teachers are willing to believe in the capacity of formerly low-achieving minority students in troubled inner-city schools to succeed. If the philosophy of inclusion is to be maximally relevant to the reform of Chapter 1 and special education, it also must include explicit reference to issues of race and ethnicity and extend to an understanding of the persistently low expectations that have been held for minority students in the name of these programs. For most urban teachers, the shift to programs that are motivating and challenging will be precisely the change for which they have been waiting. Others, unfortunately, may hang on to the beliefs that enabled them to accept lowered expectations to begin with. In planning professional development activities for teachers to support proposed changes, it will be essential to pay careful attention to those teachers who may resist change and the reasons for their resistance.

Appropriate Conceptions of Pullout Programming

In the face of the failure of special education and Chapter 1, why is it so critical to establish a culture that permits individual and small-group assistance as an integral part of school? Paired with the ethical responsibility for teachers to model acceptance of difference is the increasing evidence that some of the most powerful educational interventions available require implementation with individual students or in small groups. In the Success for All program, for example, individual reading tutoring is an integral part of the instructional model (Madden, Slavin, Karweit, Dolan, & Wasik, 1993), serving nearly a quarter of the students. Reading Recovery (Pinnell, 1989), which is based on a fundamental recognition of the capacities children bring to the task of learning to read, also requires intensive one-to-one tutoring on a daily basis. Reciprocal Teaching (Palincsar & Brown, 1984) requires small group dialogue in which teachers coach students in the development of reading comprehension.

Further, other studies are documenting the value of flexible grouping within the context of the whole class. Mason and Good (1993) used the concept of "situational adjustment" to form small, ad hoc teaching groups in mathematics that change membership depending on the particular material being covered. Similarly, Pugach and Wesson (in press) documented the use of flexible grouping techniques in a team-teaching situation made up of two fifth-grade teachers and one learning disabilities teacher that included as permanent members of these two classrooms all fifth-grade students labeled as learning disabled. In both of these studies, flexible grouping was used for remediation and enrichment alike; learning-disabled students in the integrated special education/general education team did not see themselves as being stigmatized for participating in such groups, despite the fact that groups often met in a separate room adjacent to the regular classes (Pugach & Wesson, in press). Such ad hoc grouping becomes most feasible when additional teachers are available to provide it, and the teaching resources now associated with Chapter 1 and special education provide a natural place to find them. This shift is not feasible if students who formerly received such services are simply "dumped" back into general education classes with inadequate planning and professional development for teachers (NASBE, 1992). Such change will only be successful insofar as teachers themselves honor the principle of professional collaboration in working together and model the philosophy of inclusion that should drive any special instruction provided in schools.

Given these precedents, it seems apparent that only if programs can meet the dual criteria of (a) being embedded in a healthy social classroom community in which children are not stigmatized for receiving help and (b) providing high-quality instruction with highly skilled teachers is it appropriate to have children "pulled out" for specific purposes. Sometimes those services might be for students with low-incidence disabilities; mostly they will be for providing the various kinds of academic support that should become a natural part of the educational process. But past practice should serve as a caveat regarding too quick a shift to "new and improved" pullout programs; it is simply too easy to fall into old patterns of behavior, and vigilance will be required. If the criterion of social belonging is violated, it will be difficult to capture the interest of students, no matter how appropriate the special assistance they may be given.

The Promise of Reform

For children in urban schools, the urgency of reform cannot be overstated. The attention that is currently being paid to Chapter 1 and special education places these programs in a position to exert leadership in that reform. But the full power of their influence can only be felt if these reforms proceed as joint efforts. The common point of departure ought to be overcoming precisely what has been most problematic across Chapter 1 and special education: the unintended victimization of minority children whose precarious school careers have been further fragmented as a result of participating in these special programs.

But it will only be possible to achieve this goal if both sources of victimization are addressed simultaneously, that is, the quality of the general education program and the way special assistance is designed and delivered in the context of that program. Changes in both must be intertwined if the principal problem—namely, the traditional reluctance to acknowledge natural variation in learning within general education—is to be addressed.

The reform that is contemplated is tricky politically because it encourages moving away from categorical funding driven by a seemingly well-defined deficit model of remediation. The categorical model may be easier for legislators to understand; in the case of special education, the target population has the aura of being especially well defined (and part of the special education population is in fact so identifiable). By seeking a means to retain Chapter 1 and the majority of special education funding to improve the overall programs in urban schools, funding functions more as a general financial equalizer (Rotberg, 1993) and not as categorical programming. In addition to this overall goal, it will also be necessary to protect some funds for students in low-incidence disability categories. This places special education at a particular disadvantage because its advocates have to argue simultaneously for (a) continued recognition and (b) a major shift in resource allocation. It is this discontinuous position that is likely at the root of the ambivalence many special educators feel about supporting inclusion as a reform strategy.

But despite the fear that inevitably accompanies a change of such magnitude, there are important lessons to be learned from this long period of unsuccessful experience with traditional pullout programs. Chief among them is that it is all too easy to look the other way when an unfair hand is being dealt to poor minority children in urban schools by virtue of the limited expectations set for their achievement. Aware of their situation, minority children in urban schools can be most articulate about the degree to which their isolation follows them around school. They know school is boring; they don't have the power to change it. While the political battles are being fought regarding funding, there is also a question of what ought to occur in the meantime. At the least, Chapter 1 and special education teachers need to begin developing their capacities to provide the kinds of one-to-one and small group approaches that seem to have the most promise, while working closely with their peer teachers in general education to confront the issue of building a seamless learning community among their students.

Educators probably know more today than ever before about ensuring that all children can learn—no matter what their race, ethnicity, language, or socioeconomic status. Those concerned with correcting the inequities that have resulted from Chapter 1 and special education are in a position to make the kinds of changes needed to demonstrate the depth of that knowledge. All that remains to be seen is whether we have the will to act on that knowledge for the good of the nation's forgotten children, those twice victimized in our urban schools.

Commentaries

In 1965, President Lyndon B. Johnson declared war on poverty. At that time, children in poverty remained a small portion of students in urban schools. Now over one third of the nation's urban children are living below the poverty level. Back in 1965, Title I was introduced to circumscribe the tradition of "local control" as a means of coming up with federal money that would go straight to the students. Yet by the early 1970s, a number of published reports found gross violations in the local use of federal monies, so a number of mandates were issued. Today, the problem of noncompliance has been largely solved but has been replaced with the new problem of labeling. Government programs are categorically based. Added to that is the problematic notion of margins. Disadvantaged kids were once at the margins. In the inner city, marginal kids now make up the majority. Given the new policy challenge, I find the issues addressed in Pugach's paper particularly timely.

*Kenneth K. Wong, Associate Professor of Education,
Department of Education, University of Chicago*

When outside money from a categorical grant program enters a local administrative environment, it can fundamentally alter the incentive structures and program delivery mechanisms of local administrators. Grantees are not the passive recipients of categorical largesse but active "resource mobilizers" who act to "pocket budget" external assistance to serve general administrative and economic ends. How, then, does this work with the two programs on which Dr. Pugach focuses? Special education and Chapter 1 programs are seen by school districts as unique funding "pockets" for serving students with high academic needs. School systems can exercise the greatest economic and administrative efficiency in the use of these monies when they allocate the resources first and then fill in the balance of their program with monies that are less constrained. The trick is to identify those students who can legally "fit" into these budget pockets. The more constrained the general budget, and the greater the level of overall financial and program need, the greater the incentive to "fit" more students. Is it any wonder, then, that large, financially pressed urban schools attempt to place as many children as possible into special education or Chapter 1 designations, and then use other more flexible resources for more general purposes?

Dr. Pugach has done a commendable job of identifying the educational consequences of this structure. Basically, the separation of categorical from general educational services for the disadvantaged greatly increases the likelihood that the disadvantaged will be exposed to a more narrow curriculum, be expected to achieve less than their peers, possess lowered self-esteem, and be unable to receive a coherent coordinated-services delivery arrangement that best meets their needs. Their "access to knowledge" and to the healthy peer and teacher interactions necessary for full educational development is put at risk by these services. In short, what is from a local perspective administratively rational and economically efficient is also educationally dysfunctional.

But if this situation is so bleak, then why have the traditional advocates for these groups so intently rallied for the continuation of these services?

Dr. Pugach hints at an answer that is largely two-fold. First, whatever their limitations, the categorical nature of these programs at least guarantees services to the target populations. Advocacy groups have fought long and hard for such guarantees; they will not give them up lightly, if at all. Second, there has been no sign of a readily apparent coherent alternative to the categorical program structure to serve the needs of these constituencies. Indeed, even many of those admitting the severe limitations of the categorical model are still generally persuaded that their students are better off than they would be if merely placed back into the regular instructional program—and they are probably right.

Pugach advocates new program structures that are based on such concepts as "inclusion" of disadvantaged students in the regular instructional program, high expectations for all students, and systemwide approaches to meeting the needs of the challenging populations through integrated service delivery mechanisms. What she does not address is the question of "How do we get there from here?" What will the incentives be for schools and teachers to "include" the disadvantaged in the regular instructional program, to set challenging performance expectations for them, and to work together in a systematic way to improve their performance? Three critical assumptions about categorical program service delivery must be changed and reflected in revised program provisions if this is to occur: (a) Educational needs of the most disadvantaged students can be met adequately through supplementary basic skills remediation; (b) program oversight and accountability should focus most heavily on ensuring that eligible students are legally served; and (c) the effectiveness of federal aid programs can be judged independently of the regular instructional program.

Standards-based reforms reflected in the administration's recent Elementary and Secondary Education Act (ESEA) proposal appear supportive of these types of fundamental changes in categorical grant mechanisms, at least as they affect Chapter 1; however, this will depend on how the final version of ESEA is structured. At the very least, however, an alternative, more educationally salient model for serving the needs of disadvantaged students now exists. Hopefully, it will forever change the nature of the dialogue around treating students with special educational needs so that they are viewed as fully capable of achieving outstanding academic success.

Martin E. Orland, Acting Executive Director,
National Education Goals Panel

Note

1. At the same time that we face the harsh realities of urban schools with respect to Chapter 1 and special education, it is important to acknowledge that numerous counterexamples exist in urban schools to the problematic situations used to make the arguments in this chapter. There are teachers—in special education, Chapter 1, and in general education alike—who are implementing alternative curriculums and who are working hard to overcome the enormous bureaucratic imperatives under whose shadow they work. There are principals who are moving their schools ahead despite the odds. They are working with parents and family members who are committed to their children's education at every step of the process. I work with such professionals in Milwaukee, I know they exist in countless other cities as well, and I wish to acknowledge their work even as I raise the tough issues associated with Chapter 1 and special education programs as they exist today. Despite their exemplary work, we cannot ignore the policy decisions and climate that have created difficulties for the majority of urban schools. It is to this challenge my analysis is directed.

References

Allington, R. L., & Johnston, P. (1989). Coordination, collaboration, and consistency: The redesign of compensatory and special education interventions. In R. E. Slavin, N. L. Karweit, & N. A. Madden (Eds.), *Effective programs for students at risk* (pp. 320-354). Boston: Allyn & Bacon.

Allington, R. L., & McGill-Franzen, A. (1989). School response to reading failure: Chapter 1 and special education students in grades 2, 4, & 8. *Elementary School Journal, 89,* 529-542.

Arkansas Department of Education. (1991, April). *Survey on overrepresentation of black students in special education.* Unpublished document.

Bryson, M., & Scardamalia, M. (1991). Teaching writing to students at risk for academic failure. In B. Means, C. Chelemer, & M. S. Knapp (Eds.), *Teaching advanced skills to at-risk students* (pp. 141-167). San Francisco: Jossey-Bass.

Carlson, D. L. (1989). Managing the urban school crisis: Recent trends in curricular reform. *Journal of Education, 171*(3), 89-108.

Cattau, D. (1992, March). Special ed changes face stiff opposition. *Catalyst: Voices of Chicago School Reform, 3*(6), 4.

Chinn, P. C., & Hughes, S. (1987). Representation of minority students in special education classes. *Remedial and Special Education, 8*(4), 41-46.

Cibulka, J. G. (1992). Urban education as a field of study: Problems of knowledge and power. In J. G. Cibulka, R. J. Reed, & K. K. Wong (Eds.), *The politics of urban education in the United States: The 1991 yearbook of the Politics of Education Association* (pp. 27-44). Washington, DC: Falmer.

Cloud, N. (1993). Language, culture and disability: Implications for instruction and teacher preparation. *Teacher Education and Special Education, 16*(1), 60-72.

Collins, A., Hawkins, J., & Carver, S. M. (1991). A cognitive apprenticeship for disadvantaged students. In B. Means, C. Chelemer, & M. S. Knapp (Eds.), *Teaching advanced skills to at-risk students: Views from research and practice* (pp. 216-243). San Francisco: Jossey-Bass.

Commission on Chapter 1. (1992, December 10). *Making schools work for children in poverty: A new framework prepared by the Commission on Chapter 1.* Washington, DC: American Association for Higher Education.

Forest, M., & Pearpoint, J. C. (1992). Putting all kids on the MAP. *Educational Leadership, 50*(2), 26-31.

Gartner, A., & Lipsky, D. K. (1987). Beyond special education: Toward a quality system for all students. *Harvard Educational Review, 57,* 367-395.

Guiding students to failure. (1992, August 24). *New York Times,* p. A16.

Hales, R. M., & Carlson, L. B. (1992). *Issues and trends in special education.* Lexington, KY: Federal Resource Center for Special Education.

Harry, B. (1992). Puerto Rican parents' theories of disability. *Exceptional Children, 59,* 27-40.

Heller, K. A., Holtzman, W. H., & Messick, S. (Eds.). (1982). *Placing children in special education: A strategy for equity.* Washington, DC: National Academy Press.

Herrington, C. D., & Orland, M. E. (1992). Politics and federal aid to urban school systems: The case of Chapter 1. In J. G. Cibulka, R. J.

Reed, & K. K. Wong (Eds.), *The politics of urban education in the United States: The 1991 yearbook of the Politics of Education Association* (pp. 167-179). Washington, DC: Falmer.

Hilliard, A. G. (1992). The pitfalls and promises of special education practice. *Exceptional Children, 59,* 168-172.

Madden, N. A., Slavin, R. E., Karweit, N. L., Dolan, L. J., & Wasik, B. A. (1993). Success for all: Longitudinal effects of a restructuring program for inner-city elementary schools. *American Educational Research Journal, 30,* 123-148.

Mason, D. A., & Good, T. L. (1993). Effects of two-group and whole-class teaching on regrouped elementary students' mathematical achievement. *American Educational Research Journal, 30,* 328-360.

McGill-Franzen, A., & Allington, R. L. (1991). The gridlock of low reading achievement: Perspectives on practice and policy. *Remedial and Special Education, 12*(3), 20-30.

McLaughlin, M. J., & Owings, M. F. (1992). Relationships among states' fiscal and demographic data and the implementation of P.L. 94-142. *Exceptional Children, 59,* 247-261.

Means, B., Chelemer, C., & Knapp, M. S. (1991). *Teaching advanced skills to at-risk students: Views from research and practice.* San Francisco: Jossey-Bass.

Means, B., & Knapp, M. S. (1991). Introduction: Rethinking teaching for disadvantaged students. In B. Means, C. Chelemer, & M. S. Knapp (Eds.), *Teaching advanced skills to at-risk students: Views from research and practice* (pp. 1-26). San Francisco: Jossey-Bass.

Mezzacappa, D. (1993, April). Oasis for special students. *High Strides, 5*(2), p. 4.

Milwaukee Public Schools. (1991, Summer). *One at a time, together! An integration program for the 90's.* Milwaukee, WI: Author.

National Association of State Boards of Education. (1992, October). *Winners all: A call for inclusive schools.* Alexandria, VA: Author.

Oakes, J. (1985). *Keeping track: How schools structure inequality.* New Haven, CT: Yale University Press.

O'Neil, J. (1992). On tracking and individual differences: A conversation with Jeannie Oakes. *Educational Leadership, 50*(2), 18-21.

Palincsar, A. S., & Brown, A. L. (1984). Reciprocal teaching of comprehension-fostering and comprehension-monitoring activities. *Cognition and Instruction, 1*(2), 117-175.

Palincsar, A. S., & Klenk, L. J. (1991). Dialogues promoting reading comprehension. In B. Means, C. Chelemer, & M. S. Knapp (Eds.), *Teaching advanced skills to at-risk students: Views from research and practice* (pp. 112-130). San Francisco: Jossey-Bass.

Pinnell, G. S. (1989). Reading recovery: Helping at-risk children learn to read. *Elementary School Journal, 90,* 161-182.

Pogrow, S. (1993, May 26). The forgotten question in the Chapter 1 debate. *Education Week,* pp. 36, 26.

Pugach, M. C., & Wesson, C. L. (in press). Teachers' and students' views of team teaching of general education and learning-disabled students in two fifth-grade classes. *Elementary School Journal.*

Pugach, M. C., & Warger, C. L. (1993). Curriculum considerations. In J. I. Goodlad & T. C. Lovitt (Eds.), *Integrating general and special education* (pp. 125-148). New York: Merrill/Macmillan.

Rotberg, I. C. (1993, February). *Federal policy options for improving the education of low income students* (Congressional Testimony 105). Santa Monica, CA: Rand Corporation.

Sailor, W. (1991). Special education in the restructured school. *Remedial and Special Education, 12*(6), 8-22.

Schemo, D. J. (1992, May 7). Albany says Long Island district steers minorities to special ed. *New York Times,* p. A18.

Schmidt, P. (1993, July 14). Districtwide approach enables border system to defy low expectations for L.E.P. students. *Education Week,* pp. 6-7.

Simpson, R. L., Whelan, R. J., & Zabel, R. H. (1993). Special education personnel preparation in the 21st century: Issues and strategies. *Remedial and Special Education, 14*(2), 7-22.

Singer, J. D. (1992). Are special educators' career paths special? Results from a 13 year longitudinal study. *Exceptional Children, 59,* 262-279.

Slavin, R. E., Madden, N. A., Karweit, N. L., Livermon, B. J., & Dolan, L. (1990). Success for all: First-year outcomes of a comprehensive plan for reforming urban education. *American Educational Research Journal, 27,* 255-278.

Stainback, W., & Stainback, S. (1984). A rationale for the merger of special and regular education. *Exceptional Children, 51,* 102-111.

Task Force on a National Personnel Agenda for Special Education and Related Services. (1992). *Who will teach? Who will serve?* Alexandria, VA: National Clearinghouse on Professions in Special Education.

U.S. Department of Education. (1992). *Fourteenth annual report to Congress on the implementation of the Individuals with Disabilities Act* (Vol. 1). Washington, DC: Author.

Viadero, D. (1993, June 23). Special education. *Education Week*, p. 12.

Wang, M. C., Walberg, J., & Reynolds, M. C. (1992). A scenario for better—not separate—special education. *Educational Leadership, 50*(2), 35-38.

Warger, C. L., & Pugach, M. C. (1993). A curriculum focus for collaboration. *LD Forum, 18*(4), 26-30.

Wehlage, G., Smith, G., & Lipman, P. (1992). Restructuring urban schools: The new futures experience. *American Educational Research Journal, 29,* 51-93.

Wesson, C. L., & Deno, S. L. (1989). An analysis of long term instructional plans in reading for elementary resource room students. *Remedial and Special Education, 10*(1), 21-28.

Will, M. C. (1986, November). *Educating students with learning problems— A shared responsibility.* Washington: U.S. Department of Education, Office of Special Education and Rehabilitative Services.

Ysseldyke, J. E., O'Sullivan, P. J., Thurlow, M. L., & Christenson, S. L. (1989). Qualitative differences in reading and math instruction received by handicapped students. *Remedial and Special Education, 10*(1), 14-20.

Ysseldyke, J. E., Thurlow, M., Graden, J., Wesson, C., Algozzine, B., & Deno, S. (1983). Generalizations from five years of research on assessment and decision making: The University of Minnesota Institute. *Exceptional Education Quarterly, 4*(1), 75-93.

• • • • • •

3

• • • • • •

The Plight of High-Ability Students in Urban Schools

JOSEPH S. RENZULLI

SALLY M. REIS

THOMAS P. HÉBERT

EVA I. DIAZ

In Hartford, Connecticut, Melvin Kardulis, a gifted 17-year-old high school artist and dancer, was walking home from a local video store, having completed an errand for his grandmother. Following a senseless

AUTHORS' NOTE: Research for this chapter was supported under the Javits Act Program (Grant No. R206R00001) as administered by the Office of Educational Research and Improvement, U.S. Department of Education. Grantees undertaking such projects are encouraged to express freely their professional judgment. This chapter, therefore, does not necessarily represent positions or policies of the government, and no official endorsement should be inferred.

exchange of words with another African American teenager, Melvin became the victim of a homicide. The 16-year-old youth who was charged with murder was carrying a gun for protection. The city of Hartford grieved, and the art department in Melvin's school created a multimedia exhibit on inner-city violence entitled "Martin, Malcolm and Melvin" that included a video of Melvin dancing.

It is clear that the plight of high-ability students in urban schools has been largely ignored by policy makers and researchers, for few studies and programs currently exist that focus on these students. It is imperative that a significant portion of our educational resources be invested in those young people who have high potential for making creative contributions to all fields of human endeavor. It is also imperative that opportunities for the development of high potential be extended to the vast number of young people that frequently have been excluded from educational programs for high-ability students because of race, gender, or socioeconomic background. With this agenda as its mission, the Jacob K. Javits Gifted and Talented Students Education Act funded the National Research Center on the Gifted and Talented (NRC/GT) in 1990. The NRC/GT directorate, located at the University of Connecticut, conducted a comprehensive national assessment of research needs in 1990-1991, and the results of the needs assessment served as a basis for creating research projects focusing on the highest priority topics. In response to the paucity of research providing explanations of minority students' underachievement, high-ability students from economically disadvantaged backgrounds were identified as a priority. The study discussed in this chapter addresses an important mission of NRC/GT through an examination of the secondary school experiences of high-ability students in an economically disadvantaged urban environment (Reis, Hébert, & Diaz, in preparation). It also examines differences between high-ability students who achieve and those who underachieve; these differences may enable researchers and practitioners to identify strategies to help all able students realize their potential.

This chapter, about achieving and underachieving students who attend a large urban high school in Hartford, Connecticut, is divided into two parts. The first part reviews previously conducted research about high-ability African American students and Puerto Rican students because these are the two major population groups in Hartford.

The second part explains the Schoolwide Enrichment Model (SEM). This model, developed to serve the unique needs of high-ability students, can also provide enrichment opportunities for all students in the school. The Schoolwide Enrichment Model has been under development at the University of Connecticut for the past 20 years and has been implemented in hundreds of school districts across the country, including several large urban districts.

High-Ability Students in Urban Areas

Too many apathetic students abandon high school each year to begin lives of unemployment, poverty, crime, and psychological distress. According to Hahn (1987, p. 257), "dropout rates ranging from 60 to 65 percent in Boston, Chicago, Los Angeles, Detroit and other major cities point to a situation of crisis proportions." Clifford (1990, p. 22) believes the term *dropout* may not be adequate to convey the disastrous consequences of the abandonment of school by children and adolescents; *educational suicide* may be a far more appropriate label. Clifford argues that school abandonment is not confined to a small percentage of minority students, low-ability children, or the apathetic. It is a systematic failure affecting the most gifted and knowledgeable as well as the disadvantaged, and it is threatening the social, economic, intellectual, industrial, cultural, moral, and psychological well-being of our country.

Demographic changes indicate that one in three Americans will be a person of color by the turn of the century (Banks, 1991; Hyland, 1989), and demographic reports indicate that many urban neighborhoods have become increasingly poor, minority, and non-English speaking. By 1980, 81% of all Blacks and 88% of Hispanics resided in metropolitan areas; 71% and 50%, respectively, lived in the inner cities (U.S. Bureau of the Census, 1980). In a 1991 federal census report, the city of Hartford, Connecticut, reported a population that was 38.9% African American and 31.6% Hispanic (U.S. Bureau of the Census, 1991). Related demographic studies of school-age children in the United States provide information about the graduating class of the year 2000. For example, the Hispanic population, highly concentrated in urban areas, has experienced the most dramatic growth in the last 20 years.

Currently, Hispanics have the highest dropout rate, 36%, of all major population subgroups and are disproportionately represented in a number of school programs. Hispanics constitute only 5% of those children enrolled in gifted programs (Hyland, 1989). At the high school level, Hispanics are invariably underrepresented in the honors, academic, and college-bound tracks and overrepresented in general or vocational programs (Orum, 1986).

African American students also make up a significant percentage of our urban high schools, and their underrepresentation in educational programs for the gifted is a cause for great concern. In 1977, Congresswoman Shirley Chisholm introduced legislation to include funding for gifted and talented minority and culturally different children (Davis & Rimm, 1989). In a keynote address before the National Forum on Minority and Disadvantaged Gifted and Talented, Chisholm (1978) pointed out the failure of our educational system to nurture the talents of gifted disadvantaged students, faulting American education for inadequate methods of recognizing talent among culturally different children. Historical precedents and lack of empirical data on appropriate identification processes and educational planning techniques have been noted as part of the reason for this failure (Baldwin, 1987a). Authorities in gifted education argue that the predominant use of IQ and achievement tests cannot be relied upon to assess the capabilities of this population (Baldwin, 1977; Frasier, 1989; Hilliard, 1976; Torrance, 1971). Many intervening variables such as socioeconomic deprivation and a relative perception of powerlessness should be considered by educators in locating the hidden talents of the Black child (Baldwin, 1987a).

Research on African American High-Ability Students

Research devoted to high-ability African American youth is limited. Ford and Harris (1990) examined the relevant literature on gifted children of color, particularly African American, and discovered that of 4,109 published articles on gifted youth since 1924, less than 2% (75) addressed children of color. The percentage would be even lower if one counted only those articles about gifted and talented African American youngsters. These numbers are disheartening because less information means less understanding about the academic achievement needs of students of color in our urban high schools.

Educators and researchers have, however, reached agreement on some findings regarding barriers to the recognition of and assistance for gifted African American students. For example, the number of African American students identified as gifted remains small. Several factors named as barriers in the identification of African American students include the use of definitions of giftedness that reflect middle class majority culture values and perceptions (Baldwin, 1987b); the use of standardized tests that do not assess the exceptional abilities of children of color (Davis & Rimm, 1989; Ford & Harris, 1990; Kitano & Kirby, 1986, MacMillan, 1982; Richert, Alvino, & McDonnel, 1982); low socioeconomic status attributed to differences in environmental opportunities that enhance intellectual achievement (Baldwin, 1987b; Clark, 1983; Kitano & Kirby, 1986); and cultural differences in the manifestation of gifted behaviors (Baldwin, 1985; Clark, 1983; Davis & Rimm, 1989; Ford & Harris, 1990; Frierson, 1965; Gay, 1978; Kitano & Kirby, 1986; Torrance, 1977). Current identification procedures generally have included some adjustment to accommodate these deviations from middle-class, majority-culture standards, limitations in environmental opportunities, and depressed scores on standardized tests (Frasier, 1989).

Although many researchers and practitioners acknowledge the cultural and economic factors that contribute to African American students' low achievement and marginal performance on majority-culture assessments, African American students continue to lag well behind whites in key measures of academic achievement, including SAT scores, reading proficiency, and college enrollment (Hill, 1990). Social scientists and educators have focused on the lack of success of children of color for generations, yet there is a dearth of research focusing on *achievement* within the African American population. Explaining why some African American students do well in school while others do poorly remains one of the most important and controversial problems in public education today (Cummings, 1977).

Among the many theories advanced to explain variations in the academic performance of African American youngsters, one, in particular, has gained prominence. This theory posits that variations in the quality of family life strongly influence an African American child's school performance. Though this interpretation has gained prominence and popularity among educators, there remains considerable debate over its validity. The body of scholarly literature that focuses on family-based determinants of variations in academic performance is currently known as the cultural deprivation theory.

Educational researchers who investigate the cultural deprivation theory suggest that poor academic performance among students of color can be traced to a basic failure of the socialization process in the home. Early childhood experiences in poverty environments create personality formations that may be adverse to effective achievement in the classroom as well as in all areas of life (Katz, 1969). Generally, this interpretation evolved because some Black children did poorly in school and an assumption was postulated that some aspects of their family life influenced school performance. Black children were depicted as victims of their environment, beginning school careers psychologically, socially, and physically disadvantaged. Researchers believed that these children were oriented to the present rather than to the future, to immediate needs rather than delayed gratification, and to the concrete rather than the abstract. They were believed to be handicapped by limited verbal skills, low self-esteem, and low aspirations (Dolce, 1969). Other scholars elaborated on this position and suggested that mental ability itself was greatly influenced by childhood experiences in the home (Ausubel, 1963; Deutsch & Brown, 1964).

Some evidence exists that seems to document the relationship between socioeconomic status, parental success expectations, parental encouragement to pursue higher education, variations in academic performance, and educational attainment aspirations. Generally, this research indicates that the higher the level of socioeconomic status (SES), the higher the level of parental educational attainment aspirations, and the higher the level of students' educational attainment aspirations as well as actual performance in school (Cummings, 1977). In attempting to explain specifically what it is about socioeconomic status that influences variations in achievement and aspirations, Sewell and Shah (1968) reported that high-SES parents generally not only have higher success expectations but also encourage their children to pursue higher education more frequently than do lower SES parents. Therefore some evidence suggests that the failure of lower SES parents to encourage and support their children's school activities influences their actual school performance.

Among the African American population, however, the data are unclear. Some research findings suggest that orientations toward success among Black parents and children are no different than those held by white parents and children. Other researchers suggest that if differences in achievement orientations do exist, it is only because poor African American parents often accept alternate values that are by-products of sharp contradiction between cultural ideals and the realities of urban life in poverty.

One theory that may provide insight about the underachievement of high-ability urban youth has been posited by John Ogbu (1974, 1985, 1987, 1991). Ogbu, one of the first social scientists to challenge the cultural deprivation theory mentioned above, is the leading proponent of a controversial school of thought. He argues that a critically important difference exists between immigrant minorities, people who have moved to the United States because they seek a better life, and nonimmigrant, or "caste-like," minorities, people whose status in American society is a result of slavery, conquest, or colonization. According to Ogbu, immigrant minorities such as Southeast Asians, Chinese, and Filipinos may face insurmountable barriers once they arrive but tend to see those barriers as temporary. However, caste-like minorities, such as Blacks and Mexican Americans, not only experience discrimination from the dominant white culture but are also caught in a web of inferiority and self-defeat that discourages them from living up to their potential. Caste-like minorities do not regard their situation as temporary because they tend to interpret the discrimination against them as more or less permanent and institutionalized. According to Ogbu's theory (1987), immigrants believe that education is a golden opportunity for advancement, whereas Blacks and other caste-like minorities do not trust the American educational system to educate Black children in the same way it educates white children. Ogbu (1987) believes that the mistrust stems from the exclusion of Blacks from the high-quality education received by whites and that this exclusion has hampered the academic performance of Black children. Ogbu has argued that the cultural models of the two types of minorities—immigrant and involuntary minorities—enter differentially into the process of schooling and that accordingly, school achievement is affected differently. Ogbu did not claim that all immigrant students were successful and all involuntary minorities were academically unsuccessful, but rather described what appear to be dominant patterns for each type.

Ogbu's theories (1974, 1985) have been criticized (Erickson, 1987) because they lack empirical evidence and do not explain the success of many minority students, including "caste-like" minorities. Trueba (1988) believes that Ogbu's typology of minority groups as autonomous, immigrant, or caste-like is unfounded and highly stereotypical. Trueba (1988) states, "Ogbu implies that school success and cultural assimilation (or 'crossing cultural boundaries') go together. Many minorities succeed in school without losing their cultural identity" (p. 274). However, studies that support Ogbu's theories have been conducted recently. Ethnographic research indicated that urban Black youngsters defined academic success as more appropriate for whites. Fordham (1988) and Fordham and Ogbu (1986) examined the concept of racelessness as a factor in the academic achievement of African American high school students in a high school in Washington, D.C., fictitiously called Capital High School. They reported that high-achieving students were more willing to identify with the cultural beliefs and value systems of the dominant culture than less successful students. In Capital High School, Ogbu and Fordham found that "acting white" wasn't merely doing well in school. Instead, it incorporated a variety of attitudes and behaviors, including speaking standard English, listening to white rock and roll music and white radio stations, going to the opera and the ballet, spending a lot of time in the library studying, working hard to get good grades in school, going to the Smithsonian Institution, doing volunteer work, going camping, hiking, or mountain climbing, having a cocktail party, being on time, and reading and writing poetry (Hill, 1990).

Additional studies supported Fordham and Ogbu's findings. A study by Petroni and Hirsch (1970) of Black high school students in a midwestern city illustrated the dilemma of successful minority students. Academically successful Black students at Plains High School stayed away from certain courses and extracurricular activities because of pressure from Black peers. According to Petroni and

Hirsch (1970), African American students who participated in student government, madrigals, and the senior play were likely to be shunned. More recently, Scott-Gregory (1992) reported the peer pressure not to achieve academically was the most discouraging obstacle to success faced by inner-city Black students in Oakland, California. According to Scott-Gregory, the abuse which occurs is similar to that which confronts smart, hard-working students of all colors. The ethic of some Black youth is that education is a pointless endeavor. Those who do not share these feelings, and who work hard in school, often face the ridicule and abuse of their peers.

Through case study research, Gibson (1982) analyzed how competing cultural systems affected students' performance in school. Gibson suggested that students' multiple roles and statuses interacted to influence the academic performance of middle and high school students. Gibson supported Ogbu's theory, finding that students' performance was directly affected by the relationship between the cultural patterns supported by the school and those adhered to by students.

Other social scientists attempted to explain the lack of school success for young people of color by examining social and psychological factors, family and community factors, and educational programmatic factors, and provided a multitude of theories regarding why students of color did not achieve academically (Trueba, 1988). Rabovits and Maehr (1973) investigated differential teacher expectations with respect to students' race and learning ability, finding that Black students, both "gifted" and "nongifted," received less favorable treatment than white students. Ford (1992) examined determinants of underachievement in high-ability Black students in an urban school district, and her findings suggested that psychological factors played the greatest role in underachievement. Her research differed from earlier studies because it examined the perceptions of the students themselves. Ford noted that although psychological theories offered insight to explain some of the problems that contributed to the low achievement levels of minority students, social and cultural issues must be examined.

Gender may have an additional impact on the achievement of high-ability young people. Most of the research reported, however, deals with problems of Black males. A paucity of research exists about Black females, although a study currently in progress suggests that high-ability Black females in urban high schools seldom realize their potential (Reis et al., in preparation). In their research on under-achievement, McCall, Evahn, and Kratzer (1992) supported Ogbu's findings on the cultural peer group affecting urban youngsters when they stated, "In some groups, achievement is seen as sissified for boys, and cultural norms emphasize street smarts, athletics, and survival skills rather than academic knowledge" (p. 32).

Majors and Billson (1992) suggested that the school-related prob-lems of African American males were related to issues of masculinity. According to their theory, African American men learned long ago that the classic American virtues of thrift, perseverance, and hard work did not provide them with the same tangible rewards that accrued to white men. Yet they defined their manhood in similar terms: breadwinner, provider, procreator, and protector. Without the means to adequately fulfill these roles, many became frustrated, impatient, angry, and alienated. To combat these feelings, Black males adopted a "cool pose." A ritualized expression of masculinity, involving behavior, speech, and physical and emotional posturing, suggested distance, irony, and superiority over outsiders, and deliv-ered a message of strength and control. This style created a chasm between the African American males who adopted it and other people in their communities. By acting detached, calm, fearless, aloof, and tough, they shielded themselves from supportive relation-ships. The authors indicated that Black males were more likely than any other cultural group to be recommended for special education classes, classes for the emotionally disturbed, and remedial classes, and to be labeled as mildly mentally handicapped. Some recommen-dations were justified in certain cases, but given the lack of cultural sensitivity of some teachers, counselors, and administrators, these recommendations were considered a form of subtle racism with devastating consequences for African American youth. Subtle racism was also suggested by McCall et al. (1992), who indicated that some teachers refused to take a high test score as a serious sign of academic ability when it was achieved by a student who did not look or act like most academically achieving students. An upper-middle-class student with a discrepancy between ability and performance was viewed as underachieving, but a lower class or culturally different youngster was seen as merely testing well, a situation calling for no special attention or possibly considered a fluke.

Research on High-Ability Puerto Rican Students

There are several different subgroups of Hispanics in America with similar yet sometimes distinctive characteristics. Therefore any literature review on Hispanic youth must account for these distinctions. Researchers of Hispanic students have commonly referred to the following subgroups: Mexican American, Puerto Rican, Cuban, and Central or South Americans. Three subgroups account for more than 80% of the Hispanic population. The largest group, Mexican Americans, accounts for 60.6% of the total. Puerto Ricans make up 15.1%, and Cubans account for 6.1%. Other groups, including Central or South Americans and Hispanic persons identifying themselves as Latino or Hispanic, account for 18.2% (Hyland, 1989). Each of the major subgroups has distinctive characteristics and experiences different degrees of success in American public schools. A point of differentiation among Hispanic Americans concerns regional residency: Mexican Americans reside primarily in California and Texas; Puerto Ricans reside primarily in New York, New Jersey, and other parts of the Northeast; and Cubans reside primarily in Florida (Hyland, 1989). The Hispanic population in the research conducted in Hartford, Connecticut, consists primarily of Puerto Rican youth; therefore this review of literature focuses on this group.

As American citizens since 1917, Puerto Ricans assimilated many of the attitudes and values of American society, yet were reluctant to give up the uniqueness of their own cultural identity. As American citizens, they are free to migrate to the mainland in search of employment, educational opportunities, and a better life for their children. Unfortunately, they are coming at a time when the economy of the country is in decline and when automation has eliminated most of the jobs requiring unskilled laborers. Unable to find permanent employment and establish new roots on the mainland, Puerto Ricans move back and forth from the island to the mainland according to their needs. This mobility affects the family structure and the educational performance of the children (Frenkel, 1992).

Although little research has been conducted on high-ability Puerto Rican students, identifiable family factors exist that foster high achievement among Puerto Rican youth, including parental education, high socioeconomic status, an educational environment at home, and parental involvement (Borges, 1975; Brown, Rosen, Hill, & Olivas, 1980; Torregrosa-Diaz, 1986). Researchers have also identified several factors affecting low achievement within the Puerto Rican population. Fitzpatrick (1987) and De La Rosa and Maw (1990) have found that discordance resulting from differences between mainstream and Puerto Rican cultures, poverty and low socioeconomic status, low parental education, and conflict between parents and children are all determinants of low achievement.

Ambert and Figler (1992) suggest that family life has been one of the greatest sources of strength for Puerto Ricans. For some Puerto Rican families, living in the United States represents a stressful challenge, for it involves the possibility of weakening the highly valued extended family network. Other important cultural and family values may be adversely affected. In a recent research study of 28 Puerto Rican families, Ambert and Figler (1992) found that Puerto Rican families in the United States are distinguished by a strong sense of cultural identity as Puerto Ricans; a strong sense of family membership, with a strong caring element among members of the nuclear family; a desire for more education; and a traditional view of gender roles. These findings supported the well-known Hispanic cultural value referred to as *familismo*, which tends to emphasize interdependence over independence, affiliation over confrontation, and cooperation over competition (Comas-Diaz, 1989; Falicov, 1982). Hispanic families are characterized by their focus on the collective. The needs of the family have greater priority than the needs of the individual.

The priority placed on the family may negatively affect the development of talent in the individual. Perrine (1989) indicated that the "dynamic of families in the Hispanic culture is a vital force and must be considered" (p. 15) in planning the academic experiences of high-ability Hispanic students. Perrine (1989) suggested that plans need to include parents because parental support is a critical factor in determining whether young people's capabilities are valued and nurtured. Perrine (1989) noted several factors, characteristic of the dynamic of Hispanic families, that have the potential to militate against the nurturance of giftedness in school, including family structure, parental view of the educational process, and family view of the general value of education and school success.

Perrine (1989) also indicated that the structure of the Hispanic family is critical with respect to role modeling. Male dominance in the family setting does not encourage a bright youngster's tendency for independent thought and behavior. For example, in a Hispanic family, children are embraced and cared for, but infrequently included in family decisions. Perrine (1989) also noted that due to their limited experience with education, parents of Hispanic students do not perceive participation in "school life" as their domain. Many Hispanic families, whether they have lived in the United States for generations or recently arrived, reflect a different view of parental association with the school and the duties of the teacher than do Anglo American families. Hispanic parents have enormous respect for teachers and do not believe that parents, as nonexperts in education, should make educational decisions. An additional complicating factor is that sometimes a communication problem develops in the parent-child relationship when the parents conduct their lives primarily in Spanish and their children develop a predominant facility in English. As a child matures, less discussion and interaction occurs about issues or decisions a young person faces. The family support system, which was previously important, becomes less valued by the youngster (Perrine, 1989).

Thus an understanding of the needs of Puerto Rican students is predicated upon an understanding of the value system of Hispanic families. Some research has taken this into account: for example, research on how families influence the achievement of their children includes studies of Hispanic families. A study by Soto (1986) investigated the differences on the home environment of higher and lower achieving Puerto Rican children. By using a revised version of the Majoribanks Family Environmental Schedule, Soto found statistically significant differences between the two groups regarding pressure for achievement, concern for the use of English, and parental reinforcement of aspirations. Soto (1986, 1988) found a link between home environment and achievement in school. The families of high achievers made it apparent to their children that reading was enjoyable and important, higher goals were realistic and attainable, and learning and school were important.

Hine (1991) examined several family factors that fostered high achievement among gifted Puerto Rican students. Her findings supported Soto's assertions, but she identified four additional factors that were crucial in nurturing high achievement in Puerto Rican students who had been identified as gifted and who were excelling in school: role models outside the family, outstanding teachers, consistently high teacher expectations, and an intrinsic drive to succeed.

Investigating school and classroom environments provided researchers with a better understanding of why urban youngsters may have academic difficulties. Hispanic youngsters commonly attend schools that are considered poor, highly segregated, and plagued with high dropout rates (Diaz, 1986; Orum, 1986). This type of school environment is not considered conducive to learning, and in these schools, achievement levels were low among Hispanic students. Several research teams (Bryk & Thum, 1989; Espinosa & Ochoa, 1986; Pittman & Haughwout, 1987) suggested that low achievement levels in large, urban, segregated schools were explained in part by the poor school climate and constant discipline problems among teachers and students. A study by Alvarez (1983) investigating the correlates of differential achievement among 98 inner-city Puerto Rican students discovered that school was the major contributor to achievement among low-income Puerto Rican children. Alvarez found that the impact of schools was higher than the impact of family background or personal traits. Ortiz (1988) claimed that Hispanic students were more likely to have poor schooling environments that fostered poor academic performance and were taught by teachers who set low expectation levels for students and perceived Hispanic students as slow learners (Brown et al., 1980; Meléndez, 1978). Such a negative situation was likely to hinder the educational experiences and achievement of Hispanic youth in urban environments.

Walsh (1991) asserted that a mismatch existed between the academic environment and the daily lives of Puerto Rican youngsters. For these students, school had little relation to the rest of their lives. Their learning experiences were perceived as irrelevant and unrewarding, and they developed poor attitudes and low motivation that, in turn, fostered low achievement. Thus they were often at risk of being labeled as "underachievers" or "emotionally disturbed," or as having "behavior problems." According to Passow (1972), one reason for low success among high-ability Hispanic students is that they are usually placed in programs that focus on developing abilities valued by the majority culture. In such programs, Hispanic students have to work twice as hard to succeed, overcoming obstacles of differing value systems, languages, and behaviors and inadequate academic preparation. Perrone and Aleman (1983) contend that children who grow up in minority subcultures have an achievement orientation different from that of children from the dominant culture: Children of color attribute any success to luck and any failure to personal inadequacy, and therefore tend to not believe people who try to convince them of their abilities. As early as 1973, Renzulli indicated that high-potential culturally diverse students from disadvantaged backgrounds were vitally interested in social changes that took place around them in their neighborhoods and in real-world problems in society at large. Renzulli (1973) explained,

> Thus, it is little wonder that they get "turned off" by a curriculum which deals with the exports of Brazil and the names of Columbus' ships when rallies against racism and demonstrations in Washington are the real issues with which they would like to deal. These issues provide excellent opportunities for constructing activities that promote decision making and social leadership skills. Exercises which encourage imaginative solutions to real life problems have a much greater likelihood of promoting creativity than the timeworn chores of writing a story about "what I did last summer." (p. 3)

A Study of Achievers and Underachievers

In a 2-year ethnographic study, Reis et al. (in preparation) examined the high school experiences of high-ability youth in an inner-city high school in Hartford, Connecticut. The major research questions under investigation involved how the needs of high-ability students were met in an urban setting and the factors that distinguished between high-ability youth who achieved and underachieved. Through participant observation, ethnographic interviews, and document review, the researchers attempted to describe the cultural reality of 30 high-ability students who either achieved or underachieved in school. Descriptions of culturally diverse high-ability students who achieved and underachieved have emerged from the study, as well as suggestions for meeting the needs of these high-ability young persons in an urban setting.

Initial findings from this study indicate that numerous differences exist between the young people who achieve and those who underachieve in this urban high school. The high-ability achievers were satisfied with their education and the majority of their teachers. These achievers consistently acknowledged the importance of the honors classes they took at South Central and the appropriate level of challenge within these classes. They especially appreciated "teachers who cared about them" more than teachers who were content specialists. Statements such as the following provide a powerful message to educators: "I wouldn't be here today if it weren't for Coach Brogan," or "Mrs. Lowell always has a room full of kids after school because kids go there for extra help or just to talk to her about anything." The achievers also sought and found numerous support systems including adults who cared about them, multiple extracurricular activities, religious experiences, and help with productive use of time.

The high-ability underachievers had less favorable opinions about their high school experiences, and the following reasons emerged for their underachievement: less appropriate curriculum and courses, lack of support systems, poor use of after-school time, and participation in gang-related activities. They had less sense of self-identity and little belief in themselves when compared with the achievers. The high-ability underachievers had aspirations that were not aligned with their current performance in school. Though they clearly had high ability, there seemed to be confusion or no match at all between their strength areas and their choices for the future. When their talents matched their aspirations, the plan of how to realize the goal was either unrealistic or not being followed.

Current Trends in Gifted Programs

The types of programs for the gifted that have existed over the past several decades are in serious jeopardy. Reasons for the decrease in services, as we have come to know them, have been described in detail in a number of articles (Renzulli & Reis, 1991; Treffinger, 1991; VanTassel-Baska, 1991), and researchers identify two major causes of the cutbacks taking place across the nation. First, the declining economic health of the country has placed all social, educational, and public service programs in severe competition with one another for scarce dollars. Educational programs for students with superior abilities have always received a low priority in the presence of competition with what are perceived to be more pressing needs of the overall educational system. Traditional justifications for gifted programs based on arguments about "the needs of gifted students" and even arguments with economic overtones ("the nation's greatest natural resource") simply don't exert much influence at a time when books such as Jonathan Kozol's *Savage Inequalities* (1991) point out in graphic fashion the plight of vast numbers of at-risk students.

Second, numerous school reform initiatives have called into question many of the practices typically associated with programming for students with high potentials. Ability grouping, advanced classes, and opportunities to pursue advanced content and special interests are viewed as undemocratic by some reform advocates who are heavily invested in achieving greater equity for lower achieving students. Many other states and districts are examining national trends toward total heterogeneous grouping and a standardized curriculum for all students, variously referred to as *curriculum frameworks, standards,* or *outcome-based education.* Yet few could argue that the uniqueness and individuality of every student should be respected and that learning experiences for all students should be arranged so that whatever paths students travel, and whatever distances they travel on these paths, must be appropriate to their unique abilities, interests, and learning styles. If we do not develop specific techniques for achieving this ideal, our educational system will degenerate into a homogeneous, one-size-fits-all curriculum that continues to drive down the overall performance of our entire school population.

Use of the Schoolwide Enrichment Model in Urban Areas

The programming model that we have advocated since the early 1970s has always argued for a behavioral definition of giftedness

(Renzulli, 1978, 1986) and a greater emphasis on applying gifted program know-how to larger segments of the school population (Renzulli & Reis, 1985). The present reform initiatives in general education have created an atmosphere in which there is much greater receptivity for more flexible approaches, and accordingly, we have reconfigured the Schoolwide Enrichment Model (SEM) to blend into school improvement activities that are currently taking place throughout the country. Space does not permit a detailed description of the full model; however, the following sections will describe the school structures and the service delivery components of the model. The school structures targeted by the model include the regular curriculum, the enrichment clusters, and the continuum of special services. The service delivery components include the Total Talent Portfolio, curriculum modification technique, and enrichment learning and teaching. The Total Talent Portfolio will be described in greater detail for purposes of illustration. A graphic representation of the reconfigured model is presented in Figure 3.1.

The Regular Curriculum

The regular curriculum consists of anything and everything that is a part of the predetermined goals, schedules, learning outcomes, and delivery systems of the school. The regular curriculum might be traditional, innovative, or in the process of transition, but its predominant feature is that authoritative forces (i.e., policy makers, school councils, textbook adoption committees, state regulators) have determined that the regular curriculum should be the "centerpiece" of student learning. Our efforts to influence the regular curriculum fall into three categories. First, the challenge level of required material should be differentiated through processes such as curriculum compacting, textbook content modification procedures, and group jumping strategies. Second, systematic content intensification procedures should be used to replace eliminated content with selected, in-depth learning experiences. Third, types of enrichment recommended in the Enrichment Triad Model (Renzulli, 1977b) should selectively be integrated into regular curriculum activities. Although our goal in the SEM is to influence rather than replace the regular curriculum, it is conceivable that the application of certain SEM

School Structures

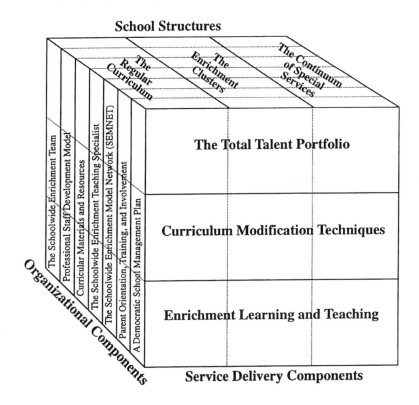

Figure 3.1. The Schoolwide Enrichment Model: Relationship Between Two Types of Components of the Model and School Structures
SOURCE: Reprinted by permission of Creative Learning Press, Inc., Mansfield Center, CT.
NOTE: Persons who are not familiar with the concepts listed in this figure should review Renzulli, 1977a, and Renzulli and Reis, 1985.

components and related staff development activities might eventually result in substantial changes in both the content and instructional processes of the entire regular curriculum.

Enrichment Clusters

The enrichment clusters are nongraded groups of students who share common interests and who come together during specially designated time blocks to pursue these interests. All teachers (including music, art, and physical education) are involved in teaching the clusters, and their involvement in any particular cluster should be based on the same type of interest assessment that is used for students in selecting clusters of choice. Community resource persons should also be invited to participate in the enrichment clusters. The organizational pattern for enrichment clusters is called *multiple/ multiple talent pools*, and the model for learning used with enrichment clusters is based on an inductive approach to the pursuit of real-world problems rather than traditional, didactic modes of teaching. This approach, entitled *enrichment learning and teaching*, is purposefully designed to create a learning environment that places a premium on the development of higher order thinking skills and the authentic application of these skills in creative and productive situations. The theory underlying this approach is based on the work of constructivist theorists such as Jean Piaget and Jerome Bruner, and applications of constructivist theory to classroom practice (e.g., Atkin & Karplus, 1962; Lampert, 1984; Lawson, 1978; Linn, Chen, & Thier, 1977). Enrichment clusters are excellent vehicles for promoting cooperativeness within the context of real-world problem solving, and also provide superlative opportunities for promoting self-concept. A major assumption underlying the use of enrichment clusters is that *every child is special if we create conditions in which that child can be a specialist within a specialty group.*

Enrichment clusters allow students and adults who share a common interest and purpose to come together for given periods of time. Like extracurricular activities and programs such as 4-H and Junior Achievement, the main rationale for participation in one or more clusters is that *students and teachers want to be there.* Selection of an enrichment cluster, however, is not a random or spontaneous process. Interest assessment procedures, examples of previous positive involvement in curricular or nonschool activities, and highly positive reactions to purposefully selected interest development activities are all used to help young people and adults make decisions about which enrichment cluster(s) they might like to select for given periods of time.

Enrichment clusters are organized around major disciplines, interdisciplinary themes, or cross-disciplinary topics (e.g., an electronic music group, or a theatrical/television production group that includes actors, writers, technical specialists, and costume designers). At the upper grade levels, when interests become more specialized, groups within the general disciplines further subdivide into more focused interest groups. These arrangements are a programmatic application of Gardner's theory of multiple intelligences (Gardner, 1983). The enrichment clusters are not intended to be the total program for talent development in a school, but they are a major vehicle for stimulating interests and developing talent potentials across the entire school population. They are also vehicles for staff development in that they provide teachers an opportunity to participate in enrichment teaching, and subsequently to analyze and compare this type of teaching with traditional methods of instruction. In this regard the model promotes a spillover effect by encouraging teachers to become better talent scouts and to apply enrichment techniques to regular classroom situations.

Continuum of Special Services

A broad range of special services is the third school structure that is targeted by the model. Although the enrichment clusters and the SEM-based modifications of the regular curriculum provide a broad range of services to meet individual needs, a program for total talent development still requires supplementary services that challenge young people who are capable of working at the highest levels of their special interest areas. These services, which cannot ordinarily be provided in enrichment clusters or the regular curriculum, typically include individual or small group counseling, direct assistance in facilitating advanced-level work, arranging for mentorships with faculty members or community persons, and making other types of connections between students and out-of-school persons, resources, and agencies. Direct assistance also involves setting up and promoting student, faculty, and parental involvement in special programs such as Future Problem Solving, Odyssey of the Mind, the Model United Nations program, and state and national essay, mathematics, and history contests. Another type of direct assistance consists of arranging out-of-school involvement for individual students in summer programs, on-campus courses, special schools, theatrical groups, scientific expeditions, and apprenticeships at places where advanced-level learning opportunities are available. Provision of these services is one of the responsibilities of the schoolwide enrichment teaching specialist or an enrichment team of teachers and parents who work together to provide various options for advanced learning.

Total Talent Portfolio

Our purpose in reconfiguring the SEM model is to offer some solutions for achieving equity and excellence that are based on the know-how that has emerged over the years on enrichment learning and teaching. The purpose of these new developments is twofold. First, we are attempting to provide schools with a systematic plan to implement and/or maintain commitments to the development of high levels of talent in young people, regardless of the direction that a school might take so far as its reform agenda is concerned. Second, we want to do everything possible to ensure that there is a viable and exciting role within the school for specially trained persons who have strong backgrounds in enrichment learning and teaching. Although we have made some changes in the role that gifted/talented teachers traditionally have played, a major part of their role remains focused on direct services to students who are targeted because of particular behavioral potential(s). But our approach to targeting has been expanded, and accordingly, we have developed procedures for examining the multiple talent potentials of a broader segment of the entire school population. To achieve this goal, we recommend the use of some existing SEM components with all students. These components include the Interest-A-Lyzer (Renzulli, 1977a, 1977b), performance-based assessment, learning styles assessment, and the preparation of a Total Talent Portfolio that is based on the factors presented in Figure 3.2. This expanded approach to identifying talent potentials is essential if we are to make genuine efforts to include more minorities and other traditionally overlooked students in a plan for *total* talent development.

The second service delivery component of the SEM is a series of curriculum modification techniques that are designed to (a) adjust levels of required learning so that all students are challenged, (b) increase the number of in-depth learning experiences, and (c) intro-

Abilities	Interests	Style Preferences			
Maximum Performance Indicators	Interest Areas	Instructional Style Preferences	Learning Environment Preferences	Thinking Style Preferences	Expression Style Preferences

Tests
  Standardized
  Teacher-Made
Course Grades
Teacher Ratings
Product Evaluation
  Written
  Oral
  Visual
  Musical
  Constructed
(Note differences between assigned and self-selected products)
Level of Participation in Learning Activities
Degree of Interaction With Others
Ref: General Tests and Measurements Literature
	Fine Arts
	Crafts
	Literary
	Historical
	Mathematical/Logical
	Physical Sciences
	Life Sciences
	Political/Judicial
	Athletic/Recreation
	Marketing/Business
	Drama/Dance
	Musical Performance
	Musical Composition
	Managerial/Business
	Photography
	Film/Video
	Computers
	Other (Specify)
	Ref: Renzulli, 1977b
		Recitation & Drill
		Peer Tutoring
		Lecture
		Lecture/Discussion
		Guided Independent Study*
		Learning/Interest Center
		Simulation, Role Playing, Drama-tization, Guided Fantasy
		Learning Games
		Replicative Reports or Projects*
		Investigative Reports or Projects*
		Unguided Independent Study*
		Internship*
		Apprenticeship*
		*With or without a mentor
		Ref: Renzulli & Smith, 1978
			Inter/Intrapersonal
			Self-Oriented
			Peer-Oriented
			Adult-Oriented
			Combined
			Physical
			Sound
			Heat
			Light
			Design
			Mobility
			Time of Day
			Food Intake
			Seating
			Ref: Amabile, 1989; Dunn, Dunn, & Price, 1975; Gardner, 1983
				Analytic (School Smart)
				Synthetic/Creative (Creative, Inventive)
				Practical/Contextual (Street Smart)
				Legislative
				Executive
				Judicial
				Ref: Sternberg, 1984, 1988, 1991
					Written
					Oral
					Manipulative
					Discussion
					Display
					Dramatization
					Artistic
					Graphic
					Commercial
					Service
					Ref: Renzulli & Reis, 1985

Figure 3.2. Dimensions of the Total Talent Portfolio

SOURCE: Reprinted by permission of Creative Learning Press, Inc., Mansfield Center, CT.

duce various types of enrichment into regular curricular experiences. The procedures used to carry out curriculum modification are curriculum compacting, textbook analysis and removal of repetitious material from textbooks, and a planned approach for introducing greater depth into regular curricular material.

Curriculum Compacting

Curriculum compacting has been described in detail in a teacher's manual (Reis, Burns, & Renzulli, 1992) and staff development manual (Starko, 1986) that are part of the resources related to the SEM. Compacting is a systematic procedure for modifying or streamlining the regular curriculum in order to eliminate repetition of previously mastered material, upgrade the challenge level of the regular curriculum, and provide time for appropriate enrichment and/or acceleration activities. Essentially, the procedure involves completing the compacting process and documenting this process on a form called the compactor. The process includes (a) defining the goals and outcomes of a particular unit or segment of instruction, (b) determining and documenting which students have already mastered most or all of a specified set of learning outcomes, or who are capable of mastering them in less time than their peers, and (c) providing replacement activities for material already mastered through the use of instructional options that enable a more challenging and productive use of the students' time. These options include content acceleration, individual or group research projects, peer teaching, and involvement in nonclassroom activities that will be discussed in the section on the continuum of services. A key feature of these options is that students will have some freedom to make decisions about the topic and the methods through which the topic will be pursued. Curriculum compacting might best be thought of as *organized common sense*, because it simply recommends the natural pattern that teachers ordinarily would follow if they were individualizing instruction or teaching in the days before textbooks were invented. Compacting might also be thought of as the mirror image of remedial procedures that have always been used in diagnostic/prescriptive models of teaching.

Textbook Analysis and Removal of Repetitious Material

The second procedure for making adjustments in regular curricular material consists of examining textbooks in order to determine which aspects of a required text can be economized upon through the textbook analysis and removal of repetitious drill and practice. The textbook is the curriculum in the overwhelming majority of today's classrooms, and despite all of the rhetoric about school and curriculum reform, the situation is not likely to change in the near future. Until high-quality textbooks are universally available, we must deal with the curriculum situation as it currently exists. Although curriculum compacting is one procedure that can be used to get an unchallenging curriculum "off the backs" of students who are in immediate need of modifications in learning, the procedure is a form of damage control; therefore we need to take a more proactive stance to overcoming the well-documented low levels of American textbooks. In other words, we must deal directly with the textbooks themselves. This is a big job, and unlike compacting, it cannot be accomplished through relatively short amounts of teacher training and an administrative commitment to make this service available to students in need. Nor can it be accomplished through the traditional top-down approach to curricular reform. Another dreaded set of state directives inevitably results in reluctant teacher participation on yet another curriculum committee and in the obligatory production of largely unused piles of spiral-bound documents that are essentially reinventions of a textbook-based status quo.

The procedures for carrying out the textbook analysis and the removal process are based on the argument that "less is better" when it comes to content selection, but it is necessary to make wise decisions when determining which material will be covered in greater depth. A prerequisite is that teacher groups, working in collaboration with curriculum specialists, must have a solid understanding of the goals and content of a particular unit of study, and of the reasons for covering given segments of material. The first step in the process might best be described as "textbook triage." Each unit of instruction is examined to determine (a) which material is needless repetition of previously covered skills and concepts, (b) which material is necessary for review, and (c) which material is important enough to cover in either a survey or an in-depth manner. These decisions obviously require an understanding of the goals and content of the curricular materials being used and some know-how about the use of criteria for making curricular modification decisions. What teachers teach is at the very heart of professional competency. The textbook analysis and removal process offers teachers an opportunity to come together as a group of professionals around specific tasks within and across grade levels and subject areas. Effective group work using this process will undoubtedly contribute to individual teacher growth so far as content mastery is concerned, and it has the added benefit of promoting the types of consultation and sharing of knowledge and experience that characterize other professions.

Increasing In-Depth Learning Experiences

Adding depth to the curriculum is a particularly troublesome task because teachers have been encouraged to add more topics to what they have been teaching rather than to discontinue teaching large numbers of prescribed topics in favor of smaller amounts of in-depth material (Floden, Porter, Schmidt, Freeman, & Schwille, 1981). State and district frameworks typically specify outcomes in terms of quantity of material, and the emphasis has generally been on content and process skills rather than conceptual understandings and applications (Porter, 1989). Introducing greater depth into the curriculum is also directly related to the issue of time (discussed later in this chapter). If the curriculum is "crowded" by superficial coverage of fragmented or compartmentalized facts and concepts, little time will be available for the in-depth study of highly representative topics in a field, key concepts that unlock deeper understandings of particular areas of study, or the pursuit of broad-based, interdisciplinary themes. Nor will time be available for learning the kinds of firsthand investigative methodologies that allow students to apply what they have learned to real-life situations. Using the strategies discussed earlier (i.e., compacting and the systematic removal of redundant and unchallenging material) opens the door to opportunities for in-depth learning; however, there is a need to implement specific strategies for content selection, and to differentiate instruction to achieve deeper understanding.

Enrichment Learning and Teaching Defined

Enrichment learning and teaching is based on the ideas of a small but influential number of philosophers, theorists, and researchers. The work of these theorists coupled with our own research and program development activities has given rise to the concept that we call enrichment learning and teaching. The best way to define this concept is in terms of the following four principles:

1. Each learner is unique; therefore all learning experiences must be examined in ways that take into account the abilities, interests, and learning styles of the individual.
2. Learning is more effective when students enjoy what they are doing; therefore learning experiences should be constructed and assessed with as much concern for enjoyment as for other goals.
3. Learning is more meaningful and enjoyable when content (i.e., knowledge) and process (i.e., thinking skills, methods of inquiry) are learned within the context of a real and present problem; therefore attention should be given to opportunities to personalize student choice in problem selection, the relevance of the problem for individual students at the time the problem is being addressed, and strategies for study.
4. Some formal instruction may be used in enrichment learning and teaching, but a major goal of this approach to learning is to enhance knowledge and thinking-skill acquisition that is gained through teacher *in*struction with applications of knowledge and skills that result from students' *con*struction of meaningfulness.

The ultimate goal of learning guided by these principles is to replace dependence and passive learning with independence and engaged learning. Although all but the most conservative educators will agree with these principles, much controversy exists about how these (or similar) principles might be applied in everyday school situations. A danger also exists that these principles may be viewed as yet another idealized list of glittering generalities that cannot easily be manifested in schools overwhelmed by the deductive model of learning. Developing a school program based on these principles is not an easy task. Over the years, however, we have achieved a fair amount of success by gaining faculty, administrative, and parental consensus on a small number of easy-to-understand concepts and related services, and by providing resources and training related to each concept and service delivery procedure.

The SEM approach is consistent with the more flexible conception of *developing* gifts and talents that has been a cornerstone of our work and our concerns for promoting more equity in special programs. It also draws upon such emerging work as Gardner's theory of multiple intelligences. We also recommend and suggest procedures for the use of more thinking-skills activities and general enrichment in the regular classroom. In the reconfigured model, the role of the gifted/talented teacher, whom we prefer to call the *schoolwide enrichment teaching specialist*, will consist of both direct services to any student engaged in "high-end" learning (e.g., individual or small group investigation, mentorships, advanced "methodological" minicourses, out-of-school experiences) and leadership activities that will infuse the know-how of enrichment learning and teaching techniques into the overall school program. A part of our work in facilitating this process is the preparation of categorical databases that list a broad array of thinking-skills activities and enrichment materials, as well as other databases on academic competitions, publishing opportunities for young people, methodological resource books and materials, summer programs, visitation sites, teleconferences, and proven staff development materials.[1] We have always argued that a large amount of gifted program activities should be made available for all students and that SEM should serve as a vehicle for sharing the know-how of enrichment learning and teaching with the entire school. The reconfigured model will push this concept even further by enlarging the role of the schoolwide enrichment team and developing genuine partnerships between SEM specialists and teachers and administrators. We still believe, however, that direct services in the form of high-level follow-up and appropriate referrals to advanced resources and services are a "lifeline" for underchallenged students with high potentials. For this reason, we will continue to advocate enrichment specialist positions as well as greater use of talent development techniques by the general faculty.

The essence of our new work is the application of SEM know-how to the overall process of school improvement, and the development of some additional know-how that addresses factors related to increasing the challenge level for all students. For example, curriculum compacting has been effectively used for high-achieving students who are underchallenged by the regular curriculum. But a large amount of research has shown that "dumbed down" textbooks and a focus on minimum-outcome-based competencies have lowered the achievement levels of large numbers of the school population. Experience has shown that the billions of dollars spent on compensatory drill and practice approaches to remediation have produced negligible results for disadvantaged students. We need to apply some of our proven techniques for compacting and enrichment to the entire curriculum, and we must replace excessive drill and practice with advanced, in-depth content and thinking skills activities for all students. Accordingly, we have identified techniques and staff development procedures for a more proactive approach to curricular modification. It is our hope that experienced gifted/talented teachers who have familiarity with compacting and staff development will provide the technical know-how and leadership to implement this process that can eventually benefit all students.

Conclusion

Providing services for high-ability students has always been a slender and tenuous thread within the fabric of American education. Administrators, policy makers, and legislators have reluctantly provided support for the development of giftedness in our schools, and they have often bought into "quick fix" approaches such as IQ cutoff scores because of expediency, tidiness, and the search for convenient ways to set limits on the amount of funds available for talent development. The results of this tradition have been very restricted opportunities for all but the few who come up with the omnipotent cutoff score that allows them to be certified as "the gifted" (Richert et al., 1982). In the process we have frequently excluded the vast talent pool that can be found in minorities, underachievers, children from low-income families, artistically talented students, and those who display the mechanical genius that can be found in vocational and technical schools. In summary, we have often excluded from our gifted programs almost everyone else who does not fit a very limited stereotype of human potential.

Because so many policy makers and state regulations minimize motivation and task commitment in favor of achievement test and intelligence test scores, we must question how these data will be interpreted by educators of urban students in their hands. Most of us were not fortunate enough to pick our parents, nor in most cases could we choose the school we attended, the nutrition we received, or a host of other factors that the trait theorists have found correlate well with school success. Unless we are bold enough to explore more flexible definitions, programs that serve our most potentially able students will continue to be found mainly in middle- and upper-class suburbs, because along with the professional fathers, designer jogging suits, and gourmet catfood, we also happen to find better slices of success on standardized tests. As the popular cliché states, "If you don't get a chance to come to bat, you don't get a chance to hit."

Commentaries

When considering the plight of inner-city students—inside or outside of school—we can all agree that it is deteriorating at an alarming rate. We can also agree that some students are more insulated than others from the impacts of negative academic and nonacademic factors (such as tracking, labeling, discrimination, and unchallenging educational expectations and experiences) by positive family, community, and other social/economic factors. Where disagreements among many educators and researchers begin to arise, however, are in the areas of which groups of students are worse off, which are most deserving or worthy at some level of special attention, and what kinds of solutions are needed. Renzulli and his colleagues (Reis, Hébert, & Diaz) do a most skillful job of cutting through these issues and isolating those strategies that ensure that all urban youth, and high-ability students in particular, experience an educational system that values and supports their gifts and diversity. I find the Schoolwide Enrichment Model (SEM) particularly commendable in its comprehensiveness, thoughtfulness, and sensitivity to the "giftedness" of all students. As an educational psychologist with a particular interest in how we enhance motivation to learn and self-regulated learning skills in all students, I am very impressed that the SEM uses students' interests and goals as the "sorting system" into enrichment clusters—not abilities or grade levels or other categories that can carry negative limits to potential.

In addition, the SEM model provides for "special services" such that the needs of all students are met holistically. From my perspective, these are not only key but are well grounded in our understanding of how best to promote optimal learning and development of human potential. Research supports that all learners need and can benefit from learning goals and environments they perceive as rich, challenging, personally relevant, accepting, and supportive. In such contexts, all students have the potential to be highly motivated learners. I believe one of our biggest challenges is to educate the public—including parents, educators, and policy makers—about what we know is best for learning and learners. If we know what maximizes learning for all students—as defined by the growing body of research and theory— how can we in good conscience do otherwise?

Barbara L. McCombs, Senior Director for the Motivation and Human Development Group, Mid-Continent Regional Educational Laboratory (McREL)

The Renzulli paper focused on the high achiever, when in fact our focus should be on high ability. Many students possess tremendous ability, but their academic achievement levels don't reflect their true ability. For this reason, I do not support gifted programs. Every child is gifted; it is up to us to develop those gifts, and schoolwide enrichment models can help us do that.

It seems to me, or at least it would be my wish, that the proposal of enrichment clusters should be initiated in schools. They need to be challenging and interesting. The argument Dr. Renzulli makes for supporting out-of-school enrichment programs is relevant not just to so-called gifted students, but rather to all students. Finally, one aspect that was blatantly missing in the Renzulli paper was the subject of racism and its impact on student achievement. Until we talk about the impact of the attitudes and dispositions on performance, we will not even begin to address the issue.

Brenda Lilienthal Welburn, Executive Director, National Association of State Boards of Education (NASBE)

Note

1. These databases and related program development activities will become part of a Schoolwide Enrichment Model Network (SEM-NET) that is available to interested persons on a subscription basis. Please write to the authors for information about how to gain access to the network.

References

Alvarez, M. D. (1983). *Puerto Ricans and academic achievement: An explanatory study of person, home and school variables among high-risk bilingual first graders.* Unpublished doctoral dissertation, New York University.

Amabile, T. M. (1983). *The social psychology of creativity.* New York: Springer-Verlag.

Ambert, A. N., & Figler, C. S. (1992). Puerto Ricans: Historical and cultural perspectives. In A. N. Ambert & M. D. Alvarez (Eds.), *Puerto Rican children on the mainland: Interdisciplinary perspectives* (pp. 17-37). New York: Garland.

Atkin, J. M., & Karplus, R. (1962). Discovery or invention. *Science Teacher, 29,* 5.

Ausubel, D. (1963). *The influence of experience on the development of intelligence.* Paper presented at the Conference on Productive Thinking in Education, NEA Project on the Academically Talented Student. Washington, DC.

Baldwin, A. Y. (1977). Tests do underpredict: A case study. *Phi Delta Kappan, 58*(8), 620-621.

Baldwin, A. Y. (1985). Issues concerning minorities. In D. Horowitz & M. O'Brien (Eds.), *The gifted and talented: Developmental perspectives* (pp. 223-249). Washington, DC: American Psychological Association.

Baldwin, A. Y. (1987a). I'm black but look at me, I am also gifted. *Gifted Child Quarterly, 31*(4), 180-185.

Baldwin, A. Y. (1987b). Undiscovered diamonds: The minority gifted child. *Journal for the Education of the Gifted, 10*(4), 271-285.

Banks, J. A. (1991). Multicultural literacy and curriculum reform. *Educational Horizons, 69*(3), 135-140.

Borges, F. (1975). *Variables associated with successful learning to read experiences of children when they enter school in Puerto Rico.* Unpublished doctoral dissertation, Lehigh University (ERIC Document Reproduction Service No. 122 237).

Brown, G. H., Rosen, N. L., Hill, S. T., & Olivas, M. A. (1980). *The condition of education for Hispanic Americans.* Washington, DC: National Center for Education Statistics.

Bryk, A. S., & Thum, Y. M. (1989). *The effects of high school organization on dropping out: An explanatory investigation* (CPRE Research Report SRR-012). New Brunswick, NJ: Rutgers University, Center for Policy Research in Education.

Chisholm, S. (1978). Address at the National Forum on the Culturally Disadvantaged Gifted Youth. *Gifted Child Today, 2*(4), 40-41.

Clark, B. (1983). *Growing up gifted* (2nd ed.). Columbus, OH: Charles Merrill.

Clifford, M. M. (1990). Students need challenge, not success. *Educational Leadership, 48*(1), 22-25.

Comas-Diaz, L. (1989). Culturally relevant issues and treatment implications for Hispanics. In D. R. Koslow & E. P. Salett (Eds.), *Crossing cultures in mental health* (pp. 31-48). Washington, DC: International Counseling Center.

Cummings, S. (1977). Explaining poor academic performance among black children. *Educational Forum, 41,* 335-346.

Davis, G. A., & Rimm, S. B. (1989). *Education of the gifted and talented* (2nd ed.). Englewood Cliffs, NJ: Prentice Hall.

De La Rosa, D., & Maw, C. E. (1990). *Hispanic education: A statistical portrait.* Washington, DC: National Council of La Raza.

Deutsch, M., & Brown, B. (1964). Social influences in Negro-White intelligence differences. *The Journal of Social Issues, 20,* 24-35.

Diaz, W. (1986). Hispanics: Challenges and opportunities. In L. Orum (Ed.), *The education of Hispanics: Status and implications.* Washington, DC: National Council of La Raza.

Dolce, C. J. (1969, January 11). The inner-city: A superintendent's view. *Saturday Review of Literature,* p. 36.

Dunn, R., Dunn, K., & Price, G. E. (1975). *Learning style inventory.* Lawrence, KS: Price Systems.

Erickson, F. (1987). Transformation and school success: The politics and culture of educational achievement. *Anthropology and Education Quarterly, 18*(4), 335-355.

Espinosa, R., & Ochoa, A. (1986). Concentration of Hispanic students in schools with low achievement: A research note. *American Journal of Education, 95,* 77-95.

Falicov, C. J. (1982). Mexican families. In M. McGoldrick, J. K. Pearce, & J. Giordano (Eds.), *Ethnicity and family therapy* (pp. 134-163). New York: Guilford.

Fitzpatrick, J. P. (1987). *Puerto Rican Americans: The meaning of migration to the mainland.* Englewood Cliffs, NJ: Prentice Hall.

Floden, R. E., Porter, A. C., Schmidt, W. H., Freeman, D. J., & Schwille, J. R. (1981). Responses to curriculum pressures: A policy-capturing study of teacher decisions about content. *Journal of Educational Psychology, 73,* 129-141.

Ford, D. Y. (1992). Determinants of underachievement as perceived by gifted, above-average, and average black students. *Roeper Review, 14*(3), 130-136.

Ford, D. Y., & Harris, J. J. (1990). On discovering the hidden treasures of gifted and talented black children. *Roeper Review, 13*(11), 27-32.

Fordham, S. (1988). Racelessness as a factor in black students' school success: Pragmatic strategy or pyrrhic victory? *Harvard Educational Review, 58*(1), 54-84.

Fordham, S., & Ogbu, J. U. (1986). Black students' school success: Coping with the "burden of 'acting White.'" *Urban Review, 18,* 176-206.

Frasier, M. M. (1989). Identification of gifted black students: Developing new perspectives. In C. J. Maker & S. W. Schiever (Eds.), *Critical issues in gifted education: Defensible programs for cultural and ethnic minorities* (pp. 213-225). Austin, TX: PRO-ED.

Frenkel, C. M. (1992). *A comparison study of Puerto Rican students who finished high school and those who abandoned their education.* Unpublished doctoral dissertation, University of Connecticut.

Frierson, E. (1965). Upper and lower status gifted children: A study of differences. *Exceptional Children, 32*(2), 83-90.

Gardner, H. (1983). *Frames of mind.* New York: Basic Books.

Gay, J. (1978). A proposed plan for identifying black gifted children. *Gifted Child Quarterly, 22*(3), 353-360.

Gibson, M. A. (1982). Reputation and respectability: How competing cultural systems affect students' performance in school. *Anthropology and Education Quarterly, 13*(3), 3-27.

Hahn, A. (1987). Reaching out to America's dropouts: What to do? *Phi Delta Kappan, 69,* 256-263.

Hill, D. (1990). A theory of success and failure. *Teacher, 1*(9), 40-45.

Hilliard, A. G. (1976). *Alternative to IQ testing: An approach to the identification of the gifted "minority" children* (Report No. 75175, ERIC Document Reproduction Service No. ED 147009). San Francisco: San Francisco State University.

Hine, C. Y. (1991) *The home environment of gifted Puerto Rican children: Family factors which support high achievement.* Unpublished doctoral dissertation, University of Connecticut.

Hyland, C. R. (1989). What we know about the fastest growing minority population: Hispanic Americans. *Educational Horizons, 67*(4), 131-135.

Katz, I. (1969). A critique of personality approaches to Negro performance, with research suggestions. *The Journal of Social Issues, 25,* 13.

Kitano, M., & Kirby, D. (1986). *Gifted education: A comprehensive view.* Boston: Little, Brown.

Kozol, J. (1991). *Savage inequalities: Children in America's schools.* New York: Crown.

Lampert, M. (1984). Thinking about teaching and teaching about thinking. *Journal of Curriculum Studies, 16*(1), 1-18.

Lawson, A. E. (1978). The development and validation of a classroom test of formal reasoning. *Journal of Research on Science Teaching, 15*(1), 11-24.

Linn, M., Chen, B., & Thier, H. (1977). Teaching children to control variables: Investigation of a free choice environment. *Journal of Research on Science Teaching, 14*(3), 249-255.

MacMillan, D. (1982). *Mental retardation in school and society* (2nd ed.). Boston: Little, Brown.

Majors, R., & Billson, J. (1992). *Cool pose: The dilemmas of Black manhood in America.* New York: Lexington.

McCall, R., Evahn, C., & Kratzer, L. (1992). *High school underachievers: What do they achieve as adults?* Newbury Park, CA: Sage.

Meléndez, S. E. (1978). *A review of the literature on the self-concept of Puerto Rican children in bilingual education and monolingual education.* Qualifying paper, Harvard University Graduate School of Education.

Ogbu, J. U. (1974). *The next generation: An ethnography of education in an urban neighborhood.* New York: Academic Press.

Ogbu, J. U. (1985). Research currents: Cultural-ecological influences on minority school learning. *Language Arts, 62*(8), 860-868.

Ogbu, J. U. (1987). Variability in minority school performance: A problem in search of an explanation. *Anthropology and Education Quarterly, 18*(4), 312-334.

Ogbu, J. U. (1991). Immigrant and involuntary minorities in comparative perspective. In M. A. Gibson & J. U. Ogbu (Eds.), *Minority status and schooling: A comparative study of immigrant and involuntary minorities* (pp. 3-33). New York: Garland.

Ortiz, F. I. (1988). Hispanic American's children's experiences in classrooms: A comparison between Hispanic and non-Hispanic children. In L. Weis (Ed.), *Class, race, and gender in American education* (pp. 63-86). Albany: State University of New York Press.

Orum, L. (1986). *The education of Hispanics: Status and implications.* Washington, DC: National Council of La Raza.

Passow, A. H. (1972). The gifted and the disadvantaged. *National Elementary Principal, 51,* 24-31.

Perrine, J. (1989). Situational identification of gifted Hispanic students. In C. J. Maker & S. W. Schiever (Eds.), *Critical issues in gifted education: Defensible programs for cultural and ethnic minorities* (pp. 5-18). Austin, TX: Pro-Ed.

Perrone, P., & Aleman, N. (1983). Educating the talented child in a pluralistic society. In D. R. Omark & J. G. Erickson (Eds.), *The bilingual exceptional child* (pp. 269-283). San Diego: College-Hill.

Petroni, F. A., & Hirsch, E. A. (1970). *Two, four, six, eight, when you gonna integrate?* New York: Behavioral Publications.

Pittman, R. B., & Haughwout, P. (1987). Influence of high school size on dropout rate. *Educational Evaluation and Policy Analysis, 9,* 337-343.

Porter, A. (1989). A curriculum out of balance: The case of elementary mathematics. *Educational Researcher, 18,* 9-15.

Rabovits, P. C., & Maehr, M. L. (1973). Pygmalion black and white. *Journal of Personality and Social Psychology, 25*(2), 210-218.

Reis, S. M., Burns, D. E., & Renzulli, J. S. (1992). *Curriculum compacting.* Mansfield, CT: Creative Learning Press.

Reis, S. M., Hébert, T., & Diaz, E. (in preparation). *An ethnographic investigation of the urban high school experiences of high ability stu-*

dents who achieve or underachieve. Storrs, CT: National Research Center on the Gifted and Talented.

Renzulli, J. S. (1973). Talented potential in minority group students. In *Talent, potential, and minority group students: The First National Conference on the Disadvantaged Gifted.* Ventura, CA: Ventura County Superintendent of Schools.

Renzulli, J. S. (1977a). *The enrichment triad model: A guide for developing defensible programs for the gifted.* Mansfield Center, CT: Creative Learning Press.

Renzulli, J. S. (1977b). *The adult interest-a-lyzer.* Mansfield Center, CT: Creative Learning Press.

Renzulli, J. S. (1978). What makes giftedness? Re-examining a definition. *Phi Delta Kappan, 60,* 180-184.

Renzulli, J. S. (1986). The three-ring conception of giftedness: A developmental model for creative productivity. In R. J. Sternberg & J. E. Davidson (Eds.), *Conceptions of giftedness* (pp. 55-92). New York: Cambridge University Press.

Renzulli, J. S., & Reis, S. M. (1985). *The schoolwide enrichment model: A comprehensive plan for educational excellence.* Mansfield Center, CT: Creative Learning Press.

Renzulli, J. S., & Reis, S. M. (1991). The reform movement and the quiet crisis in gifted education. *Gifted Child Quarterly, 35,* 26-35.

Renzulli, J. S., & Smith, L. H. (1978). *The learning styles inventory: A measure of student preference for instructional techniques.* Mansfield Center, CT: Creative Learning Press.

Richert, E., Alvino, J., & McDonnel, R. (1982). *National report on identification: Assessment and recommendation for comprehensive identification of gifted and talented youth.* Sewell, NJ: Educational Improvement Center-South.

Scott-Gregory, S. (1992, March 16). The hidden hurdle. *Time,* pp. 44-46.

Sewell, W. H., & Shah, V. P. (1968). Parents' education and children's educational aspirations and achievements. *American Sociological Review, 33,* 191-204.

Soto, L. D. (1986). *The relationship between the home environment and intrinsic versus extrinsic orientation of fifth and sixth grade Puerto Rican children.* Unpublished doctoral dissertation, Pennsylvania State University.

Soto, L. D. (1988). The home environment of higher and lower achieving Puerto Rican children. *Hispanic Journal of Behavioral Sciences, 10*(2), 161-168.

Starko, A. J. (1986). *It's about time: Inservice strategies for curriculum compacting.* Mansfield, CT: Creative Learning Press.

Sternberg, R. J. (1984). Toward a triarchic theory of human intelligence. *Behavioral and Brain Sciences, 7,* 269-287.

Sternberg, R. J. (1988). Mental self-government: A theory of intellectual styles and their development. *Human Development, 31,* 197-224.

Sternberg, R. J. (In press). Human intelligence: Its nature, use and interaction with context. In D. Detterman (Ed.), *Current directions in human intelligence.* Norwood, NJ: Ablex.

Torrance, E. P. (1971). Are the Torrance tests of creative thinking biased in favor "of disadvantaged groups"? *Gifted Child Quarterly, 15,* 75-80.

Torrance, E. P. (1977). *Discovery and nurturance of giftedness in the culturally different.* Reston, VA: Council for Exceptional Children.

Torregrosa-Diaz, V. (1986) *Biliteracy and its effects on reading achievement among bilingual Puerto Rican and Mexican American students in grades two through four.* Unpublished doctoral dissertation, Wayne State University.

Treffinger, D. J. (1991). School reform and gifted education—Opportunities and issues. *Gifted Child Quarterly, 35,* 6-11.

Trueba, H. T. (1988). Culturally based explanations of minority students' academic achievement. *Anthropology and Education Quarterly, 19*(1), 270-287.

U.S. Bureau of the Census. (1980). *Current population reports, series p-60.* Washington, DC: Author.

U.S. Bureau of the Census. (1991). *Statistical abstract of the United States* (111th ed.). Washington, DC: Author.

Van Tassel-Baska, J. (1991). Gifted education in the balance: Building relationships with general education. *Gifted Child Quarterly, 35,* 20-25.

Walsh, C. E. (1991). *Pedagogy and the struggle for voice: Issues of language, power and schooling for Puerto Ricans.* New York: Bergin & Garvey.

• • • • • •

4

• • • • • •

Street Academies and In-School
Alternatives to Suspension

ANTOINE M. GARIBALDI

During the 1960s, significant attention was placed on the improvement of the educational attainment and achievement of students who were performing below average in the nation's schools. Landmark government-sponsored studies on the "educationally disadvantaged" (Coleman et al., 1967) were also conducted that had a major impact on federal policy and sparked the movement to provide compensatory education to underachieving students throughout the nation. Simultaneously, many local education agencies were implementing desegregation plans in their school districts, and teachers and administrators in many instances had difficulty adjusting to and carrying out these reforms. Though some gains were realized (e.g., the establishment of Head Start, Title I, and other compensatory education programs), many students, especially those from nonwhite populations, were adversely affected by the systemic changes of desegregation.

Among the noticeable negative and, to some extent, unintended effects of desegregation and also the failure of many schools to adequately serve students from nonwhite populations were disproportionately high suspensions and expulsions, students' loss of interest in schooling, and large numbers of secondary dropouts. Because of each of those factors, discussion ensued in many urban areas particularly, and exploratory efforts were conceived in an attempt to develop alternatives to decrease the number of students who were dropping out and being "pushed out" of schools. Because of the significance of some of those programmatic initiatives that were established over the last 25 years, this chapter describes the development, implementation, and perceived success of two of these nationwide alternatives—street academies and in-school alternatives to suspension programs. Both alternatives, as the reader will see shortly, were primarily designed to keep students in school by providing them with nontraditional educational environments where they could receive more individualized academic and personal attention to improve not only their school performance but also their disposition to learning and their behavior in school. Much can be learned from the adaptations of these alternative schools and programs to the specific academic and social needs of their students as educators search today for ways to make a difference for similar students in rural, urban, and suburban school districts.

Street Academy Programs

One of the largest "alternative education" efforts was the creation of street academies by the National Urban League in 1966. Borrowing from a 1964 federally funded program, HARYOU, designed to decrease the number of high school dropouts and unemployed youth in Harlem, the Greater New York Urban League in 1966 adopted HARYOU's basic concept; the program's methods were developed principally by Dr. Susan Bryant, the education director of the Greater New York Urban League. Within 3 years, 26 street academies, with several in the New York City area, had been established across the country. The majority of these programs were operated by the National Urban League, and the remainder were initiated by community and religious groups in conjunction with the federal government's Model Cities Program. Sometimes referred to as "storefront" programs, the major purpose of these innovative ventures was the reintroduction of disenchanted students, most of whom were nonwhite and from low-income families, back to the educational process. Local community leaders and organizers also wanted to convincingly demonstrate that these underserved students could be better educated in a different and more sensitive environment than the public schools those youth were currently attending or had previously attended.

Even though the actual success of most street academies was questioned by school officials during the 1960s and 1970s, chiefly because few programs had collected systematic and demonstrable evidence of their students' achievement gains and graduation rates, an important report on the street academy's history and operation was written in 1977 by Vernon P. Moore. Moore served as the evaluation director of five of these programs that had been financially supported for 5 years by the Office of Experimental Schools (OES) in the Office of Education's National Institute of Education (NIE). After a period of extensive negotiations, the National Urban League received a grant from NIE in 1972 to "test" the street academy concept, and the receptivity of local school systems to the alternatives, for 5 years as an "Experimental Schools Project" in Washington, DC, South Bend, Indiana, and Oakland, California. (Washington and Oakland each had two programs in their cities.)

The Urban League had originally sought support for seven local communities, but the initial proposals were not acceptable to the OES. According to Moore (1977), "The proposed project sought more than systematic and stable funding. Among its objectives were 'to effect fundamental and systemic change within secondary education' and 'to provide viable, self-sustaining alternatives to the existing educational system'"(p. iii). Thus the academies wanted to do more than merely serve minority and poor children, 80% of whom were African American and Hispanic, who were not being adequately educated in their regular schools; they wanted to make a major impact on the delivery of educational services within school systems as well.

Personnel and the Street Academy Philosophy

Personnel were carefully selected for these programs because the program developers contended that students' behavior, attitudes, self-concepts, self-esteem, and environmental conditions had to be addressed in addition to their potential for learning. Tutoring, individualized instruction, group "rap" sessions, and counseling, therefore, were critical components of the academy curricula. Street academy teachers, approximately three fourths of whom held a college degree, with a little less than half having official certifications to teach, not only understood the needs of their students but also recognized the importance of "reaching" these students before they totally abandoned the goal of obtaining a high school education. As George Gaudette, Director of the Washington Street Academy, stated in the 1970s, "We're dealing with students everyone else has given up on. If we can turn their attitudes around, turn them back on education, and make them believe they have as much right to success of the dollar as anyone else, then we have succeeded" (Jones, n.d., circa 1976, p. 4). Gaudette's previous statement aptly summarized and corroborated Vernon Moore's description of the philosophical foundation of the Street Academy, and the commitment that teachers had to the program's mission:

> Underlying the general Street Academy program was the concept that *all students are educable*. This emphatically included low-income racial and ethnic minority students, whether underachievers, dropouts, or students who have been pushed out of public schools. These students could be retrieved. They could be helped by education programs to acquire the coping abilities, knowledge, and competency required to successfully live as productive citizens. For this to happen, it was demanded that programs be structured around such students and possess understanding, sympathetic and humanistic environments and individually accountable personnel. (Moore, 1977, p. ii)

Educability had a holistic meaning in street academy programs because students were assisted with their development, through the teaching of values and socially appropriate behavior, as well as their learning. Additionally, students were considered "retrievable" because they had only rejected "schooling," and not "education." (Moore, 1977, p. 2) All of the programs primarily served secondary school students, even though there were also students in their early 20s, and they were prepared academically either to go to college, to obtain a G.E.D., or to enter the workforce.

Curricula

The curricula of most of the street academies were broader than the core subjects of reading, writing, and mathematics, and the courses were taught using lesson plans and materials that were culturally relevant to the students and that could be integrated into specific disciplines. Moreover, the academies incorporated remediation into course content instead of teaching students in ability groups or using "tracking" approaches. The latter strategy of improving basic skills by integrating enrichment material into the curriculum served another purpose as well—namely, the elimination of stigmas that these students had become all too familiar with in their public school classrooms. The teachers and administrators therefore focused their attention on developing students' coping abilities and knowledge so they could become productive citizens. Personal growth and the attainment of individual objectives were given high priority in the teaching and learning process so that students could set their own goals and internalize the social behaviors that were taught at the academy. Respect and trust by students toward teachers were extremely important, and the empathy of teachers toward students was critical in meeting individual and academy-related goals. Student-to-teacher ratios, moreover, were very small in most street academy classrooms (e.g., no more than 15:1 in the program that the author directed, and a maximum of approximately 40 students served at any given time); counselors were much more accessible to students and usually available during the entire day; and the student population was small enough that all students were known by the entire staff. Those features helped to emphasize a sense of community within the programs and also fostered a commitment to the academy's mission by students, teachers, and administrators.

Support Personnel and Career Development Programs

To augment the work of counselors, and school psychologists in some programs, most academies also employed "street workers," whose chief responsibility was to identify students who were not in school or who were not functioning well in school. These individuals contacted truant students, attempted to find out why they were not in school, and subsequently recruited them to attend the street academy. Acting as a social worker, the street worker would contact parents at home and assist the academy staff with the development of the student's needs assessment. Because the students' reasons for being out of school typically were more than education related, these needs assessments were comprehensive and focused intensively on the student's home situation and personal/behavioral problems. In the author's program in St. Paul during the mid-1970s, for example, many of the students were referred through the juvenile justice system because funding came from the state of Minnesota. These students had typically been involved in minor infractions of the law and were placed on juvenile probation; enrollment in school was a major requirement of their probation, and the academy was viewed as an ideal environment for them to receive individualized and small group counseling in combination with their academic work. Probation officers therefore contacted the school on a regular basis to monitor and verify students' attendance. In this particular instance, referring students to a local alternative school was a much more constructive, and cost-effective, educational option than referral to a juvenile detention center.

Career counseling was a major component of the academies' educational program because many students were interested in part-time, and eventually full-time, employment. Thus the career counselor at the South Bend Street Academy, for example, helped students to develop their long-range goals and identify their career interests. The Washington, DC, program also had a staff of career counselors, career instructors, and job development coordinators. And Oakland's Career Guidance Program operated in the same way as Washington, DC's, but the entire staff was responsible for the successful implementation of the job-related activities offered. Students participated in field trips to work sites; some were given part-time jobs through the Urban League Employment Office; guest speakers were invited to reinforce the necessity of basic skills and the development of specific technical skills for different occupations; and the role of positive attitudes toward work was integrated into the regular academic content. Where possible, parents were also involved in the programs so they could be familiar with their son's or daughter's progress and encourage him or her to stay in school.

In addition to the formal academic curricula, many programs also offered day care services for student mothers and special services for unwed mothers, as well as career/college planning, job counseling, health referral services, and assistance with legal problems. "Regular" counseling had a pivotal place in street academy programs because a large number of students had been suspended or expelled. Some cocurricular activities were also a part of street academy programs, but they usually ranged from elective courses offered at the academy or in the local school system to work opportunities in day care or senior citizen centers. (Moore, 1977, p. 10)

Cooperative Interactions With Local Schools

Cooperation with the local public schools was essential for the majority of the street academies. Books and school materials were needed; students and street academy teachers found it useful to consult with the teachers, counselors, and administrators at the "home" school; lunch was provided by some of the local districts; and, most important, many students wished to return to and graduate from their "home" high schools. However, some programs sought to establish their own independence and recognition by awarding their own diploma. This was not an easy task in most local communities because, as mentioned earlier, most of the personnel were not certified as teachers and the curricula were not always consistent with local and state requirements for graduation. Some street academy staff also believed that having the authority to grant their own diplomas would counter some of the negative characterizations of these programs as "places where the bad kids were." Those labels were eventually discarded as educators and parents saw street academy students who were previously considered "incorrigible" graduate from high school.

Funding Sources

Each street academy operated differently organizationally depending on the source(s) of funding and the purpose for which it was established. In the author's program in St. Paul, the original proposal was written by an assistant dean of education at the University of Minnesota who was also a member of the St. Paul Urban League Board of Directors and a professor of educational psychology. With the specific goal of returning students to school who had already dropped out, been expelled, and/or been placed on juvenile probation, funding was sought and obtained from the Governor's Commission on Crime Prevention and Control for 3 years (1973-1976). The establishment of the street academy in St. Paul, therefore, was seen as an important intervention strategy to reduce the number of juvenile offenses and premature departures from school due to crime, expulsion, or suspension. The University of Minnesota's College of Education served as the grant's administrative agent, and the Urban League acted as the governance authority. The goal of the grant beyond the funding period was to obtain adoption by and funding support from the local public school system. That goal was achieved, and the program continues to exist as a part of the St. Paul Public Schools.

Measures of Success

Beyond the primary goal of positively effecting change in all students served, success of the street academies was measured in four ways: (a) attainment of a General Equivalency Diploma (G.E.D.); (b) return to the student's home high school; (c) graduation from the home high school; or (d) graduation from the street academy, if the program had the authority to issue diplomas. In general, the programs were very successful by the above standards because two major goals were to assist students with their readjustment to the traditional/regular school environment and also with their personal development.

Graduation was achieved in a variety of programs, such as in St. Paul, where 27 students received diplomas from the local school district in the first 3 years of operation. Almost half (45%) of the students in the five "demonstration programs" funded by the Office of Experimental Schools had the expectation of obtaining a G.E.D., and more than half (55%) had the intention of "getting a job" when they left the academy (Moore, 1977, p. 56). Thus a great deal of emphasis was placed on improving students' reading and mathematics skills, for pretests showed that many were reading at the mid-fifth-grade level even though most were in 9th or 10th grade, and many had been out of school at least 6 months. Moore's 1977 evaluation report indicated that statistically significant gains had been achieved in both reading and mathematics; students also showed increased "self-esteem and efficacy" and "became less dependent on external approval of their attitudes," as measured by their responses on two attitudinal measures (i.e., Gurin's Multi-Dimensional I-E Test [Gurin, et al., 1969] and Crowne and Marlowe's Social Desirability Scale [Crowne & Marlowe, 1969]). Additionally, two thirds to three fourths of the students rated their street academy teachers and performance, respectively, as "excellent" or "good" compared to their self-assessments of previous public school teachers and their performance as "poor" or "fair." The following statement by a 19-year-old student, quoted in a report by Lewis P. Jones in the mid-1970s, summarizes well most students' feelings about their street academy staff:

> At my high school there was one counselor for a whole lot of us. Here the counselors single us out. When we want a conference it's not hard to get, and they check on our grades. The teachers are good because they take their time and tune into us. They don't just put it on the board. Here I don't have to put up with hassles. I'm not just one in a million. (p. 10)

Street academies thus offered many youth more than an educational alternative or choice to obtain their high school diploma; the academies provided most with their last formal educational opportunity before they chose to drop out altogether.

In-School Alternatives to Suspension

During the 1970s also, a great deal of attention was focused on the large numbers of students who were being suspended and expelled from school. Data collected by the Office for Civil Rights (OCR) during the 1972-1973 school year, and analyzed more closely by the Children's Defense Fund (CDF) in 1975, demonstrated the severity of the suspension issue. Of approximately 24 million students enrolled in the schools surveyed, almost 37,000 were expelled and slightly more than 930,000 were suspended at least once, for an average of 4 days each. Nonwhite students made up only 38% of the total enrollment but accounted for 43% of the expulsions, 49% of the suspensions (black students accounted for 47%), and more than half of the 3.5 million days lost by suspension (CDF, 1975; U.S. Department of Education Office for Civil Rights, 1993). Moreover, nonwhite students were suspended for an average of 4.3 days per suspension, compared to 3.5 days for white students. The data also showed other inequities in the disciplinary system.[1] The above evidence was so alarming that surveys and analyses were conducted in school districts across the country to determine why so many students, and especially those who were nonwhite, were being suspended and expelled.

In response to the OCR and CDF analyses, the National Association of Secondary School Principals (NASSP) in 1975 surveyed a portion of its membership and asserted that suspensions were being used by principals as a "sanction of last resort" (Neill, 1976). All of the school administrators in the sample stated that they "held conferences with students prior to suspension, except in the most extraordinary circumstances"; 86%, that they sent letters home; 73%, that they used some form of student referral system; 46%, that they used detentions, and 34%, that they used in-school suspensions. Also, 93% affirmed that students in their schools were given the opportunity to appeal adverse decisions (O'Neill, 1976). Given such a thorough consideration of out-of-school suspensions, there was great concern that administrators and teachers might have been using suspensions arbitrarily, unilaterally, and sometimes for nebulous reasons more often referred to as "insubordination."[2]

Because students lost credit for missed school work and also valuable instruction time, many schools and school systems created in-school alternatives to suspension. These programs were designed to keep students in school for the remainder of the day and provide them with academic instruction commensurate with that of their classmates. Students also received the necessary counseling to help them function better in the classroom and at school. In-school alternatives benefited both the student and the school—no academic instruction/credit was lost because assignments were given by the students' teachers, and schools' budgets were not affected by low daily attendance rates. The latter factor was extremely important because general operating revenues are typically based on average daily attendance rates. These alternative programs, which numbered in the thousands, were much more prevalent than many educators realized, as this author discovered when he organized a national conference on the topic in 1978 while working specifically on this initiative at the National Institute of Education (Garibaldi, 1979). Because their programmatic designs vary considerably, a descriptive summary of several of the more common models of in-school alternatives to suspension that were developed during the 1970s is provided below. Many of these models continue to be used today in school districts across the country.[3]

Varieties of In-School Alternatives to Suspension

The three most common models of in-school alternatives to suspension that existed during the 1970s were (a) time-out rooms, (b) in-school suspension centers, and (c) counseling/guidance programs. The models were preventive and prescriptive in orientation and attempted to assist students academically and/or behaviorally before they were involved in more serious infractions of school policy that would have led to permanent exclusion or a school transfer.

Time-out rooms were designed to do exactly what their labels suggested. Students were sent to a vacant classroom or room adjacent to the principal's office, where they were temporarily left unattended until a staff person inquired about the reason for their referral. This person served also as a facilitator between the student and the sending teacher in cases where an interpersonal conflict had precipitated the referral. Students were usually referred for one class period, and there was no formal instruction. However, the student was assigned work by the homeroom teacher, and the time-out room monitor assisted the pupil if there were questions about the assigned work. In most cases, referral back to regular classes was determined by the assistant principal after careful deliberation with the monitor.

An alternate possibility was that the monitor might help the student to draft a behavioral contract that committed him or her to more positive behavior after returning to class. That agreement was signed in the presence of the teacher and sometimes by a parent as well.

As the author learned from visits to schools with time-out rooms, many time-out rooms left much to be desired. Some rooms were located in basements, dingy cellars, or remote areas of the school building where no interaction could conceivably occur. In those instances, the time-out room was no more than a detention center and took on the characteristics of the corresponding intervention used often in clinical therapy.

In-school suspension centers, the second most common program, differed substantially from, and offered more extensive services than, time-out rooms. Placement was for longer periods (on the average 3 days), formal instruction was provided, and the staff was larger (usually comprising a counselor, a "master teacher," and a social worker). The additional staff in this model was the key factor that differentiated this program from all other types. If students were from the same grade, the master teacher could prepare daily lessons with the help of homeroom teachers in each of the students' subject areas. In the case of students from different grade levels, daily assignments were provided by each instructor and monitored by the master teacher, who helped the students when the academic material was not understood. A highly able and experienced teacher who was competent in many subjects played a pivotal role in this type of program. Moreover, students benefited substantially from individualized attention. The counselor had the responsibility of supplementing classroom activities by exposing students to audiovisual materials and games on decision making and values clarification, or by planning group guidance sessions that gave the students an opportunity to vent their frustrations about the school or their own academic performance. These experiences helped to facilitate a more positive relationship between the sending teacher and the student in trouble. The role of the social worker can be best described as a liaison between the home and the school. The social worker formalized contact between the parents of the referred student and the teachers and administrators of the school. He or she made regular visits to the parents at home or at work. This kind of rapport kept students on guard, even though they knew that the social worker was not a truant or probation officer. Generally, the staff of this type of program were special people who possessed (a) high tolerance levels, (b) unswerving commitment to the needs and problems of students, and (c) a certain savvy for working as "brokers" between students and school personnel. This was not easy, because they had to take some risks— sometimes by suggesting that the teacher, rather than the student, might need help. There was usually an average daily enrollment of 15 students in this type of program, and reassignment of a student to regular classes was a shared decision made by parents, administrators, teachers, and the in-school suspension center staff.

The third common type of alternative to suspension was the guidance program. This supplemental counseling model differed significantly from time-out rooms and in-school suspension centers because comparable facilities were not needed, and the amount of time spent by students was dependent upon the seriousness of the infraction (which determined the length of a daily or weekly counseling session). The "success" of these varied intervention models was determined by the readiness of the students to see that their misbehavior had interfered with the classroom instruction of their peers. Depending upon the students' problems and the expertise of the counselors, interventions such as nondirective counseling, Glasser's reality therapy, transactional analysis, values clarification, or Kohlberg's moral reasoning model were used. Because only one or two full-time persons were used in these programs, the services of graduate school interns in psychology, volunteer para-counselors, social workers from the community, and sometimes parents complemented the staff. The referral process in these programs was less rigid than in the other two models previously discussed, and teachers as well as parents were able to refer students.

The three types of programs mentioned above were not the only varieties of alternatives to suspension used in the schools during the late 1970s. Some schools used ombudspersons, hall monitors and pupil problem teams, work-study programs, Saturday and evening schools, after-school detention centers, and peer counseling programs. "School survival" courses were also incorporated into the regular curriculum of some schools. School system budgets, which were usually very restrictive, and the results of needs assessments on rates of suspensions typically dictated what type(s) of programs were implemented. Some districts were able to operate one or more of these programs cheaply by using unassigned staff and with materials that were already available to the individual schools. However, the majority of the in-school suspension programs were supported totally or partially by a myriad of federal entitlement programs such as the Emergency School Assistance Act (ESAA), the Vocational and Career Education Act, Titles IV-B and IV-C of the Elementary and Secondary Education Act (ESEA) that supplemented counseling and guidance services, and the Law Enforcement Assistance Administration (LEAA). With fewer of these government programs available to school districts today, financial support to implement any of the above programs would have to come totally from the district's general operating budget.

Discussion

The most important conclusion to be drawn from the previous discussion of street academy programs and in-school alternatives to suspension is that both alternatives have served the beneficial purpose of keeping students in school despite their disenchantment with the educational process, their attitudinal and behavioral problems, and/or their low levels of performance. But both programs were and have not been, nor were they ever intended to be, perfect. Instead, they were temporary efforts designed to address the needs and concerns of adolescent and young adult students who would have ordinarily dropped out or have been pushed out of school.

Having had direct experience as a street academy director for 3 years and as a primary researcher of in-school alternatives to suspension since the late 1970s, this author can strongly assert that many educators expect most alternative programs to produce overwhelming results within short periods of time before they are willing to recognize their viability. Both types of programs have been beneficial to students, school districts, and ultimately local communities, but the administrators and teachers who staff these alternatives have always had to work hard to make sure that these programs did not become "dumping grounds" for students labeled as "difficult" by their regular schools' personnel. Thus, in the case of some street academies, it was always important that the school that referred the student to the program accepted the responsibility to take students back when they appeared ready to return. This type of agreement formed the basis for a close collaboration between both of the schools involved, and students received a clear message that the two educational units were working together. That cooperation made it easy to thoroughly address the academic and personal needs of all students so that they could receive the best possible assistance from teachers and counselors. With 1991 high school dropout rates of African American, Hispanic, and white students between the ages of 14 and 24 estimated at 11.3%, 29.5%, and 10.5% (U.S. Bureau of the Census, 1992, Table No. 460), respectively, the reinstitution or expansion of street academies and other alternative schools deserves serious consideration if school districts are unable to serve these more than 4 million students.

Likewise, in-school alternative to suspension programs are still useful today and appear to be making a "comeback" in some districts. However, it is extremely important that the programs be constructive and prescriptive in their philosophical orientation rather than punitive, and that the due process of the student not be violated simply because an in-school alternative exists within the school or the district. Furthermore, it is imperative today that school districts thoroughly review *who suspends* and *for what reasons*, because a larger than expected number of African American students particularly are "pushed out" of school by suspension. According to a 1990 Elementary and Secondary School Civil Rights Survey conducted by the U.S. Department of Education's Office of Civil Rights (1993), African American students represented 32% of all suspensions nationwide and accounted for 35% of all students labeled as "educable mentally retarded," but these students' representation of total enrollment in the nation's schools is only 16%. (Suspension rates for Hispanic and Native American students were the same as their national enrollment percentages—8% and 1%, respectively—and the suspension estimate for white students was 54% compared to their 68% total enrollment.) Even though in-school alternatives are viable responses to out-of-school suspension, they are not the answer to all classroom or discipline problems. Suspensions are indeed necessary sometimes, but many teachers also need help with managing their classrooms and should obtain assistance from school psychologists, counselors, and even their fellow teachers.

The appropriate role and status of alternatives such as street academies and in-school alternatives to suspension and expulsion must be determined today by careful dialogue among teachers, administrators, and educational policy makers. The type of students discussed in this chapter need a tremendous amount of personal attention, reinforcement, and opportunities to bolster their self-concepts and self-esteem. All, however, are not "marginal" students. Some are very able but are disenchanted with the traditional educational environment. Thus we must take advantage of the experiences and lessons of alternative schools and attempt to incorporate into traditional schools' culture, organization, and structure many of the critical elements that contributed to the former programs' success. Chief among those key factors was the recognition that the root causes of students' academic, social, or personal difficulties must be identified early and remedied immediately in order to change their educational performance and their attitudes. If we truly believe that all students have the potential to learn, more must be done to bolster the personal and academic self-concepts of those who are at either end of "the margins," those considered to be "at risk" and those typically referred to as "gifted and talented."

Commentaries

My intention is to discuss this issue in order to come up with some kind of action. My initial reaction to the research was, "Why am I reading about these two programs done 20 years ago?" Because, I discovered, it is absolutely fascinating that nothing is different. Dr. Garibaldi's points of discussion are absolutely the same as those arising from studies that are being done now in the Houston Independent School District; 1991-1992 data are no different from the 1972-1973 data. Students at the margins, including those who simply don't fit in, those who maintain continual tardiness, and so forth, force us to ask, "What kind of research needs to take place?" Those kids also fit in many other categories. I suggest separating the issue of alternative schools and street academies from the issue of in-school suspen-

sions, in that the reasons for them are completely different. The motivation for alternative schools may be financial, for instance. This is very different from alternatives to suspension, which simply maintain the status quo. The people who benefit the most are not the marginal students—it is the other students, those not involved in trouble, and the teachers.

Whether or not alternative schools are part of the school district, they enroll disproportionate numbers of nonwhite youth. In the Houston district we had approximately 14,000 students who were involved in disciplinary actions—fewer than 7% of the entire population. The numbers of students who are repeat offenders are probably similar to Dr. Garibaldi's, in that 61% were sent one time to in-school suspensions. What this says is that this method is fairly effective. Hispanic students did receive the highest rate of suspension. If the remedy for misbehavior is expulsion, then we need to ask questions about methods. At each level, African American students were given the highest percentage of disciplinary action. These are important data for us to consider (i.e., how we have structured middle schools and discipline within middle schools). Almost 20% of all middle school students were referred for disciplinary action. They are being referred to assignment centers, they are being kicked out, and so on. I ask, then, "What are we expecting of middle school kids?"

We must consider success and efficiency. We need to do away with the notion that these things are temporary—some kids will always need things done differently. But why kids need things to be different, now this is an area we need to explore.

Harriet Arvey, Assistant Superintendent of Pupil Services, Houston Independent School District

As important as the questions are that surfaced in this work, I want to suggest that perhaps we can't get there from here. Root causes should perhaps have been the focus of this research, for until we address this, I am not sure that a few more case studies will make all that much difference. Many of our kids are finding that schools are not for them—or that they are not right for the schools. It is a rational model. If you see your purpose as being able to provide the schools with alternatives—such as junior guidance classes in New York, that is, middle school intervention—you will see a much larger number of disturbing cases than you will see disturbed students.

We are responding more to children who are disturbing us than to those who are disturbed. But suppose the purpose is to hone academics? It is not from that population that we are getting youngsters who are exemplars. These students are returning to schools, pretty much, still at the margins. School itself remains relatively unchanged.

We need answers to the problems of school wastage. Could it be that if we changed our strategies children would remain in school? Empowering children must be part of the solution. We must focus on strategies for dealing with a system that was not necessarily designed for them, and then teach kids how to deal with those environments. We must determine what it is they need, and how to raise hell when they are not getting it. For most any of these kinds of changes, we need massive investments in staff development.

For 10 years now I have been talking about the lack of utility in didactic instruction. There is a mismatch between what schools are about and what kids need. Tensions are created when purposes of schools don't serve the needs of students. Most of what we do in school is about conservation. The kids who are failing don't need conservation, they need radical change, they need revolution. Some people do think of schooling and education as revolutionary activity. The hegemonic culture, the dominant culture, is in conflict. We must think about incorporating into this culture a subculture that is resistant to the dominant culture. Some years ago John Ogbu wrote a little book, focusing on kids as young as 9, 10, and 11, who recognized the benefits/rewards of graduating from high school. He speculated about the relationship of the lack of investment in education and the kids' perceptions of rewards. If a student doesn't think it is worth doing, doesn't see it out there, then that means we are engaging in a futile pursuit. We must place emphasis on political socialization—this may fulfill the purposes of helping the young people to better learn to work together for common causes.

Edmund W. Gordon, Professor Emeritus, Yale University

Notes

1. The Children's Defense Fund also points out that Black students were suspended at twice the rates of whites overall, that Black students at the secondary and elementary level were suspended three times as often as whites (12.8% vs. 4.1% at the secondary level,

and 1.5% vs. 0.5% at the elementary level), and that Black students were multiply suspended (i.e., three times or more) at a rate of 42% compared to 27% for white students. (See also Garibaldi and Bartley, 1990.)

2. *Insubordination* is a discretionary category generally used by teachers to refer students for suspension. Refusal to do homework or classwork, verbal assaults on teachers by students, and other types of misbehavior usually fall within this category.

3. Most of the extant literature on in-school alternatives to suspension provides descriptive information on individual programs (see National School Public Relations Association, 1976, and the National Association of Secondary School Principals' *NASSP Bulletin*, January 1977).

References

Children's Defense Fund. (1975). *School suspensions: Are they helping children?* Washington, DC: Washington Research Project.

Crowne, D. P., & Marlowe, D. (1969). A new scale of social desirability independent of psychopathology. *Journal of Consulting Psychology, 24*(4), 349-354.

Coleman, J. S., Campbell, E. Q., Hobson, C. J., McPartland, J., Mood, A. M., Weinfeld, F. D., & York, R. L. (1967). *Equality of educational opportunity.* Washington, DC: Government Printing Office.

Garibaldi, A. M. (1979). In-school alternatives to suspension: Trendy educational innovations. *Urban Review, 11*(2).

Garibaldi, A. M., & Bartley, M. (1990). Black school pushouts and dropouts: Strategies for reduction. *Urban League Review,* Summer/Winter. [Also in W. DeMarcell & E. W. Chunn (Eds.), *Black education: A quest for equity and excellence* (pp. 227-235). New Brunswick, NJ: Transaction.]

Gurin, P., Gurin, G., Lao, C. C., & Beattie, M. (1969). Internal-external control in the motivational dynamics of Negro youth. *Journal of Social Issues, 25,* 29-53.

Jones, L. P. (n.d., circa 1976). *The street academy experience: An experiment in alternative education for inner-city youth.* Unpublished manuscript.

Moore, V. P. (1977). *The street academy: The five-year experience* (Final report submitted to the National Institute of Education's Office of Experimental Schools for Contract No. 400-75-0032). New York: National Urban League Research Department.

Neill, S. B. (1976). *Suspensions and expulsions: Current trends in school policies and programs.* Arlington, VA: National School Public Relations Association.

U.S. Bureau of the Census. (1992). *Statistical abstract of the United States 1992* (Current Population Reports, series P-20). Washington, DC: Author.

U.S. Department of Education Office for Civil Rights. (1993, February). *1990 Elementary and Secondary School Civil Rights Survey, adjusted national estimated data.* Washington, DC: Author.

• • • • • •

5

• • • • • •

Alternatives and Marginal Students

MARY ANNE RAYWID

This chapter is a report on the current state of alternative education, particularly as it pertains to marginal or at-risk students. It offers information and analysis regarding what alternative schools are, how effective they are, how they fare in relation to other efforts to deal with the at-risk population, and the past and present of the alternative education movement.

But the chapter is also, in effect, an argument. It shows that many of the most promising proposals for improving the education of at-risk students—as well as many of the most popular reform recommendations for the education of all students—have drawn on the practice of alternative schools. However, these school improvement efforts import only selected features of that practice, thus divesting them of their transformational potential. Alternatives can and do yield

AUTHOR'S NOTE: The author wishes to thank the following individuals for their comments and suggestions on an earlier version of this chapter: Michelle Fine, Sy Fliegel, Joe Nathan, Gil Schmerler, Alan Singer, Mary Ellen Sweeney—and most especially Gregory A. Smith.

"restructured" education—but only because they restructure along multiple lines: organizational, environmental, and programmatic.

Background

Alternative schools in this country now date back for more than a quarter of a century. Although they have undergone periodic evolutions, they have remained a marginal phenomenon within the educational system. But they have also remained an active concept that continues to affect many youngsters. Both by design and by happenstance, an increasing number of the students most directly affected by alternatives are the disadvantaged youngsters populating urban schools.

The first public alternative schools, launched in the late 1960s, were mostly inspired by the ideas and events of that decade. Those that enrolled largely white, middle-class students and were found largely in small towns or suburbs—like the Village School in Great Neck, New York, Murray Road in Newton, Massachusetts, and the Wilson Open Campus School in Mankato, Minnesota—were typically influenced by the humanistic impulses and liberation theme of the 1960s. Those in the South, and in northern cities, tended to reflect the civil rights emphases of the time and were focused on giving poor and minority youngsters the educations previously denied them. There were also alternatives launched with the sociopolitical optimism that it was possible to refashion the world and its institutions and build a new society (Raywid, 1981).

Many of these first public school alternatives owed much to the "free" schools and the "freedom" schools that had emerged earlier in the decade within the private sector. The free schools echoed the ideas of progressive education or of A. S. Neill, and the freedom schools, launched initially in the South in the wake of the voter registration drives of the early 1960s, were aimed at individual and group empowerment.

Even if indirectly, these alternative schools generally represented a critique of the educational system; the notion of an alternative implied that some group of kids or some set of ideas was not receiving appropriate attention in conventional schools. Some alternatives openly saw themselves as the vanguard and model for the education of the future. Others saw themselves as an alternative to bureaucracy and a demonstration of a different, more humane way to organize human activity, without hierarchy, restrictive regulation, or monitoring (Duke, 1976; Nirenberg, 1977).

In the early 1970s, the federal Experimental Schools Program (ESP), seeking ways to refashion entire school systems, funded three districts to create multiple alternative schools. The program, launched in 1971, sponsored such systems in Minneapolis, in Berkeley, California, and in Tacoma, Washington. Although ESP was more concerned with establishing models for school change than with enhancing educational effectiveness, a pedagogically oriented rationale for improving outcomes through such systemwide options appeared with Mario Fantini's (1973) *Public Schools of Choice*. Fantini argued that different youngsters need different kinds of school environments if they are to succeed. A year later, David Tyack's *The One Best System* (1974) lent support to this idea by underscoring the arbitrariness logic of the assumption that there is one best way—or even one feasible way—to organize and deliver education. Both these books were invoked to urge that alternative schools become the norm and that all public schools in effect become alternatives to all of the others. The new "best system" would be marked by diversity and choice, with families selecting the school program and environment they found most compatible.

In 1976, the federal government offered yet another stimulus to the alternatives and options idea when it began funding magnet schools under the Emergency School Aid Assistance Act. Today the nation has 2,652 magnet schools offering 3,222 magnet programs (Steel, Levine, Rossell, & Armor, 1993). There have from the start been important differences between magnet and alternative schools, although some observers initially saw magnets as alternative schools created to stimulate voluntary racial desegregation. But alternatives were the forebears of the magnet genre, and many of the schools calling themselves "alternatives" have been funded as magnet schools.

At the same time that the alternatives idea was finding sponsorship by interests advocating change at the system or district level, a number of people seeking solutions to specific problems and for distinctive populations had begun turning to alternative schools as an answer. Thus there were initiatives for alternatives in the interests of preventing school vandalism and violence, juvenile crime and delinquency, and finally students' dropping out.

Thus from the start there has been ambiguity as to the purpose and intended audiences of alternative schools. Was it an idea for schools or for school systems? For all students or only for populations with special needs? To be available by choice or by assigned placements? Despite these ambiguities, however, two enduring consistencies have characterized most alternative schools: First, they have been designed to respond to a group not optimally served by the regular program; second, they have therefore represented varying degrees of departure from standard school organization, programs, and environments. The first of these traits has often linked alternative schools with unsuccessful, "disadvantaged," "marginal," or "at-risk" students. The second has often linked alternatives with innovative and creative practices and organization. And particular alternative schools have varied according to which of these two traits has loomed largest for them.

The audience question becomes particularly urgent under present demographic conditions. Although some alternatives say quite explicitly, "It is our school and its way of teaching that is alternative, not our students" (Schwarz, 1993, p. 1), many feel that alternatives are schools for some rather than all. Yet the line dividing "special needs" students, the "educationally disadvantaged," and the "at-risk" or "marginal" from the rest of the student population has become blurred. Indeed, given the minority majorities that dominate urban public schools, the number of youngsters living at and below poverty levels, and the educational backgrounds of many parents, a large majority of students in urban schools fall within the at-risk category.

Within its High School Division, New York City has a separate Alternative Schools Office that administers more than 35 schools and 300 programs. There is no official definition of *alternative*, however, and the only relevant source suggests merely that "most serve students not likely to succeed in high school or who have previously dropped out" (Phillips, 1992, p. 3). Phillips also noted that structurally, alternatives are small, many are nongraded, they employ some form of school-based management, many of their teachers teach outside their certified areas in interdisciplinary programs, and most teachers function as student advisors. Programmatically, "all are committed to unique principles and practices of schooling," and most pursue action learning and external learning opportunities. The list reflects features typical of alternative schools elsewhere as well.

Definitional Problems

So what is alternative education? The literature contains a dozen or more attempts to define it, identify its key characteristics, or name the elements important to its success (see, for example, Doob, 1977; Duke, 1978; Morley, 1991; Sweeney, 1988). In the absence of a standard definition, what will be offered here are some properties enumerated in definitional attempts to date, an identification of some boundaries, and a description of three distinct types of alternative schools.

Most descriptions emphasize smallness, personalization, interpersonal relationships, and a primary focus on students as human beings (Deal & Nolan, 1978; Loria, 1989; Morley, 1991; Wheelock & Sweeney, 1989). Organizationally, most call attention to flexibility, autonomy, the frequency of extended and diffuse staff roles, and to the alternative as a distinct administrative unit with its own separate identity and mission. Many analysts also note innovative and nontraditional curricular organization, instructional strategies, and governance patterns as traits.

Differences in the definitions are generally a matter of emphasis. Some conceptions make a specifically oriented school culture most central (e.g., Sweeney, 1988), some stress a particular school climate (e.g., Morley, 1991), and others have an organizational and structural focus (e.g., Raywid, 1988). The absence of a definition makes it necessary to specify boundaries distinguishing alternative schools from other programs and arrangements. First, an alternative school differs from a magnet school in that magnets specifically serve a desegregation purpose (Steel et al., 1993). The two also differ in that alternative schools are typically home-grown arrangements developed and independently operated by their immediate staff, whereas magnets are typically centrally inspired and remain centrally coordinated. Accordingly, alternatives may show substantially more organizational departure and innovation than magnets. Nevertheless, a great many alternative schools have been classified as magnets (for grant purposes), and some magnet schools—for example, some career academies—have been characterized as alternatives (Wehlage, Rutter, Smith, Lesko, & Fernandez, 1989).

An alternative school may be a school within a school or a minischool (the former being part of a larger school, the latter constituting a separate school in its own right, even if housed within a building with another school or schools), but it differs from a house plan. A house plan is an administrative arrangement intended to downscale a large school by dividing it into units. It assigns students and teachers to separate units, but these units are not differentiated as to mission, and there may be few if any programmatic differences from house to house. Mission and program distinctiveness are, by contrast, typical features of alternative schools.

An alternative school differs in several ways from an assigned "track." First of all, alternative schools are usually a student option (with one important exception to be discussed below), and students are thus free to move in and out of an alternative school, whereas such freedom is not part of track placement. Second, tracks may incidentally group students into the same classes, but there is ordinarily no intent to make an entity out of the group.

Alternative schools—or at least one type thereof—are likely to differ from programs explicitly targeted as dropout prevention, or programs for at-risk students, in seeking a range of students and deliberate heterogeneity as to ability and school motivation.

Alternative School Types

Not surprisingly, given their history and their diverse purposes, alternative schools represent programs of very different sorts. There are three distinct ideal types, with individual schools approximating these to varying degrees.

Type I alternatives are the ideological progeny of the early 1960s programs. They intend to make school engaging, challenging, and fulfilling for all involved. Their efforts have yielded a number of innovations and creative programs and arrangements that are now widely urged as general school improvement measures. These schools reflect organizational and administrative departures from the traditional, as well as programmatic innovations, and they may be our clearest examples of "restructured" schools (Hawley, 1991).

Type I alternatives are schools of choice, and they are usually extremely popular. Perhaps the best known examples are East Harlem's District 4 schools and the Central Park East schools to which the Spanish Harlem district gave rise. Type I alternatives are sometimes programmatically similar to magnet schools in that they are likely to reflect themes or emphases pertaining to content or instructional strategy or both.

Type II alternative schools, by contrast, are programs to which students are "sentenced," usually as a last chance prior to expulsion. Variants include in-school suspension programs, "cool-out" rooms, and longer term placements for the behaviorally disruptive. But one of the distinctive characteristics of the Type II program is that it is assumed to be temporary and promises "time off for good behavior." Under the title of "alternative schools," there are many such programs in the South, particularly in Florida and Texas (Bureau of Compensatory Education, 1980).

Typically, behavioral modification in one form or another is the Type II program's focus, and there is no attempt to modify curriculum or pedagogy. In fact, in-school suspension programs often try to have students perform the work of the regular classes. The assignments are likely to be a lot more solitary, however, and designed strictly for individual completion. Type II alternatives where students remain for a longer time may instead offer an academic curriculum that is "basics" oriented with an emphasis on factual knowledge and elementary skills.

Type III programs, meanwhile, are generally nonpunitive and more positive and compassionate in orientation. They are designed for students presumed to need extra help, remediation, or rehabilitation—usually academic and/or social/emotional. If jail is the best metaphor for Type II alternatives, therapy is appropriate for Type III programs. In theory, after sufficient treatment, successful students will be able to return to the mainstream and continue in the regular program. Predictably, then, Type III alternatives often focus on remedial work with high-structure tasks. They frequently also attempt to generate the conditions that will stimulate social and emotional growth—a matter often seen as calling for a focus on the school as community (Foley & Crull, 1984; Wehlage, Rutter, Smith, Lesko, & Fernandez, 1989).

Alternative schools are usually identifiable as one or another of these three ideal types, although particular programs can appear something of a mix. A compassionate staff, for example, may give a Type II program overtones of Type III, despite official purposes. Or a committed Type III staff may undertake a bit of the programmatic innovation that distinguishes a Type I alternative. But even so, the genre goes far in determining an alternative school's silhouette and central features.

First, the genre determines the program's raison d'être and hence the expectations that govern it and the criteria by which it will be evaluated. Second, the genre will also determine whether student affiliation is by choice or assignment. Type I alternatives are options, or programs of choice. Type II are not. Type III programs often include some combination of referral with student right to reject but not initiate the placement. The difference is important because the choice feature is clearly associated with positive results (Crain, Heebner, & Si, 1992; Larson & Allen, 1988; Musumeci & Szczypkowski, 1991) and is also considered particularly advantageous with marginal students—by virtue of both their previous negative school experiences and the conviction of many of them that they can exercise little influence over what befalls them (Butler-Por, 1987).

Third, and perhaps most far-reaching, Type I alternatives assume that by changing a school's program and environment, one can alter the behavior, performance, and achievement of those associated with it. Type II and Type III alternatives assume, by contrast, that a lack of educational success is due to deficiency on the part of the student, whether characterological, emotional, intellectual, or something else. The result is that Type II and Type III alternatives sustain the service delivery mission orientation associated with bureaucracy, whereas Type I alternatives are committed to responsiveness—that is, to providing the essentials for facilitating the success of their charges.

It might seem that Type II is not really an alternative at all and is simply irrelevant to the challenge of making a positive difference for students at risk. However, a strange ambiguity often seems to mark school efforts to deal with education-resistant students. The school's response frequently combines punishment and support. For instance, sometimes the infractions that send students to the Type II in-school suspension programs include truancy. Thus the punitive response is explicitly invoked as a means of encouraging attendance and preventing dropping out. (The success potential of such a strategy is contingent, of course, upon strong student motivation—which is just what seems to be missing. But the irony may be lost in the face of our ambivalence toward these youngsters.) We often tend toward ambivalence with respect to students who fail to respond positively to our efforts. We want to help as well as punish the most defiant, and we may harbor serious misgivings even about those to whom we can respond with compassion. Even in Type III programs, as well as in Type II, arrangements often suggest negative judgments about students and "blaming the victim."

The ambivalence present at the policy level can be seen in an evaluation of Florida's alternative education programs that insisted the programs were for "disinterested" and "unsuccessful" students, as well as for the "disruptive" (Office of Planning and Budgeting, 1981). Legislation proposed in Florida named "intervention centers" and "in-school suspension programs" as two types of educational alternatives, along with "other alternatives to suspension or expulsion" (Bureau of Compensatory Education, 1980, p. 143). At the same time, the committee recommending such arrangements insisted the programs must be "positive, not punitive" (p. 18). And a national survey of alternatives for disruptive youth concluded, "Alternative [school] climate should reflect the philosophy that it's better and easier in the normal, comprehensive school environment, which encourages students to want to return to the regular school setting as soon as possible" (Garrison, 1987, p. 22). Thus there seem to be a number of contradictions and mixed signals.

The Research Record

We turn now to the track record of alternative schools—how well they work and how successful they are. We will look briefly at Types II and III and then focus on Type I because it is the variety with the most clear positive findings. Subsequently we shall review the findings on several core features associated with alternatives.

Type II Schools

The record of Type II schools suggests that they often serve no purpose beyond ridding conventional classrooms of disruptive youngsters. As we shall see, the attributes that make for positive effects are not highly correlated with those of the programs to which students are sent for poor behavior. The latter programs that report benefits tend to fashion themselves more as therapeutic than as penal settings—associating them with Type III rather than Type II alternatives (Gold & Mann, 1984).

According to a study by Florida's Office of the Governor, there were almost 58,000 assignments of youngsters to in-school suspension programs during the 1979-1980 school year (the total does not represent 58,000 students, but instances, and a number of youngsters may have been sent to in-school suspension several times during the year). Analyses of multiple districts showed no correlation between the existence of such programs and local levels of dropouts, referrals, corporal punishment, suspension, or expulsion (Office of Planning and Budgeting, 1981). Thus the programs were helping with none of the problems that Type II alternatives had been launched to solve.

Type III Schools

The record of Type III programs is stronger. These alternatives are based on the assumption that students can be helped to succeed in the "regular" school. They tend to stress personal social/emotional development, reeducation, and academic remediation. The environments they provide are typically small, supportive, with positive student-adult relationships, and considerable amounts of individual attention. Student behavior typically improves under such circumstances, with increased attendance and fewer disciplinary incidents (Gold & Mann, 1984). Academic gains are also attributed to these programs, in terms of credit accumulation and/or knowledge and skills acquired. However, the changes often last only as long as the student remains in the alternative school. Only the Gold and Mann (1984) study reports gains persisting as long as a year after return to the "regular" school. Other studies have found that once students return, the problems recur (Frazer & Baenen, 1988; McCann & Landi, 1986). The studies typically conclude that the programs have failed to bring about the improvements sought—rarely, if ever, that the students involved can succeed in an alternative school environment. Thus evidence that supports the need for such variants is often read as testimony to their failure.

Type I Schools

A different picture emerges from studies of Type I alternative schools. There are numerous stories of dramatic gains and turn-arounds for youngsters who had detested school; of problem students, some previously classified handicapped, whose problematic behavior disappeared in the alternative school setting; and of impressive academic gains (see Raywid, 1984, 1989). There are also stories of alternative schools that are outstandingly effective, marked by extraordinary student accomplishment and high levels of commitment on the part of all constituents, teachers, students, and parents. Not all schools, of course, meet with this sort of success, but it is not uncommon for researchers and evaluators to receive testimony to individual transformations like the following:

> Rickie flourished at the Media Academy, in an environment in which teachers were willing to reach out to him as a person. "I learned more this year than any other year of school," he said of his first year at the Academy. . . . "I had never experienced this before where the teachers are close and encourage me. I was just a C+/B- student, but now I am an A/B student." (Wehlage et al., 1989, pp. 166-167)

> I've seen more positive growth in my son in six weeks, than in a year and a half of intensive counseling. SAIL teachers are tuned into the language that Bryan speaks. . . . He's constantly telling me about new things he has learned and amazing ways that people relate to him. We both just can't believe it. I no longer have to force him out of bed—he wouldn't miss a day for the world. (Wood, 1989, pp. 197-198)

It is also not uncommon to discover evidence of school transformation, as distinct from that of individual students. Wehlage, Smith, and Lipman (1992) define a transformed or successfully restructured school as one displaying second-order change, harmonious student-adult relations, engaging curriculum and instruction, reallocated staff roles and responsibilities, and the use of community resources. They reported the following about 6 of the 14 alternative schools they studied:

> Teachers have assumed the additional roles of counselor, confidante, and friends, and efforts are made to bond the students to the school, to the teaching staff, and to one another. Course content is more closely tied to the needs of the students in these programs, and efforts are made to make the courses more engaging and relevant. Greater emphasis is placed on hands-on and experiential learning and students are given greater responsibility for their own success. More attention is paid to the individual needs and concerns of students, in and outside of class. Teachers work together to govern the school and make critical decisions about curriculum and school policy. . . . A climate of innovation and experimentation is common. (Wehlage et al., 1989, p. 172)

Thus there is reason to believe that alternatives represent an effective way to transform schools as well as individual students (Hawley, 1991). There is also evidence that they can transform entire districts.

To date, the unchallenged model of district-wide alternatives is Manhattan's Community School District 4 in East or Spanish Harlem. With its 95% minority population, its high poverty levels (80% of the students are on free or reduced-cost lunches), and its history of school failure, virtually its whole population qualifies as disadvantaged and at risk. As of 1973 the district—the one scoring worst throughout the city on a number of academic indicators—began encouraging the development of programs they came to identify as "alternative concept schools." These were schools launched by groups of interested teachers who did not have a detailed blueprint guiding their development. As described by their many chroniclers (Domanico, 1989; Elmore, 1988; Fliegel, 1993; Harrington & Cookson, 1992; Kutner &

Salganik, 1986; Rogers & Chung, 1983), the programs shared these features:

1. They were small.
2. They were designed, both programmatically and organizationally, by those who were going to operate them.
3. They took their character—or theme or "focus"—from the particular strengths and interests of the teachers who conceived them.
4. Their teachers all chose the program—with the plan that subsequent teachers would be selected with the input of present staff.
5. Their students and their families chose the program.
6. Each program was administered by a teacher-director.
7. Their small size denied them much auxiliary, specialized staff (e.g., librarians, counselors, deans).
8. All of the early programs were housed as minischools in buildings dominated by much larger programs.
9. The superintendent acted so as to sustain the autonomy and protect the integrity of the minischools within each of their buildings.
10. All of the programs enjoyed considerable autonomy from district interference, and the administration also buffered them from demands of citywide school officials.

These programs emerged one at a time, as small groups of teachers stepped forward with a proposal. In 1974, three opened. In the next 3 years, there were six more, and in the following 3 years, an additional six. By 1983 there were 21 such programs at the junior high and elementary school level. At that point the district opened all junior high schools to choice and ended neighborhood assignments.

The "alternative concept" programs were invited and then supported by an enterprising, reform-minded young superintendent hoping to turn things around. He deliberately cultivated innovation and risk taking among those within the district, and due to both the loose coupling of the city system and the neglect sometimes accorded causes presumed hopeless, District 4 remained largely ignored for a number of years.

Meanwhile, the program's development was fostered by continuity in leadership. When Tony Alvarado, the initiating superintendent, left in 1983 to become New York City Schools Chancellor, he was succeeded by Carlos Medina, who had been his assistant. Sy Fliegel, who had been director of the alternative schools, continued to perform that function. When Medina named Fliegel the deputy superintendent, John Falco, who had founded one of the original alternative schools, became and still serves as alternative schools director.

Student achievement has risen strikingly. Compared to 15% in 1974, by 1988 62% of District 4 students were reading above grade level (Fliegel, 1993). As of 1983, 49% of the district's students were scoring above grade level in math (Domanico, 1989). There are also indications that District 4 is successfully fostering English acquisition, for it reports fewer students in programs for the limited English proficient than do any of the other nine districts in the city where 50% or more of the students are Latino (Domanico, 1989). Still another indicator is the record of district youngsters accepted by selective high schools. Fewer than 9% of the city's students are admitted to these schools, yet in 1987, 22% of District 4's eighth-grade graduates entered such high schools, and in 1990, 20% did so (Fliegel, 1993).

District 4 operates two high schools, both of which far surpass city averages for graduation rates. At the Manhattan Center for Science and Mathematics, more than half the students earn Regents diplomas. Of the 245 students graduating in 1988, 241 went on to higher education (Fliegel, 1993). The figures for Central Park East Secondary School appear equally impressive. A recent study shows that 80% of the ninth-grade entrants graduate from the school, with most of the departers having transferred or moved out of the city. The dropout rate is 5%. Moreover, more than 90% of CPESS graduates go directly to college, and early indications are that most will complete it—at 4-year, residential institutions (Schwarz, 1993).

Factors Associated With Success. Wehlage et al. (1989) offer a good framework for examining the record of Type I alternatives. They conclude that to succeed with at-risk youngsters, schools must be "communities of support" in two senses: They must be carefully sustained as communities with which youngsters want to be affiliated—that is, places successfully evoking bonding of students to the school; and they must be places where students are genuinely educationally engaged—that is, places where they are attentively involved with school and classroom activities.

A third facet or dimension of an effective alternative school is its organizational context and conditions.[1] First of all, alternative schools must be small (Gregory & Smith, 1987; Sweeney, 1988; Wehlage et al., 1989). In fact, small schools or the downscaling of large ones is now being widely and generally recommended for all students (Bryk & Driscoll, 1988; Fowler & Walberg, 1991; Oxley & McCabe, 1990). Further, alternatives must be cohesive units with their own separate space, programs, students, and staff. Human relationships within the school are the critical component, particularly the relationships between students and adults and, most particularly, between students and teachers (Foley & Crull, 1984; Gold & Mann, 1984; Raywid, 1982). Role definitions for teachers become broader, less specialized, and more diffuse than in most schools, enabling them to interact more extensively with students and in multiple capacities—friend, confidant, mentor, advisor (Bryk & Driscoll, 1988). This in turn calls for structures that generate and sustain such relationships, and probably most alternatives large enough to need them have thus devised small advisories and "family" groups. Sustaining such relationships and responding to individuals also requires organizational flexibility and a minimum of formality.

Alternative schools prefer social control through norms as opposed to rules and regulations (Raywid, 1990). Choice is pivotal for several reasons. First, it facilitates the assembling of a group sharing some educationally related concern, thus enabling the school's mission to find support (Hill, Foster, & Gendler, 1990). Second, it facilitates strong affiliation and heightens the sense of membership (Bryk & Driscoll, 1988; Erickson, 1982). Third, a continuing emphasis on choice—not only in gaining entrance, but within the program—maximizes motivation and commitment, as well as teaches responsibility (Kaczynski, 1989; Trickett, 1991). Finally, choice is important to avoid the stigmatizing of alternatives.

Another key to success is teacher design of programs (both curricular and instructional) and teacher participation in setting school policy (Duke, 1976; Rosenholtz, 1989; Sweeney, 1983). These functions create greater mutual interdependence among teachers and thus generate more collaborative interaction (Center for Research on the Context of Secondary School Teaching, 1993), assuring a sense of staff ownership and collective responsibility (Rosenholtz, 1989). Relatedly, there is often a flattened hierarchy and a downplaying of status differences. A democratic, empowerment, or shared decision-making theme is likely to characterize staff relationships within the school and often to include students (Trickett, 1991).

Such organizational differences matter. A study comparing 12 alternatives confirmed that student perceptions of and reactions to an alternative environment were related to its organizational characteristics (Stevens, 1985). Not surprisingly, then, alternatives are cited as prime illustrations of restructured schools (Wehlage et al., 1992). A longitudinal study of professional community within schools is finding its clearest and most positive case in a New York City alternative school (Raywid, 1993), and a second study concluded that a Michigan alternative school came closer to exhibiting the characteristics of professional community than any of the other 15 schools studied. Teachers in the Michigan school have a greater influence on policy than at any other site, teacher collaboration time is more extensive, they have high marks for principal leadership, and job satisfaction is among the highest encountered (Center for Research on the Context of Secondary School Teaching, 1993).

Alternative schools must be "membership" institutions, or places with which students want to affiliate; this is perhaps one of their strongest accomplishments. Bryk and Driscoll (1988) demonstrated the importance of a strong communal orientation to commitment, effort, accomplishment, and satisfaction for both teachers and students. Further, Wehlage et al. (1989), as well as others (e.g., Gold & Mann, 1984) claim that the bonding of youngsters to school and staff is particularly important for at-risk students.

A national survey (Raywid, 1982) found that alternative schools identify the personal relationships the school fosters as their most distinctive feature, more critical than curriculum or instructional strategies. In many alternative schools, an advisory system assures that every student is known well to at least one adult (Wehlage et al, 1989), often through forming a close-knit group to which students belong throughout their stay in the school. These groups meet often (daily in some schools) and may pursue out-of-school activities together as well as in-school discussions.

Virtually all alternatives emphasize student/teacher relationships; some also stress student-to-student relationships. In a school where both kinds of relationships are stressed, the emphasis on the school as community is probably stronger and its effects more powerful and pronounced—but there is no explicit evidence to this effect.

There is, however, considerable evidence that alternative schools take pains to personalize the arrangements and practices that mark them, from longtime teacher assignments to students' daily classwork. Assignments are often tailored to individuals as a means of sparking response. To cite an imaginative instance, one alternative school turned a dreaded annual library research project into something much more palatable by having it start with the selection of a front-page story from the *New York Times* on the day the student was born (Raywid, 1993).

Several other alternative school features reflect their more personalized nature. Virtually all address holistic aims, including emotional and social as well as academic development (Sweeney, 1988). Students are known and treated as individuals, and the staff remains aware of the directions in which their students' lives are moving. This calls for a sustained concern with meeting the needs of students, which students acknowledge by reporting that teachers in alternative schools "care." Studies find that even the lowest scoring alternative schools are in closer sync with what youngsters (and their teachers) think they need than the highest scoring comprehensive high schools (Gregory & Smith, 1987).

The alternative school commitment to the preferences of students and teachers constitutes a kind of empowerment for all. In some alternatives this is manifested in the machinery of democracy, either in group meetings offering all a direct voice or in representative bodies. In others, the strength of individuals is shown by the influence that strongly felt concerns exert over decisions. People feel that their concerns will be considered by the decision makers, whether or not they are part of that group.

The alternative school record is less consistent with respect to the sort of academic student engagement that Wehlage and colleagues expect of the effective alternative school. Perhaps this is the clearest manifestation of the effects of the difference between Type I and Type III programs—the former assuming that new schools are needed, the latter striving to improve students. Thus Type I alternatives are typically marked by considerable instructional creativity, whereas Type III more typically emphasize the basics. Thus in some alternative schools, staff focus heavily on individual problems and on the resocialization process, with less emphasis on knowledge, skills, or work habits that might prepare them for postsecondary education (Smith, 1988).

For instance, Trickett (1991), who wrote a history of 14 years in the life of a New Haven alternative school, barely mentions academic work and engagement. Gold and Mann (1984) emphasize the importance of students experiencing success but say little about the instructional programs conducive to it. Yet the record explored in these pages shows a number of alternative schools whose students are highly accomplished academically, and for whom authentic academic engagement is a major emphasis.

Type I alternatives often emphasize making curriculum compelling and challenging and trying to invite students into learning. In the high school "SWS" program at the Wheatley School on Long Island, for instance, recent classes have included such titles as "Literary Dogs" (featuring 11 short stories about dogs), "The German Question," "Male Versus Female Perspective and Aesthetic in Two American Novels," and "Constitutional Quarrels." Last year the district's superintendent taught a course on multiple interpretations of the Cinderella myth. History is often organized in this alternative school as separate courses on individuals (e.g., Stalin), incidents (e.g., Watergate and Nixon), or decades (e.g., a course on the 1920s that includes sociological and cultural fare as well as economic and political history). During last spring's final 7-week module, the 75 students enrolled wrote and rewrote more than 700 papers, including a comparison of Norman Podhoretz and James Baldwin on racism, and Bruno Bettelheim and Hannah Arendt on victimization.

In other Type I alternatives, the focus is on experiential learning. The City-As-School programs that have now been established all over the nation were among the first alternative school attempts to render school learning accessible other than primarily through books.

"Challenge" programs, in which learning is pursued and documented through student design and completion of distinct "passages," represent another form of experience-focused learning (Gregory & Smith, 1987; Williams, 1993). The instructional orientation seeking to combine academics with work-related efforts, yielding a tangible product, is another. At the Media Academy in Oakland, California, for instance, students "major" in print and electronic journalism, and they regularly produce two newspapers (Wehlage et al., 1989). Service learning has also long been associated with alternative schools. One of the earliest such efforts was the Consumer Action Service developed at the St. Paul Open School, in which students took on the cases of disgruntled consumers and successfully resolved 70% of the cases (Nathan, 1992). Students at the Jefferson County Open School in Colorado make an annual 2-week trip to the Navajo Reservation to plant fruit trees. This year two groups also went to assist in flood relief in Missouri (Colorado Options in Education, 1993).

The Lessons of Two Failed Ventures. At this point, having looked at the components and considerations associated with success, let us turn to two ventures that did not succeed, the dropout prevention initiative in New York City and the New Futures project conducted in four cities. As these projects suggest, one advantage of alternative schools over other strategies appears to lie in their capacity to provide a systemic or total school environment approach to dropout prevention. A second associated advantage lies in the relative capacity of alternatives to successfully introduce transformative change in schools.

Between 1984 and 1990 there were two extensive dropout prevention programs operating in New York City, one state sponsored and one city sponsored. Together they involved 36 high schools, 98 middle schools, and 5 elementary schools. The first 4 years of the 6-year project cost approximately $120 million (Meyer, 1990). An extensive evaluation concluded that neither of the two programs had accomplished very much, in that there were few gains in student attendance, retention, or courses passed (Grannis, 1992). Indeed, some students had gone backward in these respects. The city's own evaluation concluded flatly that "the programs failed to meet their goals" and recommended that the projects be extensively redesigned in order to restructure the schools involved (Meyer, 1990).

Both evaluations identified the problem as a piecemeal approach that made the changes introduced mere supplements to existing programs and arrangements rather than a revamping of them. Guidelines and accountability procedures focused on the adoption of discrete measures rather than on outcomes, and few schools showed evidence of extensive, fundamental, or far-reaching changes (Grannis, 1992; Meyer, 1990). The evaluators agreed that "a comprehensive restructuring of students' school experiences" was necessary and that houses or alternative schools should be created for all students.

According to the recommendations, school organization as well as program must be transformed if school is to affect the attitudes and achievement levels of marginal students. Evidence in support of this conclusion comes also from a recent study of New York City's career magnet schools, which enroll almost a third of the city's high school students (Crain et al., 1992). Employing an experimental design, this study looked at the impacts of career magnet schools on weaker students (those whose academic records were too weak to meet the programs' usual criteria and who gained admission through a lottery).

These students were paired with other, comparable students who applied but were not admitted to the career magnets. The study found that average readers were more successful in the magnet schools than in comprehensive high schools. They accumulated more credits, had bigger reading gains, and were more likely to remain in school. But the findings of another set of comparisons may be even more significant. Some of the career magnets are separate schools in which all the students enrolled are youngsters who have chosen the program. Others are schools within schools housed in, but very minimally separated from, comprehensive high schools. (Magnet and nonmagnet students are enrolled in the same classes.) The programs that separated their magnet and nonmagnet students were substantially more effective with respect to both dropout prevention and educational accomplishment (Crain et al., 1992).

The investigators posit curricular explanations: "Those programs which take their career commitment most seriously are the ones that show the strongest educational outcomes" (Crain et al., 1992, p. 32). Equally plausible, however, is that the schools within schools fell short of significantly altering the experience of school. School organization and school environment were not transformed. Nonseparation means that school culture and climate, and hence student sense of affiliation, change very little.

Analysis of another failed effort suggests why such efforts fail despite major infusions of resources. The Annie Casey Foundation has invested $40 million over a 5-year period in order to alter the life chances of at-risk youth, an effort known as the "New Futures" project (Wehlage et al., 1992). Changing educational practice was a major component of the program, which has been carried out in four cities. In fact, the grantor was explicit in expecting long-term transformations of both an organizational and instructional nature. Yet at the end of the first 3 years, an evaluation team concluded that "a school restructuring process likely to lead to improved outcomes for at-risk youth has not yet begun." Nor, they add, are the sorts of change necessary even "on the horizon" (Wehlage, Smith, & Lipman, 1991, pp. 18, 35).

Why? There were at least two explanations, one a consequence of the other. First, even the more radical of the specific changes had been implemented as supplements or add-ons to existing structures and practices rather than as replacements of them. This meant that negative factors like poor adult/student relationships and a negative school climate continued to prevail, with "highly punitive discipline policies, an overemphasis on control, and frequent adversarial relations between students and teachers" (Wehlage et al., 1992, p. 85). Also, the group exposed to the changes remained small. The school's fundamental definition, the way staff went about their business, and the students' basic experience of school all remained unchanged.

The second, underlying reason why the restructuring had not really begun was that staff remained unconvinced of its necessity. The problem, they continued to assume, lay with the students and not the school. Thus staff continued to identify causes of difficulty as individuals' personal problems and to call for idiosyncratic solutions.

This is a landmark study on change—and on how even the most radical or potentially restructuring of arrangements can be rendered innocuous and minimally disturbing of business as usual. It suggests that to try to change structure without changing culture is likely to prove futile. The study is also a testament to the importance of school climate. Despite efforts to improve things for the youngsters involved, adult/student relationships remained largely adversarial, and the hoped-for consequences of the efforts never materialized. The study also suggests that the conservative, change-resistant method of improving is to add on more discrete services—more forms of support and remediation—as dispensed by more specialists. Success demands systemic change, a total school transformation.

Together, these studies make powerful recommendations on how to make schools viable for marginal students. The New Futures evaluation suggests that the culture of a school must rest on a sincere staff conviction that all youngsters can be educated if the right conditions are supplied them—and on a moral commitment to doing so. The New York City dropout prevention program suggests that piecemeal adoption of components will not suffice, regardless of their potential. A systemic approach is required, in the sense that a school's various systems must be alternative—in terms of program, structure, organization, the allocation of roles and responsibilities, interaction patterns, and so forth—in order to accomplish more than superficial and peripheral change.

Although none of these studies explicitly recommended the wide-scale adoption of alternative schools, they clearly underscore a major strength of Type I alternative schools: They represent the combining of the necessary components.

The Alternative Schools Movement and Its Influence

Given the evidence we have examined, then, it might be asked what sort of support alternative schools enjoy and why they are not more prevalent. We turn first to the present status of the alternative education movement and its influence, and then to the factors that constrain it.

Today several indicators would signal a live and healthy alternative schools movement. A number of state conferences and at least two national conferences of alternative schools assemble annually, the latter typically drawing as many as 400 people. The alternative education periodical *Changing Schools* has been published for more than 20 years. There are currently 21 state associations of alternative schools, according to an annual directory now in its fourth edition

(Thrasher, 1993). These state groups are organized into a confederation titled the International Affiliation of Alternative School Associations and Personnel. A national survey of public and private alternatives is currently underway, and a major publisher will carry the resulting alternative school handbook.

Yet despite such signs of institutionalization, and despite the advantages and accomplishments of alternative schools, there may be less of an identifiable alternative school movement today than there was earlier. The movement has from the start been divided into at least three types of schools that differ fundamentally. The Type I population is further fragmented into the National Coalition of Alternative Community Schools, the Progressive School Association, and those associated primarily with holistic education or with invitational education.

According to at least one analyst, this fragmentation is probably good news as well as bad. It may be harder—though not impossible—to find the Type I alternatives that appeared so rapidly 20 years ago, with their "accent on freedom, responsibility, and involvement" (Schmerler, 1983, p. 5). On the other hand, many more youngsters are now benefiting from their message. Much that these schools have stood for has now either been adopted by, or is widely urged for, the mainstream.

Several contemporary urban reform initiatives are influenced by alternative schools and show how they have affected the mainstream. The first is New York City's small high schools initiative. Thirty-four such schools opened in 1993, with an additional 27 scheduled for September 1994. The schools differ considerably in content and style, but all are separate, autonomous minischools; all emphasize a particular theme; and all reflect close ties to some community or other group outside themselves (Berger, 1992). All have been chosen by their students and staff. Not all have explicitly fashioned themselves as alternatives, but a number have (Henderson & Raywid, 1994).

Two other initiatives show the imprint of alternatives. In 1987, the New York City Board of Education mandated the division of all ninth grades into "houses," in order to provide "the opportunity to personalize the school experience, gaining the advantages of a small school while addressing the academic and social needs of entering

high school students" (Oxley & McCabe, 1989. p. i). A study examining the first-year experience of the plan observed that it has "the
potential to serve as the centerpiece of needed restructuring at the
high school level" (p. 4).

But the same researchers, in a second-year study (Oxley & McCabe,
1990), noted that none of the schools investigated had adopted all the
elements necessary for optimum success, which they summarized
this way:

> Well-conceived house plans subdivide schools into physically
> discrete smaller units creating intimate environments that pro-
> mote interaction among staff and students. They take advan-
> tage of the opportunities provided by the smaller settings and
> work groups to create cohesive educational programs rein-
> forced by interdisciplinary teaching; enable staff to offer per-
> sonal, ongoing support to students and each other; involve staff
> and students in the decision-making process; and encourage
> wide participation in extra-curricular activities. (p. v)

These recommendations would make each house very much like
an alternative school. The only typical Type I alternative school
features omitted are a particular theme or focus and affiliation by
choice. In fact, in the house plan it would appear that neither staff
nor student interests need to be involved in the determination of
assignments. Neither is the decision whether to move in the direction
of houses left to choice, for the ninth-grade organization was mandated citywide, and the extension of that organization to other grades
is within the prerogative of principals.

Similarly, Philadelphia is attempting to launch "charters" in 22
neighborhood high schools. To date, 15 of these schools have been
entirely broken up into charters, or schools within schools, with the
rest containing only one or two of the charters (Chira, 1993). A total
of 94 charters now exist, each consisting of 200 to 400 students, with
10 to 12 core teachers.

> The charter faculty enjoy a common preparation period daily,
> share responsibility for a cohort of students, and invent
> curriculum, pedagogies and assessment strategies that re-

flect a commitment to a common intellectual project. Students travel together to classes, and across their four years in high school. With teachers, counselors and parents they constitute a semi-autonomous community within a building of charters. (Fine, 1993, p. 7)

Fine (1993), a codesigner of the initiative, reports that not all 94 of the charters represent fully transformed schools—most are still in process. But, she notes, "None is worse than the full, anonymous bureaucratic school out of which it was designed" (p. 23). The effort, she reports, has been informed by the research of Wehlage et al. (1989) on alternative schools, and by Oxley and McCabe (1990).

At the same time that such alternatives influences are visible, the alternative education sponsorship and context are likely to be downplayed. Educational discussion, as well as research, is currently likely to recommend attributes central to alternative schools—for example, advisories, service learning, the school within a school or minischool arrangement, choice, focus, personalization, and community—but with bare mention of the alternative school of which these are components or qualities. In consequence, alternative school features and tenets are playing a more extensive role in reform efforts than their lack of prominence would suggest.

A number of features that alternatives have pioneered, such as service learning, performance and portfolio assessment, and school community building, are being recommended by reformers who may not even be aware of the origins. Researchers also downplay it. For example, *Reducing the Risk* (Wehlage et al., 1989) began with a national search for schools effective in dropout prevention. Of the 14 exemplary schools they selected for intensive study, all but 3 are clearly alternative schools. In fact, the authors consider all 14 to be alternative schools (Wehlage et al., 1992). But nowhere in their study is that elaborated or the genre explored.

A Lack of Institutional Legitimacy

Given the various successes, why the low profile? Why don't alternative schools enjoy a more prominent and positive image, and why haven't they been more widely adopted? One analyst calls alternatives the Cinderella of the era: a school type that seemed to have most of the very features and qualities being sought, but that apparently remained undiscovered (Gregory, 1985). Why? It would appear, as Wehlage et al. (1989) put it, that even after 25 years, alternatives have not achieved institutional legitimacy. At least five reasons may be involved.

First, alternative education has an image problem. The widespread and frequent failure to distinguish among the three types of alternative schools identified in this chapter not only blurs their images into an erroneous composite but tars some extraordinarily successful programs with the records of others that are nothing like them. Although this has long been recognized as a problem (Hamer & Ampadu, 1982), it persists. But even the successful Type I alternatives have image problems. They are likely to be seen as fringe or flaky or student-indulgent by virtue of their departures.

Second, although not all alternative school students have been unsuccessful in their prior school(s), many have. This sort of enrollment bias is probably inescapable as long as there remains a regular program because those for whom conventional school seems a poor fit will obviously be those most drawn to the alternatives. The result, however, is to attach stigma to alternative schools—as programs for losers, misfits, misbehavers. And although, as we have seen, it is only Type II alternatives that assume a judgmental and negative stance vis-à-vis their students, negative judgments toward alternatives students and schools are sometimes revealed in the behavior of people outside the program—in the relevant recommendations of counselors and in the criticism by other teachers of the coddling of indifferent students. As one study of alternative schools put it, their students arrive having been "expelled to a friendlier place" (Gold & Mann, 1984).

According to the conventional wisdom at least, the rest of the population can presumably get along fine in the conventional school. Traditionally, the "loser" stigma has not only been attached to unsuccessful students; the teachers who teach such students and the schools that enroll them have also been accorded relatively low status. It is ironic that succeeding with the students who pose the most demanding of pedagogical challenges earns a teacher less stature than succeeding with students whose success is most likely! But because this is the case (Finley, 1984; Talbert & Ennis, 1990), alternatives occupy a low-status position in the educational hierarchy, making them unlikely candidates for widespread emulation.

Third, as the foregoing analysis has suggested, Type I alternative schools differ extensively from "regular" schools with respect to their organizational features. The experience with magnet schools would suggest that school systems are none too anxious to sponsor even programmatic divergence and diversity, with many doing so only in the presence or threat of court desegregation orders. Organizational variety and diversity are even harder for large systems to tolerate than programmatic departures. Divergence, after all, jeopardizes the most touted advantages of a bureaucracy: common standards, uniformity, fairness, and equity. Thus the organizational departures implicit in the alternative school concept may be one reason why education officials often appear to want to keep such programs to an absolute minimum.

Fourth, Type I alternative schools pose a challenge to the popular Effective Schools approach, which seeks improvement via the strengthening of bureaucracy and intensified application of its principles, tighter coupling, more assertive leadership, firmer control, and more frequent monitoring (Boyan, 1988; Clark, Lotto, & Astuto, 1984). By contrast, Type I alternatives typically represent less status differentiation, less experience of control, social rather than regulatory control, symbolic leadership over managerial, and more individual teacher autonomy and collective responsibility (Raywid, 1990).

Fifth, people view alternative schools as a threat to or an indictment of regular school practice, thus generating ambivalence or worse, even with respect to clearly successful practice. But the public as well as education professionals seem strongly ambivalent about alternative schools. Consider the following seeming contradictions. Perhaps the nation's single most celebrated principal is Deborah Meier of the alternative Central Park East Secondary School, yet the country is not clamoring for more alternative schools. Strangely, the film that probably has won more public approbation for schools than any other—*Why Do These Kids Love School?*—describes alternative schools. The film has won prizes and showings not accorded other films about school, and it often elicits intensely positive viewer response (Raywid, 1993). Yet it deals exclusively with a genre that is not itself the object of wide public appeal.

At the same time, despite this low status, many educational arrangements and practices pioneered in alternative schools are now being recommended for all schools—including teacher empowerment, personalization, cross-disciplinary instruction, a theme or focus, minischools, alternative assessment, service learning, and advisories or "family" groups.

Conclusion

It remains to be seen whether alternative schools will gain the institutional legitimacy that will probably be necessary for widespread adoption as such, or whether the more likely prospect is additional borrowings and permutations. The answer may lie in part in the outcomes of the sorts of adaptations now underway in Philadelphia's charters and in the New York house plan arrangement. They represent a number of modifications when viewed alongside the Type I alternative school.

Neither of the two plans makes choice a key feature, although both student and staff choice has played a part in some (but not all) of Philadelphia's charters. None of the New York house plans provides for student choice. Nor is focus or programmatic distinctiveness viewed necessary for a charter or house. Moreover, these initiatives do not pursue the autonomy or degree of separateness that New York's alternative schools and its new miniature high schools represent. It will be instructive to see whether the full separation that the minischools insist on proves a factor in the comparative success of the three initiatives: New York's new small high schools, its house plan, and Philadelphia's charters.

A final difference may also prove significant: Both New York's house plan and Philadelphia's charters are mandated arrangements, in which at least some participants are bound to be lukewarm to negative players. New York's minischools, by contrast, are staffed only by teachers who have chosen to be there.

Whatever the results may be, the alternative school model will likely be kept alive by a combination of its successes and the current problems plaguing education, as well as by present and imminent demographic changes. As an analyst speculated a decade ago,

> We may view alternative education as a small movement that has passed its peak. . . . Or we may, if we accept the broadest definition . . . see the movement as a growing and ever-more-powerful force in American education. Either way, for the long-range salvation of education in this country, alternative schools—or at least the philosophies and processes they represent—will play a crucial role in the future. (Schmerler, 1983, p. 5)

Commentaries

Schools operate like systems, systems that are embedded in larger systems. Living systems are resilient and self-preserving; they are often averse to change. Adding on does not change a system. I would summarize what succeeded and what did not in the following way:

Most innovations fail, not because they didn't work, but because they were never fully implemented. Why do alternative schools (Type I, as described by Raywid) work? First, they create relationships with caring adults who happen to be educators. Second, they foster self-efficacy. These schools deliberately attempt to foster resilience in children. They have certain features that can be emphasized, but caring is not enough—this is the same lesson that people have learned about parenting. Alternative schools work better for everyone—if you can find a good fit. In terms of cost-effectiveness of alternative schools, I would certainly expect that it would be not only better, but also less expensive.

Why is it that certain concepts as advanced by Raywid have not been adopted after all this time? We may be reaching a critical stage. We are approaching the 21st century looking into the rearview mirror instead of looking ahead. But change sometimes occurs rapidly—and that may be the case here.

Ann Masten, Professor of Child Psychology,
Institute of Child Development, University of Minnesota

Dr. Raywid's paper provides a thoughtful and solid review of American alternative schools. She offers insight into the social, political, and educational concerns that gave birth to alternative schools, and explores the variety of assumptions about school learning that undergird different types of alternative schools. But what stands out sorely in the discussions surrounding her work, and that of other presenters, are omissions in several major areas. The first has to do with vested interests of the populations to be served, specifically, low-income parents and parents of color. What is the end goal to all of this care and concern that we have for poor children and children of color? Even when our systems do work well, they do not work the same for everybody in light of racism, sexism, classism, and minimal appreciation of cultural/linguistic diversity. The exclusion of the populations most affected leaves us trying to solve problems with only half of the needed capacity. We simply will not be capable of making serious inroads into educational problem solving for at-risk students until we include and meaningfully involve as equal partners the people for whom we make these decisions.

The second issue concerns the impediment of our own self-interests in the current educational system. We as "others" who are doing the planning, the evaluation, and the thinking are being served by the nature of the questions we are asking. Where and how are the interests of low-income and culturally diverse families being served? With our current top-down analyses from legislators, teachers, and so on, we are missing the bottom half—not the lower half, simply the other half, which involves bottom-up analyses. What are the issues of the populations that have not been represented so far? For instance, if I am an African American parent sending my child to an inner-city school, some of my questions would be: "Why do you continually fail to educate my child? Why don't you fund the school properly? How come the schools in our communities do not have the same quality of teachers, educational materials, equipment, and variety of educational opportunities and exposures as the schools across town?" We must add this "bottom-up" analysis to all problem identification and goal setting. Whose interests are being served by our efforts to restructure?

In the Los Angeles school district, 85% of students in the public schools are children of color. Is the goal, then that 85% of the Los Angeles workforce should be people of color? Will Los Angeles colleges have 85% representation of people of color? Will the white unemployment rate rise? In working out

restructuring goals, we have to be honest—our choices and actions poten-
tially embody serious and profound conflicts of interest.

The third substantive issue to be addressed is history. The concept of
students "at risk" has a history that has been affected by larger social forces
such as racism, sexism, cultural ethnocentrism, and social class bias. How
have we deleted these root influences from the content and structure of our
proposed ideas for restructuring? Dr. Raywid provides examples of schools
that have failed. In one of these schools, negative program elements had not
been removed and new components were merely added on. The students'
basic experience of school remained unchanged, and the staff remained
unconvinced that it was necessary to change. Staff perceived "the problem"
as residing within the student; it was the student who had to be "fixed," not
the content or structure of the educational system serving that student. To
what extent are our proposals mere add-ons with underlying negative social
forces left intact?

As part of the solution, first, parents and communities must be included
at every step—this includes poor parents, parents of color, and affected
communities. These groups need to be meaningfully involved in all aspects
of any effort to make the educational system work for all children. Second,
our cultural problems are so embedded that we need to find some neutral
persons (even outside of this country) who can offer candid, disinvested
analyses and recommendations. We are too close, too vested in existing
structures, to do the job equitably.

Pauline Brooks, Project Director, National Center for
Research on Evaluation, Standards, and Student Testing,
University of California, Los Angeles

Note

1. It should be noted that many indications recommend these
concerns not only for at-risk youngsters or urban schools, but for all
youngsters and schools. As Wehlage et al. (1989) phrased it, "[W]e
believe that what is good for at-risk students is usually good for other
students as well; given this, we view the implications of our research
as pertinent to the improvement of most schools" (p. 5).

References

Berger, J. (1992, August 6). Plan seeks small schools with themes. *New York Times*, p. B1+.

Boyan, N. J. (Ed.). (1988). *School effects: Handbook of research on educational administration*. New York: Longman.

Bryk, A., & Driscoll, M. E. (1988). *The high school as community: Contextual influences and consequences for students and teachers*. Madison, WI: National Center on Effective Secondary Schools.

Bureau of Compensatory Education. (1980). *Alternative education: Planning and implementing successful programs*. Tallahassee: Florida Department of Education.

Butler-Por, N. (1987). *Underachievers in school: Issues and intervention*. New York: John Wiley.

Center for Research on the Context of Secondary School Teaching. (1993). Report of survey findings to Horizons High School, Wyoming, Michigan, March, 1991. In S. A. Williams (Ed.), *Restructuring through curriculum innovation* (pp. 79-83). Bloomington, IN: Phi Delta Kappa.

Chira, S. (1993, July 14). Is smaller better? Educators say yes for high school. *New York Times*, p. A1.

Clark, D. L., Lotto, L., & Astuto, T. A. (1984, Summer). Effective schools and school improvement: A comparative analysis of two lines of inquiry. *Educational Administration Quarterly, 20*(3), 41-68.

Colorado Options in Education. (1993, October 8), pp. 4-5.

Crain, R. L., Heebner, A., & Si, Y. P. (1992). *The effectiveness of New York City's career magnet schools: An evaluation of ninth grade performance using an experimental design*. Berkeley: National Center for Research in Vocational Education.

Deal, T. E., & Nolan, R. R. (1978). An overview of alternative schools. In T. E. Deal & R. R. Nolan (Eds.), *Alternative schools: Ideologies, realities, guidelines* (pp. 1-17). Chicago: Nelson-Hall.

Domanico, R. J. (1989). *Model for choice: A report on Manhattan's District 4*. New York: Manhattan Institute for Policy Research.

Doob, H. S. (1977). *Evaluations of alternative schools*. Arlington, VA: Educational Research Service.

Duke, D. L. (1976, May). Challenge to bureaucracy: The contemporary alternative school. *Journal of Educational Thought, 10*(1), pp. 34-48.

Duke, D. L. (1978). *The retransformation of the school: The emergence of contemporary alternative schools in the United States.* Chicago: Nelson-Hall.

Elmore, R. F. (1988). *Community District 4, New York City.* Unpublished manuscript, Center for Policy Research in Education.

Erickson, D. (1982). *The British Columbia story: Antecedents and consequences of aid to private schools.* Los Angeles: Institute for the Study of Private Schools.

Fantini, M. D. (1973). *Public schools of choice.* New York: Simon & Schuster.

Fine, M. (1993). *Chart[er]ing urban school reform.* Unpublished manuscript.

Finley, M. K. (1984). Teachers and tracking in a comprehensive high school. *Sociology of Education, 57*(4), 233-243.

Fliegel, S. (1993). *Miracle in East Harlem: The fight for choice in public education.* New York: Times Books.

Foley, E. M., & Crull, P. (1984). *Educating the at-risk adolescent: More lessons from alternative high schools.* New York: Public Education Association.

Foley, E. M., & McConnaughy, S. B. (1982). *Towards school improvement: Lessons from alternative high schools.* New York: Public Education Association.

Fowler, H. J., & Walberg, H. (1991, Summer). School size, characteristics, and outcomes. *Educational Evaluation and Policy Analysis, 13*(2), 189-202.

Frazer, L. H., & Baenen, N. R. (1988). *An alternative for high-risk students: The school-community guidance center evaluation, 1987-88.* Austin, TX: Office of Research & Evaluation, Austin Independent School District.

Garrison, R. W. (1987). *Alternative schools for disruptive youth.* Malibu, CA: Pepperdine University, National School Safety Center.

Gold, M., & Mann, D. W. (1984). *Expelled to a friendlier place: A study of effective alternative schools.* Ann Arbor: University of Michigan Press.

Grannis, J. C. (1992). *Educational reforms for at-risk students: New York City case study.* New York: Institute for Urban and Minority Education, Teachers College, Columbia University.

Gregory, T. B. (1985, Fall). Alternative school as Cinderella: What the reform reports look at and don't say. *Changing Schools, 13*(3), 2-4.

Gregory, T. B., & Smith, G. R. (1987). *High schools as communities: The small school reconsidered.* Bloomington, IN: Phi Delta Kappa.

Hamer, I. S., Jr., & Ampadu, M. (1982, April). Research and alternative schools: A critique of "Strategies for working with problem students." *Urban Education, 17*(1), 3-12.

Harrington, D., & Cookson, P. W., Jr. (1992). School reform in East Harlem: Alternative schools vs. "schools of choice." In G. A. Hess (Ed.), *Empowering teachers and parents: School restructuring through the eyes of anthropologists* (pp. 177-186). Westport, CT: Bergin & Garvey.

Hawley, W. D. (1991). Public policy and public commitments to enable school restructuring: Lessons from the high school in the community. Introduction to E. J. Trickett, *Living an idea: Empowerment and the evolution of an alternative high school* (pp. v-xi). Brookline, MA: Brookline Books.

Henderson, H., & Raywid, M. A. (1994, Winter). "Small" revolution in New York City. *Journal of Negro Education, 63*(1), 28-45.

Hill, P. T., Foster, G. E., & Gendler, T. (1990). *High schools with character.* Santa Monica, CA: Rand.

Kaczynski, D. J. (1989, March 29). *Traditional high school dropouts: A qualitative study at an alternative high school.* San Francisco: American Educational Research Association.

Korn, C. V. (1991). *Alternative American schools: Ideals in action.* Albany: State University of New York Press.

Kutner, M., & Salganik, L. (1986). *Educational choice in New York District 4.* Unpublished manuscript.

Larson, J., & Allen, B. (1988). *A microscope on magnet schools: 1983 to 1986: Vol. 2. Pupil and parent outcomes.* Rockville, MD: Montgomery County Public Schools.

Loria, O. C. (1989). *Survey of alternative schools: Keys to successful school redesign.* Unpublished manuscript, Midcontinent Regional Educational Laboratory.

McCann, T., & Landi, H. (1986, Spring/Summer). Researchers cite program value. *Changing Schools, 14*(2), 2-5.

Meyer, C. (1990). *Dropout prevention initiatives FY 1986 to 1990: Lessons from the research.* New York: Division of Strategic Planning/Research and Development, New York City Public Schools.

Morley, R. E. (1991, August). *Alternative education.* Clemson, SC: National Dropout Prevention Center.

Musumeci, M., & Szczypkowski, R. (1991). *Final report, New York State magnet school evaluation study.* Larchmont, NY: Magi Educational Services.

Nathan, J. (1992). *Free to teach: Achieving equity and excellence in schools* (2nd ed.). Cleveland: Pilgrim.

Nirenberg, J. (1977, Winter). A comparison of the management systems of traditional and alternative public high schools. *Educational Administration Quarterly, 13,* 86-104.

Office of Planning and Budgeting. (1981). *An evaluation of the Florida State Alternative Education Program.* Tallahassee: Executive Office of the Governor.

Oxley, D., & McCabe, J. G. (1989). *Making big high schools smaller.* New York: Public Education Association.

Oxley, D. & McCabe, J. G. (1990). *Restructuring neighborhood high schools: The house plan solution.* New York: Public Education Association.

Phillips, S. E. (1992, Spring). Alternative education in New York City: What is it? *Options,* p. 3.

Raywid, M. A. (1981, April). The first decade of public school alternatives. *Phi Delta Kappan,* 551-554.

Raywid, M. A. (1982). *The current status of schools of choice in public secondary education.* Hempstead, NY: Project on Alternatives in Education, Hofstra University.

Raywid, M. A. (1984, April). Synthesis of research on schools of choice. *Educational Leadership, 70-78.*

Raywid, M. A. (1988). Why are alternatives successful? *Holistic Education Review, 1*(2), 27-28.

Raywid, M. A. (1989). The mounting case for schools of choice. In J. Nathan (Ed.), *Public schools by choice* (pp. 13-40). Minneapolis: Free Spirit.

Raywid, M. A. (1990). Rethinking school governance. In R. F. Elmore (Ed.), *Restructuring schools* (pp. 152-205). San Francisco: Jossey-Bass.

Raywid, M. A. (1993, October). Professional community and its yield at Metro Academy. In K. S. Louis & S. D. Kruse (Ed.), *Professionalism in schools: A communitarian perspective* (pp. 29-61). Madison, WI: Center for the Organization and Restructuring of Schools.

Rogers, D., & Chung, N. H. (1983). *Livingston Street revisited.* New York: New York University Press.

Rosenholtz, S. (1989). *Teachers' workplace: The social organization of schools.* New York: Longman.

Schmerler, G. (1983, Spring). Alternatives strong! *Changing Schools, 11*(2), 5.

Schwarz, P. (1993, May 17). Dear students, parents and staff. *Central Park East Secondary School Newsletter,* 1-2.

Smith, G. A. (1988). *Adjustment before learning: The curricular dilemma in programs for at-risk students.* Unpublished paper, National Center on Effective Secondary Schools, University of Wisconsin at Madison.

Steel, L., Levine, R. E., Rossell, C. H., & Armor, D. J. (1993). *Magnet schools and desegregation, quality, and choice. Final report.* Palo Alto, CA: American Institutes for Research.

Stevens, M. (1985, Spring). Characteristics of alternative schools. *American Educational Research Journal, 22*(1), 135-148.

Sweeney, M. E. (1983). *An exploratory functional-structural analysis of American urban traditional and alternative secondary public schools.* Unpublished dissertation, Portland State University, Portland, OR.

Sweeney, M. E. (1988, Summer). Alternative education and "alternative" schools. *Holistic Education Review, 1*(2), 22-25.

Talbert, J. E., & Ennis, M. (1990, April). *Teacher tracking: Exacerbating inequalities in the high school.* Boston: American Educational Research Association.

Thrasher, R. (1993). *Patterns: A directory for state alternative education associations, 1993-1994.* Denver: Colorado Department of Education and Colorado Options in Education.

Trickett, E. J. (1991). *Living an idea: Empowerment and the evolution of an alternative high school.* Brookline, MA: Brookline.

Tyack, D. B. (1974). *The one best system.* Cambridge, MA: Harvard University Press.

Wehlage, G. G., Rutter, R. A., Smith, G. A., Lesko, N., & Fernandez, R. R. (1989). *Reducing the risk: Schools as communities of support.* London: Falmer.

Wehlage, G., Smith, G., & Lipman, P. (1991, May). *Restructuring urban schools: The new futures experience.* Unpublished manuscript, National Center on Organization and Restructuring of Schools, University of Wisconsin.

Wehlage, G., Smith, G., & Lipman, P. (1992). Restructuring urban schools: The New Futures experience. *American Educational Research Journal, 29*(1), 51-93.

Wells, A. S. (1993). *Time to choose: America at the crossroads of school choice policy.* New York: Hill & Wang.

Wheelock, A., & Sweeney, M. E. (1989). Alternative education: A vehicle for school reform. *Changing Schools, 17*(2), 1, 4-6.

Williams, S. A. (Ed.). (1993). *Restructuring through curriculum innovation. Exemplary practice series.* Bloomington, IN: Phi Delta Kappa.

Wood, R. (1989). SAIL: A pioneer for schools of choice in Florida. In J. Nathan (Ed.), *Public schools by choice* (pp. 181-202). Minneapolis: Free Spirit.

• • • • • •

6

• • • • • •

The Impact of Linguistic and Cultural Diversity on America's Schools

A Need for New Policy

EUGENE E. GARCIA

If you were to visit Mrs. Margaret Tanner's classroom in sunny southern California, you would see a fifth-grade classroom much like any other. The physical plant in which she teaches was built in the late 1950s, and it looks like a school— there are classrooms, a cafeteria, playgrounds. The number of students the school serves has remained around 600 since its opening, although for a 5-year stretch in the late 1970s the school served over 900 students and operated split morning and afternoon sessions. Mrs. Tanner has had as few as 19 students in her classroom and as many as 35, but on the average the daily attendance in her classroom has remained at about 26 to 28 students.

Mrs. Tanner has taught her fifth graders in this classroom for 21 years. She is quite a dedicated and committed teacher. However, she is quick to describe the greatest challenge to that professional commitment—the challenge of cultural diversity in her student body. When she took that initial fifth-grade assignment, she was teaching in one of many Los Angeles suburbs, and her students and her community was almost all middle class, white, English speaking, third- to fourth-generation European immigrants. They were all much like herself.

In that short first decade of her professional career, the Los Angeles metropolitan area extended itself beyond her suburb to create new suburbs, and her community became a haven for recently arrived Mexican immigrants and other Spanish-speaking immigrants from the southwestern United States. In that decade, the majority of students in her class changed. African American students speaking a distinct English dialect, most of them immigrants from the southern United States, joined students who spoke Spanish in their working-class homes and commuted regularly between the United States and Mexico. Their immigrant parents, like the parents of her students earlier, had come to this locale to find employment and achieve a higher standard of living. Although they were not like her, she felt just as committed to these new students as she had felt toward her first students.

In the last decade, further shifts in the population have dramatically changed the nature of her student body. More and more, she teaches students who speak a variety of languages in their homes and communities: Spanish, Vietnamese, Russian, Hmong, Chinese, and Farsi. The communities from which these students originate are made up of first- and second-generation Mexican immigrants and first-generation Vietnamese, Hmong, Chinese, Iranian, Russian, and Central American refugees. Many of these families have come to seek employment and a better standard of living; others have escaped their politically volatile and often violent nations of origin. Mrs. Tanner is quick to point out that her commitment and determination to serve these students is no less, maybe even greater than ever before. But she will also be the first to admit that the diversification of her student body has challenged, to the very core, her own conceptualization of her role as teacher and the skills necessary to achieve effective instruction.

Mrs. Tanner's circumstances are not rare in this country. The challenges of a culturally and linguistically diverse student population are soon to be the norm rather than the exception for our new teachers of the 21st century. Student populations that were once minorities in Mrs. Tanner's classroom became for her the majority. We need no crystal ball to see that the future for U.S. schools will mirror the changes that have occurred in Mrs. Tanner's classroom. Minorities will become majorities, particularly in highly populated metropolitan areas of this country—areas where the majority of our students are concentrated—and where the majority of this country's students will either succeed or fail. Mrs. Tanner is a pioneer, a representative of things to come: Our assumptions of teaching, learning, and schooling will be challenged as hers have been. But our commitment to this diverse student population, like hers, must never waver.

The initiatives targeted at culturally and linguistically diverse students have at times been synonymous with the schooling endeavors aimed at poor, lower-class, at-risk, underachieving, and dropout students. As Gonzalez (1990) has documented, children of immigrants are usually perceived as the foreigners and intruders who speak a different language or dialect and hold values significantly different from the American mainstream. Such perceptions have led policy makers (including the U.S. Supreme Court) to highlight the most salient characteristic of these students, the racial and language differences, in their attempts to address the historical academic underachievement of immigrant populations. This chapter will include an expanded discussion of risk factors for their underachievement both within and outside the schooling arena, along with demographic data of particular relevance to their schooling.

The Magnitude of Cultural Diversity Among U.S. Students Today

Immigration Trends: Roots of Diversity

From 1981 through 1990 more than 7 million people immigrated to the United States, marking a 63% increase in the immigrant population over the previous decade (Table 6.1). Apart from the sheer magnitude in the numbers of immigrants to the United States, what are the characteristics of this population? That is, in relative terms,

TABLE 6.1 Immigration to the United States by Region 1820-1990, With Special Emphasis on 1971-1980 and 1981-1990

Region and Country of Origin	1820-1990 (Total 171 Years)	1971-1980	1981-1990
All countries	56,994,014	4,493,314	7,338,062
Europe	37,101,060	800,368	761,550
Austria-Hungary	4,342,782	16,028	24,885
Austria	1,828,946	9,478	18,340
Hungary	1,667,760	6,550	6,545
Belgium	210,556	5,329	7,066
Czechoslovakia	145,801	6,023	7,227
Denmark	370,412	4,439	5,370
France	787,587	25,069	32,353
Germany	7,083,465	74,414	91,961
Greece	703,904	92,369	38,377
Ireland	4,725,133	11,490	31,969
Italy	5,373,108	129,368	67,254
Netherlands	374,232	10,492	12,238
Norway-Sweden	2,145,954	10,472	15,182
Norway	801,224	3,941	4,164
Sweden	1,284,475	6,531	11,018
Poland	606,336	37,234	83,252
Portugal	501,261	101,710	40,431
Romania	204,841	12,393	30,857
Soviet Union	3,443,706	38,961	57,677
Spain	285,148	39,141	20,433
Switzerland	359,439	8,235	8,849
United Kingdom	5,119,150	137,374	159,173
Yugoslavia	136,271	30,540	18,762
Other Europe	181,974	9,287	8,234
Asia	5,019,180	1,588,178	2,738,157
China	914,376	124,326	346,747
Hong Kong	302,230	113,467	98,215
India	455,716	164,134	250,786
Iran	176,851	45,136	116,172
Israel	137,540	37,713	44,273
Japan	462,244	49,775	47,085
Korea	642,248	267,638	333,746
Philippines	1,026,653	354,987	548,764

continued

TABLE 6.1 Continued

Region and Country of Origin	1820-1990 (Total 171 Years)	1971-1980	1981-1990
Turkey	412,327	13,399	23,233
Vietnam	458,277	172,820	280,782
Other Asia	1,030,718	244,783	648,354
America	13,067,548	1,982,735	3,615,255
Canada & Newfoundland	4,295,585	169,939	156,938
Mexico	3,888,729	640,294	1,655,843
Caribbean	2,703,177	741,126	872,051
Cuba	748,710	264,863	144,578
Dominican Republic	510,136	148,135	252,035
Haiti	234,757	56,335	138,379
Jamaica	429,500	137,577	208,148
Other Caribbean	780,074	134,216	128,911
Central America	819,628	134,640	468,088
El Salvador	274,667	34,436	213,539
Other Central America	544,961	100,204	254,549
South America	1,250,303	295,741	461,847
Argentina	131,118	29,897	27,327
Colombia	295,353	77,347	122,849
Ecuador	155,767	50,077	56,315
Other South America	668,065	138,420	255,356
Other America	110,126	995	458
Africa	334,145	80,779	176,893
Oceania	204,622	41,242	45,205
Not specified	267,459	12	1,032

SOURCE: U.S. Bureau of the Census, (1975, 1990).

from which countries does this population originate? And, perhaps more important, what are the greatest changes and emerging immigration trends?

During the two decades from 1974-1994, Mexico has remained the country of origin for the majority of U.S. immigrants. Mexican immigrants outnumber those from any other single nation of origin by over a million for this time period. Immigrants from the Philippines rank second, with those from China, Korea, and Vietnam following close behind. In terms of the greatest numbers, this ranking of countries of origin has remained relatively stable since 1971, with the exception of Cuba. The United States has seen a decline of Cuban immigrants in the 1980s.

During the past two decades, certain countries of origin have exhibited high growth rates in migrations to the United States. In the last 10 years, for example, more than six times as many Salvadorans have fled to the United States from war-torn El Salvador as in the previous decade. Irish immigration has increased 178%. The numbers of Iranian and Haitian immigrants have more than doubled. Eastern European countries, such as Hungary, Poland, and Romania have averaged approximately a 100% increase, and the Vietnamese community continues to grow at a rate 62% greater than in the previous decade. Mexico, however, because of a rapid growth trend (immigration from Mexico has almost tripled since 1980) ranks first in actual numbers of immigrants, and translates into perhaps the greatest impact on the U.S. population.

These statistics describe a U.S. immigrant population made up of vastly different peoples, which is not only rapidly growing but rapidly diverging as well. In short, we always have been and continue to be a nation of immigrants.

Future Projections of Student Cultural Diversity

To document the racial and ethnic heterogeneity of our country's population, the U.S. Census Bureau has constructed a set of highly confusing terms that place individuals in separate exclusionary categories: white, white non-Hispanic, black, Hispanic (with some five subcategories of Hispanics). Unfortunately, these terms are for the most part highly ambiguous and nonrepresentative of the true heterogeneity that the Bureau diligently seeks to document. Therefore these categories are useful only as the most superficial reflection of our nation's true diversity. Racially and culturally we are not "pure" stock, and any separation by the Census Bureau, the Center for Educational Statistics, or other social institutions that attempt to address the complexity of our diverse population is apt to be misleading.

At the student level, the most comprehensive report with regard to this growth trend, *The Road to College: Educational Progress by Race and Ethnicity*, was published in 1991 by the College Board and the Western Interstate Commission for Higher Education. This report indicates that the U.S. nonwhite and Hispanic student population will increase from 10.4 million in 1985-1986 to 13.7 million in 1994-1995. These pupils will constitute 34% of public elementary and secondary school enrollment in 1994-1995, up from 29% in 1985-1986. Whites' enrollment, meanwhile, will rise from 25.8 million to 27 million, and their share of the student population will drop from 71% to 66% in 1994-1995.

Figures 6.1 and 6.2 graphically display this astounding student demographic shift. Figure 6.1 presents actual nonwhite and Hispanic K through 12 public school enrollments from 1976 to 1986 and projected enrollments (calculated using the derived changes in enrollment from 1976 to 1986 as a base) by decade through 2026. Figure 6.2 presents similar data by focusing on the percentage of total nonwhite and Hispanic student enrollments. Nonwhite and Hispanic student enrollment will grow from 10 million in 1976 to nearly 45 million in 2026. These students will grow from 23% to 70% of our nation's school enrollment during this relatively short time period. *In 2026, we will have the exact inverse of student representation as we knew it in 1990 when white students made up 70% of our enrolled K through 12 student body.*

Of distinctive educational significance is the reality that in 1986, 30 to 35% (3 million) of nonwhite and Hispanic students were identified as residing in homes in which English was not the primary language (August & Garcia, 1988). If we use these figures and extrapolate from the projections displayed in Figures 6.1 and 6.2, by the year 2000, our schools will be the home for 6 million students with limited proficiency in English. By the year 2026, that number will conservatively approximate 15 million students or somewhere in the vicinity of 25% of total elementary and secondary school enrollments. In the decades to come, it will be virtually impossible for a professional educator to serve in a public school setting, and prob-

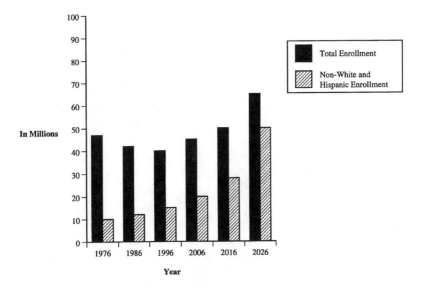

Figure 6.1. K-12 Public School Enrollment Projections: Total Versus Nonwhite and Hispanic Enrollment
SOURCE: U.S. Department of Education. Office for Civil Rights, *Directory of Elementary and Secondary School Districts and Schools in Selected Districts: 1976-1977;* and 1984 and 1986 Elementary and Secondary School Civil Rights Survey. As cited in U.S. Department of Education, National Center for Education Statistics. *The Condition of Education, 1991, Vol. 1, p. 68, Elementary and Secondary Education.* Washington, DC: 1991.

ably any private school context, in which his or her students are not racially, culturally and/or linguistically diverse.

The Language Minority Student

Within this demographic discussion of student diversity, one distinctive subpopulation will receive selective attention due to its growing size, both relatively and absolutely, and its precarious situation within our educational institutions. These students come to the schooling process without the language within which that process is embedded. As the previous demographic data have indicated, some

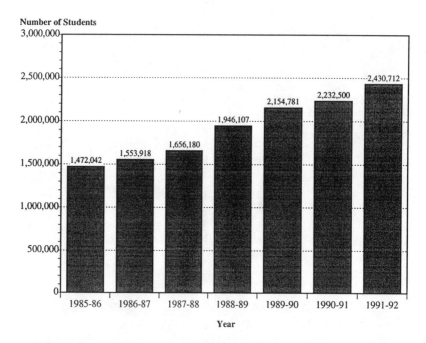

Figure 6.2. Trends in Enrollment of Students With Limited English Proficiency (LEP), 1985-86 to 1991-92
SOURCE: U.S. Department of Education, Office of Bilingual Education and Language Minority Affairs, Reports to U.S. Congress (July 1, 1994).

15% of U.S. student enrollment K through 12 will be made up of this category of students in the next two decades. By 2026, they are projected to make up nearly a quarter of our student body. Moreover, they present a special challenge to our educational institutions due to their linguistic diversity. Much of what we do in the formal teaching/learning enterprise requires effective communication of specific facts, concepts, ideas, and problem-solving strategies. Yet these students come to that teaching/learning enterprise not lacking communication abilities, but with a diverse set of communication abilities that do not match those of the school.

As one searches for a comprehensive definition of the language minority student, a continuum of definitional attempts unfolds. At one end of the continuum are general definitions, such as "students who come from homes in which a language other than English is spoken." At the other end of that continuum are highly operationalized definitions, such as "students who scored in the first quartile on a standardized test of English language proficiency." Regardless of the definition adopted, it is apparent that these students come in a variety of linguistic shapes and forms. The language minority population in the United States continues to be linguistically heterogeneous, with over 100 distinct language groups identified. Even in the largest language minority ethnic group, the Hispanic, some members are monolingual Spanish speakers and others are to some degree bilingual. Other non-English-speaking minority groups in the United States are similarly heterogeneous. Further, non-English speakers are not only linguistically distinct but also culturally distinct. Thus describing the typical language minority student is highly problematic. We might agree, however, that the student (a) is characterized by substantive participation in a non-English-speaking social environment; (b) has acquired the normal communicative abilities of that social environment; and (c) is exposed to a substantive English-speaking environment, probably for the first time, during the formal schooling process.

Estimates of the number of language minority students have been compiled by the federal government on several occasions (Development Associates, 1984; O'Malley, 1981; Waggoner, 1991). These estimates differ because of the definition adopted for identifying these students, the particular measure used to obtained the estimate, and the statistical treatment used to generalize beyond the actual sample obtained. For example, O'Malley (1981) defined the language minority student population by using a specific cutoff score on an English language proficiency test administered to a stratified sample of students. Development Associates (1984) estimated the population by using reports from a stratified sample of local school districts. Therefore estimates of language minority students have ranged between 1,300,000 (Development Associates, 1984) to 3,600,000 (O'Malley, 1981), and the population has the following attributes:

1. The total number of language minority children aged 5 to 14 approximated 2.52 million in 1976, with a drop to 2.39 million in 1980 and a projected gradual increase to 3.40 million in the year 2000 (Waggoner, 1984). In 1983, this population was more

conservatively estimated to be 1.29 million (Development Associates, 1984). Recall that this divergence in estimates reflects the procedures used to obtain language minority "counts" and estimates.

2. The majority of these children reside throughout the United States, but with distinct geographical clustering. For example, about 75% of language minority children are found in Arizona, Colorado, California, Florida, New Jersey, New Mexico, New York, and Texas (Development Associates, 1984; O'Malley, 1981; Waggoner, 1991).

3. Of the estimated number of language minority children in 1978, 72% were of Spanish language background, 2% other European language, 5% Asian language, and 1% Native American language. However, such distributions will change due to differential growth rates, and by the year 2000, the proportion of Spanish language background children is projected to be about 77% of the total (O'Malley, 1981). Estimates by Development Associates (1984) for students in grades K through 6 indicate that 76% were of Spanish language background, 8% Southeast Asian (e.g., Vietnamese, Cambodian, Hmong), 5% other European, 5% East Asian (e.g., Chinese, Korean), and 5% other (e.g., Arabic, Navaho).

4. For the national school districts sample in the 19 most highly affected states used by Development Associates (1984), 17% of the total K through 6 student population was estimated to be language minority in these states.

Regardless of differing estimates, a significant number of students from language backgrounds other than English are served by U.S. schools. Moreover, this population is expected to increase steadily in the future. The challenge these students present to U.S. educational institutions will continue to increase concomitantly.

What Types of Educational Programs Serve These Students?

For a school district staff with language minority students there are many possible program options: transitional bilingual education, maintenance bilingual education, English as a second language, immersion, sheltered English, and submersion, to name a few (Government Accounting Office, 1987). Ultimately, staff will reject program labels and instead answer the following questions:

1. What are the native language (L1) and second language (L2) characteristics of the students, families, and community(ies) we serve?
2. What model of instruction is desired?
   a) How do we choose to use L1 and L2 as media of instruction?
   b) How do we choose to handle the instruction of L1 and L2?
3. What staff and resources are necessary to implement the desired instruction?

These program initiatives can be differentiated by the way they use the native language and English during instruction. Development Associates (1984) surveyed 333 school districts in the 19 states that serve over 80% of language minority students in the United States. For grades K through 5, they report the following salient features regarding the use of language(s) during the instruction of language minority students:

1. Ninety-three percent of the schools reported that the use of English predominated in their programs; conversely, 7% indicated that the use of the native language predominated.
2. Sixty percent of the sampled schools reported that both the native language and English were used during instruction.
3. Thirty percent of the sampled schools reported minimal or no use of the native language during instruction.

Two thirds of these schools have chosen to use some form of bilingual curriculum to serve this population of students. However, some one third of these schools minimize or altogether ignore native language use in their instruction of language minority students. Recall that some two thirds to three fourths of language minority students in this country are of Spanish-speaking backgrounds. Programs that serve these students have been characterized primarily as bilingual transitional education. These programs transition students from early-grade, Spanish-emphasis instruction to later-grade, English-emphasis instruction, and eventually to English-only instruction.

For the one third of the students receiving little or no instruction in the native language, two alternative types of instructional approaches are likely to predominate: ESL and sheltered English. Each of these program types depends on the primary use of English during instruction but does not ignore the fact that the students served are limited in English proficiency. However, these programs do not require instructional personnel who speak the native language of the student. Moreover, these programs are suited to classrooms in which there is no substantial number of students from one non-English-speaking group, but instead may have a heterogeneous non-English-background student population (Ovando & Collier, 1985).

School district staff have been creative in developing a wide range of language minority student programs. They have answered the above questions differentially for different language groups (Spanish, Vietnamese, Chinese, etc.), different grade levels within a school, different subgroups of language minority students within a classroom, and even different levels of language proficiency. The result has been a broad and at times perplexing variety of program models. Such diversity in program types is a clear realization of the diversity of students and of the professional expertise that is currently available to serve this particularly diverse student body. It is best understood as a response to diversity within diversity.

Who Will Educate Our Diverse Population?

The previous demographic information has indicated that the rapidly increasing diversity in our schools is a recent but explosive and long-term phenomenon. Teachers, administrators, and other educational professionals receiving their training over a decade ago were not encumbered by the challenges facing preservice teaching candidates today. They did not need to be ready to respond to the challenge presented by a highly diverse student body. Moreover, few individuals from the ranks of the emerging majority succeeded academically themselves a decade ago, and so were not and are not in the teaching profession. In fact, for the 1987-1988 school year, of the 2.6 million public and private school teachers and the 103,000 school administrators, over 88% were white, and less than 12% were nonwhite and Hispanic (8% Black, 3% Hispanic, and less than 1% Native American, Alaskan Native, and Asian or Pacific Islander). In this same academic year, nonwhite and Hispanic academic enrollment was at 30% (National Center for Education Statistics [NCES], 1991).

Characteristics of Effective Teachers

It remains evident that the vast majority of school teachers and administrators are white and will continue to be white in the near future, whereas the proportion of nonwhite and Hispanic students continues to increase rapidly (NCES, 1991). Although it is difficult to identify specific attributes of teachers that have served a diverse student body effectively, recent efforts have attempted to do so. Unlike earlier reports that have identified and described effective programs, recent efforts have sought out effective programs and/or schools, then attempted to describe the specific instructional and attitudinal character of the teacher (Carter & Chatfield, 1986; Pease-Alvarez, Espinoza, & Garcia, 1991; Tikunoff, 1983; Villegas, 1991). Dwyer (1991) identifies four domains in which good teachers excel: (a) content knowledge, (b) teaching for student learning, (c) creating a classroom community for student learning, and (d) teacher professionalism. Villegas (1991) has extended these four domains when the student population served by the teacher is culturally and linguistically diverse. She suggests that good teachers in these classroom contexts are required to incorporate culturally responsive pedagogy.

A concern for the effectiveness of teachers is not new. From the earliest days of education program evaluation, the quality of the instructional staff has been considered a significant feature. Unfortunately, for programs serving minority students, the evaluation of effectiveness has taken second place to an empirical concern regarding the significance of the multicultural aspect of the curriculum and, for students with limited English-speaking ability, the use or nonuse of the students' native language and the academic development of the English language (August & Garcia, 1988). Very little attention is given to the attributes of the professional and paraprofessional staff who implement the myriad models and program types omnipresent in the service of these students in compensatory education programs. Typically, attention to the characteristics of such a staff is restricted only to the years of service and extent of formal educational training received (Olsen, 1988). Yet most educational researchers will grant that the effect of any instructional intervention is directly related to the quality of that intervention's implementation by the instructor(s). A recent report issued by the California Commission on Teacher Credentialing (1991) verified that a disproportionate number of poor and minority students are taught during their entire school career by the least qualified teachers, because of high teacher turnover, larger numbers of misassigned teachers, and classrooms staffed by teachers holding only emergency (temporary and not state-approved) credentials.

Training Teachers to Teach Culturally Diverse Students

Professional teaching organizations such as the National Education Association (NEA), American Federation of Teachers (AFT), and National Association for the Education of Young Children (NAEYC), to name a few of the largest, have addressed the specific need for teachers to receive special training in areas that relate to teaching the growing diverse student body. Certification agencies such as the National Council for Accreditation of Teacher Education (NCATE) and the California Commission on Teaching Credentialing have included particular provisions related to multicultural education that institutions of higher education must implement if they are to be accredited as teacher training institutions and their graduates considered positively as candidates for state teacher credentialing.

Unfortunately, even with this quite universal acceptance of the specific need to train and assess teachers with regard to their competence in teaching culturally diverse students, the present modes of training and assessment are highly problematic. The data are clear with regard to the problems of individual assessment of teacher professional competence. Present professional assessment can be criticized on several levels (McGahie, 1991; Shimberg, 1983; Sternberg & Wagner, 1986):

1. Professional competence evaluations usually address only a narrow range of practice situations. Professionals engage in very complex planning, development, implementation, problem solving, and crisis management. These endeavors do not usually require technical skills and knowledge that are easily measured. Garcia's (1991) discussion of effective language minority teachers exemplifies this complexity.

2. Professional competence evaluations are biased toward assessing formally acquired knowledge, probably because of the preponderance of similar assessment of student academic achievement. We assess teachers much as we assess students, even though we have differing expectations regarding these populations.

3. Despite the presumed importance of practice skills, professional competence assessments devote little attention to their assessment. With regard to teachers of highly diverse students, we do have some understanding of specific skills that might be necessary, although because of the lack of specific research in this domain, it remains difficult to articulate the exact skills that would be recommended as candidates for assessment.

4. Almost no attention is given to what has been identified as the disposition and affective domains of the teacher. In recent analysis of effective teachers, these attributes were shown to be as significant as content knowledge and practice skills (Pease-Alvarez et al., 1991; Villegas, 1991).

In short, we currently lack any definitive body of research and knowledge regarding the constructs that exemplify good teachers in general and good teachers of culturally diverse students specifically. That knowledge base is developing, but it is not yet substantive (Garcia, 1991).

The teaching expertise of those professionals charged with meeting the challenges of diversity is increasing but is not yet at the optimal level. We are beginning to react to that challenge. Many of you are reading this volume because of your interest, your concern, and specific professional obligations that will be yours in teaching or related educational professions. It is important to recognize that we are struggling together in this enterprise. We are far from achieving the instructional expertise that will effectively meet the growing challenges of diversity.

Summary

Trying to make sense of demographic data within the realm of education and related domains is like trying to make sense out of baseball by exploring only the vast array of statistics that we as Americans compile about our national sport. As we all know, no one can obtain a clear understanding of the game just by examining those statistics, no matter how comprehensive, strategic, or ingenious the compilations are. The same is true for the education of culturally diverse students in this country. However, much like baseball, education is an important part of our social fabric. Most of us have been to school. In fact, most of us have spent a majority of our early lives in formal schooling activities. And we use demographic statistics much as we use baseball statistics, to help us understand the nature of the enterprise through the description of the status or well-being of the teams and individual players. In the broad-stroke analysis presented in this chapter, specific status indicators for specific groups and individuals have been presented with the understanding that such description can add some depth, but not total understanding, to the challenge facing today's and tomorrow's educators.

What do these descriptive data tell us about that challenge? Continuing with the baseball metaphor, we can state that within a relatively short time the number of students who will populate our schools—who will play the game—will be radically different with regard to race, culture, and language. In less than two decades, half of our students will be nonwhite and Hispanic, with half of those students speaking a language other than English on their first day of school. A teacher receiving a teaching credential today will probably be responsible for the education of a more diverse student body than any teacher at any time in the history of formal education. This will be true at all levels of education. This growing population of students will undertake their schooling with several strikes against them. They are and will be coming to bat from social and economic circumstances that probably will leave them more vulnerable to the various pitches that they will be asked to hit. Those pitches include a more competitive global climate in which educational success is an absolute must and a world in which our fundamental knowledge base is growing exponentially.

They are likely to be equipped, not with the best that money can buy, but only with the least that society is willing to divert from other endeavors or to differentially spend on especially valued players. They are likely to be coached by individuals who do not meet the highest standards or by coaches who themselves are learning the game as they are given major coaching responsibilities. Moreover, many of these players will require coaching in a language that is not their own. They will need to acquire the knowledge of the game along with the language and culture in which the game is immersed.

Yet these same data unequivocally indicate that the future of the game rests with them. As they become the majority of players, their success is our success and their failure is our failure. They must succeed. We have no other alternative short of disbanding the game. Mrs. Tanner is living this challenge and is not about to give up. She serves as our model for the professionalism and dedication needed to meet it. However, without broader responsiveness by the systems that support her work, that professionalism and dedication will not be enough. It is this responsiveness of the U.S. Department of Education in partnership with state and local education agencies that I wish to address.

New National Policy

Rationales for changes in national policy are often related to crisis intervention: We have a problem and we must address it quickly by directing resources to that problem area. The present reassessment of national policy for linguistically and culturally diverse students and families is driven by some of this same rationale. The specific challenge of serving these populations continues to be significant for U.S. schools. Regardless of the significance of the challenge, the resources to meet it continue to lag behind the demographic realities. However, "crisis" policy corrections are often short-sighted, inflexible, minimally cohesive and integrated, and uninformed by a strong knowledge base, whether conceptual, empirical, or related to practice wisdom. The main national vehicles, Title I and Title VII of the Elementary and Secondary Education Act, to address the crisis related to linguistically and culturally diverse students have suffered from these disadvantages. Therefore the following recommendations are made regarding the development of new policy:

1. The new knowledge base, both conceptual and empirical, must be central to any proposed changes.
2. Consultation with the field is critical so as to capitalize on existing policy, administrative, curricular, and instructional practice wisdom.
3. Policies and programs must be cohesive so as to integrate efficiently the services that are to be provided—this cohesiveness must reflect the educational partnership between national, state, and local educational policy and programming.
4. The demographic and budgetary realities that are present today and will exist throughout this decade must be acknowledged and must influence new directions.

The following discussion will articulate the new proposed policy directions, primarily those related to Title VII—most commonly referred to as the Bilingual Education Act—and attempts to implement substantively new policy directions that are in line with the above presuppositions.

Knowledge Base

We have a new knowledge base. Recent research has redefined the nature of our linguistically and culturally diverse students' educational vulnerability. It has destroyed both stereotypes and myths and laid a foundation upon which to reconceptualize present educational practices and launch new initiatives (Garcia, 1991). This foundation recognizes the homogeneity and heterogeneity within and between such populations. No one set of descriptions or prescriptions will suffice. However, it is worthwhile to consider a set of intertwined commonalities that deserves particular attention. This foundation has been established by recent research documenting educationally effective practices with linguistically and culturally diverse students in selected sites throughout the United States. These descriptive studies identified specific schools and classrooms that served "minority" students and were particularly academically successful. The case study approach adopted by these studies included examination of preschool, elementary, and high school classrooms. Teachers, principals, parents, and students were interviewed and specific classroom observations were conducted that assessed the dynamics of the instructional process.

The results of these studies provide important insights with regard to general instructional organization, literacy development, academic achievement in content areas like math and science, and the perspectives of the student, teachers, administrators, and parents. Interviews with classroom teachers, principals, and parents reveal an interesting set of perspectives regarding the education of the students in these schools. Effective classroom teachers were highly committed to the educational success of their students; perceived themselves as instructional innovators using new learning theories and instructional philosophies to guide their practice; continued to be involved in professional development activities including participation in small group support networks; had a strong, demonstrated commitment to student-home communication (several teachers were using a weekly parent interaction format); and felt that they had the autonomy to create or change the instruction and curriculum in their classrooms, even if it did not meet the exact district guidelines. They had high academic expectations for all their students ("everyone will learn to read in my classroom") and also served as an advocate for their students. They rejected any conclusion that their students were intellectually or academically disadvantaged.

In summary, effective curricula, instructional strategies, and teaching staffs recognize that academic learning has its roots in sharing expertise and experiences through multiple processes of communication. Effective curricula provide abundant and diverse opportunities for speaking, listening, reading, and writing, along with scaffolding to help guide students through the learning process. However, effective schools for diverse students encourage students to take risks, construct meaning, and seek reinterpretations of knowledge within compatible social contexts. Within this knowledge-driven curriculum, skills are tools for acquiring knowledge, not a fundamental target of teaching events. It is recognized that any attempt to address the needs of these students in a compensatory or "subtractive" way is counterproductive. Effective approaches to these students are additive—they incorporate the recognition that students come with rich intellectual, linguistic, and cultural attributes that serve as a foundation for further linguistic, academic, and social development in our schools.

Practice Wisdom

Too often in the heat of legislation and policy development, such development becomes highly centralized in interest groups, professional policy personnel, and the realities of the political process. Therefore present policy proposals have taken into consideration long-term, multiple consultations. For linguistically and culturally diverse students, the usual policy players have been consulted. These include the National Association for Bilingual Education and the Mexican American Legal Defense Fund, each of which has made specific legislative recommendations of major proportions, and other educational groups that have made recommendations related to their own interests and expertise. Of particular significance is the work of the Stanford Working Group. This group, funded by the Carnegie Corporation of New York, began recently to consult widely with various individuals representing a broad spectrum of theoretical, practice, and policy expertise. In recently published reports and in various forums, they have put forward a comprehensive analysis and articulated recommendations for any new policy and legislation related to linguistically and culturally diverse populations.

This type of consultation has shaped present policy proposals. To neglect it would be to negate the importance of shared wisdom from various established perspectives. Moreover, any proposed changes must themselves be embraced by those individuals and organizations that are currently in the field if they are to become implemented effectively.

Cohesiveness

The proposed policy directions have attempted to view the provision of services to students in a comprehensive and integrated manner. Through the introduction of new major legislation in *Education 2000*, the U.S. Department of Education set the stage for the formal development and implementation of national goals and standards. Then, with the introduction of the Educate America Act, the reauthorization of the Elementary and Secondary Education Act (ESEA), the goals and standards initiatives were aligned with specific resource allocation policies, on the understanding that U.S. Department of Education, state, and local agency efforts must be integrated to enhance effectiveness and efficiency. Moreover, the national role must allow flexibility at the state and local level while requiring that all children achieve at the highest levels.

Title VII reauthorizations, as a component of the ESEA, also follow the directives of alignment. Thus Title VII is not seen as yet another program aimed at meeting an educational crisis in U.S. education, but as a key component of an integrated effort to address this educational need. Specifically, Title VII will continue to serve the missions of leadership and national, state, and local capacity building with regard to educational services, professional development, and research related to our culturally and linguistically diverse populations. However, other programs, particularly Title I, will more directly increase the direct services needed by all our students living in poverty, including those with limited English proficiency.

Demographic and Budgetary Realities

Over the past decade, increases in actual student enrollments of students with limited English proficiency are evident (see Figure 6.3). In the last 6 years, that increase is near 70%, or some 1 million students. There is no reason to believe that this trend will subside. However, it is important to also recognize that the national presence and the diversity of this population is substantial (see Figure 6.4). Since the mid-1980s, 10 new states have been added to the count of those states with more than 2% of their student population identified as having limited English proficiency. Today, 20 states can be counted

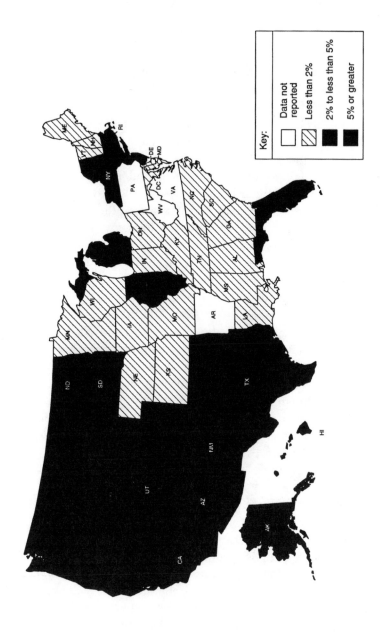

Figure 6.3. Percentage Limited English Proficiency (LEP) Enrollment by State, 1991-1992
NOTE: The District of Columbia has 3.8% LEP enrollment and Puerto Rico has 5% LSP enrollment.

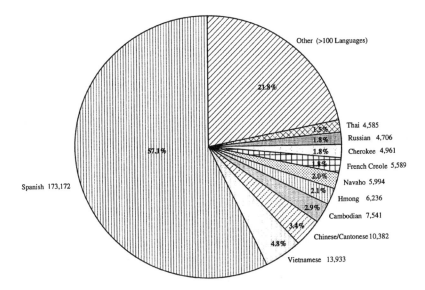

Figure 6.4. Title VII Part A Programs: Number of Limited English Proficiency (LEP) Students Served, by Most Common Language Groups Served

in such a category, and half of these states have student populations that vary between 5% and 25%. Moreover, the number of non-English-language students served is quite diverse. More than 100 language groups are currently represented in programs funded through Title VII.

Unfortunately, the fiscal resources that can be marshaled to meet the growing and diverse demands of this population are likely to not be enhanced in any significant way. National, state, and local funding allocations for these populations have not grown in proportion to the population. Although new proposals with regard to the disposition of Title I funds to high poverty areas should bring more resources to linguistically and culturally diverse students, those resources will not be significantly enhanced. Consequently present resources must be used more efficiently.

Specific Changes in Title VII

Title VII is currently divided into three specific parts. Part A programs provide funding to local districts for the development of instructional service and general capacity building; six categories of discretionary grants are provided to local educational agencies. Part B programs include national research activities and efforts to provide general information (through the National Clearinghouse on Bilingual Education), technical assistance (through 16 regional Multifunctional Resource Centers) and specific program evaluation assistance (through 2 regional Evaluation Assistance Centers) to Part A grantees. Part C programs provide resources to institutions of higher education and other educational and community agencies to provide preservice, inservice, and related professional development activities. The configuration of these programs was articulated in the 1984 reauthorization and continued in the 1988 reauthorization of Title VII.

In line with present proposals in the Department of Education, the new knowledge base, consultation with the field, the demographic realities, and budgetary realities, the following changes are proposed in the Title VII reauthorizations for 1994:

Part A
- Current six programs replaced by three new programs
  1. Enhancement Grants—2-year start-ups
  2. Comprehensive School Grants—5-year
  3. Comprehensive District Grants—5-year
- State agency review

Part B
- Required consultation with field and enhanced coordination for research activities
- Program evaluation simplified and directed at program improvement and dissemination
- More emphasis on Academic Excellence Programs: state plans required, expanded role
- Multifunctional and Evaluation Centers merge with overall ESEA efforts

Part C
- Renewed emphasis on professional development
- Teacher preparation and doctoral preparation continued; postdoctoral opportunities created

Part D
- Immigrant education changes from a formula-based funding activity to a Title VII discretionary program

These changes are closely consistent with recommendations made by the Carnegie Working Group, the National Association for Bilingual Education, and the Congressional Hispanic Caucus. Although there are differences, the main tenets of all the proposals indicate that Title VII must continue to provide national leadership and national, state, and local capacity-building opportunities in programs that recognize the importance of language and cultural diversity as a national resource and that assist in the development of educational equity and excellence. Moreover, given the limited resources for Title VII activities, resources from other national programs, specifically Title I, state educational agencies, and local educational agencies must be integrated in ways that achieve systemic educational reform. As a country we cannot afford to do less.

Commentaries

Dr. Garcia's work is indeed revolutionary. It has been a long time since we have had such a knowledgeable, research-oriented leader. In contrast, another such leader out in Tucson in a variety of ways insulted many of us. For example, in response to one person's commentary, this leader clenched her fists and said, "If you think I am going to endorse bilingual education, you are mistaken—I will never support it."

I have approached Dr. Garcia's research from the framework of my field, which is language planning. I have been involved in the pursuit of language policy development for quite a while. The challenge is based on one set of ideas: language as problem; language as resource; and language as right. There is a problem to be solved here, one that we must identify and treat. Title VII, the Bilingual Education Act, highlights transitional bilingual education. More precisely stated, however, the goal is development of English monolinguals. In fact, the mentality of the United States directs that if you speak anything other than English, you have a problem.

Many of us who look at Title VII don't even think of it as a bilingual education program; we think of it as a program to teach people English. The "Bilingual Education Act" is a euphemism for English immersion. Why do we call that a bilingual program? When teachers look at students walking into their classrooms, they think, "Oh no, here comes another one of those special education, language barrier, etc." What is being forgotten here is that the students are entering classrooms within communities. These children come in with something already—you do not have to start from scratch.

Richard Ruiz, Acting Department Chair, Department of Language, Reading, and Culture, University of Arizona

What I suggest is a very different orientation to talking about social context and its effects on children's learning. There are significant numbers of bilinguals. The student populations will never again look as they have in the past. Creating classroom communities where all children can become literate must become a central educational issue in light of the rapidly changing student population. Preparing children for life in a multilingual and multicultural society also requires preparing teachers to imagine new contexts for learning in which children develop a much more comprehensive set of literacy skills in both the first and second language.

It is a call to a new way of thinking for those states that have not challenged their own assumptions about how children learn. They possess very traditional understandings, and deficit models of understanding that influence the policy and decision makers. Many of the students in Los Angeles schools are Mexican immigrant students, many of whom go back to Mexico regularly. Transmigration is a common phenomenon. One sees the same graffiti in the Mexican villages as in the U.S. cities. The implications are that we simply will not be able to go on comparing these students with European American children.

A more appropriate response is necessary. Policies must move from bilingualism and monolingualism to biliteracy. Biliteracy far better addresses the realities of these kids' lives. Recognition is an important first step toward a definition of biliterate children—this applies to all immigrant groups, and requires challenging current attitudes. This leads to my second point, that the new knowledge base discussed by Dr. Garcia suggests that children's views are the result of the context in which they have learned—they develop contextualized understandings of things. Teachers must recognize that they are the authorities but that they do not have to be authoritarian. This new paradigm for teachers allows the teacher to act as a researcher in the classroom. There is high congruency between teachers' beliefs and their teaching styles. Teachers recognize prior experiences of students as important and significant. However, I am discouraged by the anti-immigrant feeling in my state (California). Much parent interaction within school and strengthened linkages between school and community remain vital elements of concern and action as we strive to improve current programs.

The list of potential remedies is endless, and yet there is little mention of the need to challenge the beliefs that underlie the national and local educational policies and practices that inform language instruction—to reexamine educational beliefs and practices in cross-cultural contexts. Nor is there significant discussion of how the current solutions proposed may be from the wrong solution set, or of how the questions and issues in education may be different in the 21st century.

Kris D. Gutierrez, Professor,
University of California at Los Angeles

References

August, D., & Garcia, E. (1988). *Language minority education in the United States: Research, policy and practice.* Chicago: Charles C Thomas.

California Commission on Teacher Credentialing. (1991). *Teacher credentialing in California: A special report.* Sacramento: Author.

Carter, T. P., & Chatfield, M. L. (1986). Effective bilingual schools: Implications for policy and practice. *American Journal of Education, 95*(1), 200-234.

College Board and the Western Interstate Commission for Higher Education (1991). *The road to college: Educational progress by race and ethnicity.* New York: College Board.

Development Associates. (1984). *Final report, descriptive study phase of the national longitudinal evaluation of the effectiveness of services for language minority limited english proficient students.* Arlington, VA: Author.

Dwyer, C. (1991). *Language, culture and writing* (Working paper 13). Berkeley: University of California, Center for the Study of Writing.

Garcia, E. (1991). Bilingualism, second language acquisition in academic contexts. In A. Ambert (Ed.), *Bilingual education and English as a second language: A research annual* (pp. 181-217). New York: Garland.

Gonzalez, G. (1990). *Chicano education in the segregation era: 1915-1945.* Philadelphia: Balch Institute.

McGahie, W. C. (1991). Professional competence evaluation. *Educational Researcher, 20*(1), 3-9.

National Center for Education Statistics. (1991). *The condition of education* (Vols. 1 and 2). Washington, DC: U.S. Department of Education.

Olsen, L. (1988). *Crossing the schoolhouse border: Immigrant students and the California public schools.* San Francisco: California Tomorrow Policy Research.

O'Malley, M. J. (1981). *Children's English and services study: Language minority children with limited English proficiency in the United States.* Rosslyn, VA: National Clearinghouse for Bilingual Education.

Ovando, C., & Collier, V. (1985). *Bilingual and ESL classrooms: Teaching in multicultural contexts.* New York: McGraw-Hill.

Pease-Alvarez, L., Espinoza, P., & Garcia, E. (1991). Effective schooling in preschool settings: A case study of LEP students in early childhood. *Early Childhood Research Quarterly, 6,*(3), 153-164.

Shimberg, B. (1983). What is competence? How can it be assessed? In M. R. Stern (Ed.), *Power and conflict in continuing professional education* (pp. 17-37). Belmont, CA: Wadsworth.

Sternberg, R. J., & Wagner, R. K. (Eds.). (1986). *Practical intelligence.* New York: Cambridge University Press.

Tikunoff, W. J. (1983). *Compatibility of the SBIF features with other research on instruction of LEP students.* San Francisco: Far West Laboratory (SBIF-83-4.8/10).

U.S. Bureau of the Census. (1975). *Historical Statistics of the United States, colonial times to 1970.* Washington, DC: Author.

U.S. Bureau of the Census. (1990). *Statistical abstract of the United States, 1991.* Washington, DC: Author.

U.S. Government Accounting Office. (1987, March). *Research evidence on bilingual education* (GAO/PEMD-87 12BR). Washington, DC: Author.

Villegas, A. M. (1991). *Culturally responsive pedagogy for the 1990s and beyond.* Princeton, NJ: Educational Testing Service.

Waggoner, D. (1984). The need for bilingual education: Estimates from the 1980 census. *NABE Journal, 8,* 1-14.

Waggoner, D. (1991). *Language minority census newsletter.* Washington, DC: Waggoner Incorporated.

Waggoner, D. (Ed.). (1992, July, September). *Numbers and needs: Ethnic and linguistic minorities in the U.S.* Available from Numbers and Needs, Box G1HB, 3900 Watson Place NW, Washington DC 20016.

Epilogue

A Summary of Recommendations

MAYNARD C. REYNOLDS

MARGARET C. WANG

HERBERT J. WALBERG

This chapter was prepared following the invitational conference of October 14-15, 1993, on Making a Difference for Students at Risk.[1] The conference was held to address policy and school reform issues

AUTHORS' NOTE: The conference, Making a Difference for Students at Risk, was sponsored by the National Center on Education in the Inner Cities at the Temple University Center for Research in Human Development and Education in collaboration with the National Research Center on Cultural Diversity and Second Language Learning at the University of California at Santa Cruz. The conference was supported by the Office of Educational Research and Improvement (OERI) of the U.S. Department of Education. The opinions expressed by the conferees, as discussed in this chapter, do not necessarily reflect the position of OERI, and no official endorsement should be inferred.

surrounding categorization and labeling of students in need of "supplemental" and/or "special" education and related support services, particularly those in "at-risk" circumstances. Conference attendees represented the broad spectrum of persons concerned with education, including teachers, administrators, researchers, policy makers, and representatives from advocacy agencies and professional organizations (see the List of Participants in Appendix A).

Although the complete conference proceedings will be published at a later date, this brief summary presents a number of the suggestions and recommendations made at the conference. Some were generated by presenters and others by the conference organizers (see the conference agenda in Appendix B). Participants devoted much of the conference time to small work groups, where ideas and policy recommendations were generated. Proposals from all sources are summarized here. None of them was voted on formally by the full set of conferees, and there were disagreements on some matters, so we cannot presume here to represent the views of all conference participants. However, this epilogue reflects the tenor and some specifics of the conference proceedings, considering all voices—speakers, organizers, and conferees.

On one overarching matter we can be certain: The conference touched upon deeply felt and significant issues. Finding ways to harness all the major resources and expertise in our nation's cities to improve education and life circumstances of children, youth, and families is one of the most pressing needs of our time. It is "at the margins" of inner-city schools that we encounter the most calamitous situation in education in this country. Here is where failure and disorder are at an extreme and threaten to overtake whole communities. Here is where disregard for the schools is most obvious. Even in urban universities, many researchers have abandoned inner-city schools at the margins; as a result, data are thin or missing entirely. This is surely one place where basic reform of the schools must be centered.

Of particular concern is education's neglect of students from minority families. Conferees repeatedly expressed the view that in the 30 years since the beginnings of the War on Poverty and in the 40 years since the *Brown* decision, practically nothing rewarding or enhancing has occurred in the education of minority children. In fact, we are little, if at all, beyond where we started. Special programs launched over recent decades are fragmented and ineffective, and there is still much segregation by race. The recurring theme running through the conference was that the urgent need for reform of inner-city education, especially for young minority men, cannot be overstated.

It was also clear that problems of schooling vary significantly from city to city. The influx of immigrant children from Mexico and the various Asian nations into Los Angeles contrasts sharply with the virtually all-black schools of parts of Detroit, New York, and Philadelphia. Flexibility in federal and state rules and regulations will be required to permit local adaptations in school reform efforts.

One major conference theme focused on the need for schools to be totally inclusive and thoroughly integrated. Many were concerned that when students are set aside in resource rooms, special classes, or special schools, there is a strong tendency to lower the educational standards for these marginalized groups. But conferees stressed that the goals of inclusion and integration should apply to more than just students. If bureaucratic structures in government, professional associations, and advocacy groups remain fragmented, it will be difficult to achieve the goal of integration for students.

No single idea achieved wider consensus at the conference than one relating to terminology—in particular, the negative labels attached to many students. The current identifiers for categories of children were described as "bankrupt" at best; yet there remains some resistance to changes in classification procedures. It appears that some of the hard-won victories on behalf of various categories of students and the related special funding streams will now be defended by those who feel rewarded by narrowly framed programs, even those with labels.

This conference may have been the first in which representatives of a wide range of categorical programs met together. Conferees expressed the need for continuing dialogue in the broad framework of the conference. In the discussion groups, it was clear that individual conferees represented quite separate constituency groups; yet there was recognition that cross-category dialogue produced rich new ideas and that a concerting of voices and of programs was needed.

A particularly challenging idea, expressed quite persuasively early in the conference, was that major changes in inner-city education may happen quite suddenly. Sometimes situations reach a critical stage at which changes occur rapidly, and, it was proposed, we may have reached that point in inner-city education.

Recommendations

Outlined below are some of the ideas emerging from the conference that might characterize desirable changes—whether rapid or gradual. In preparing these summaries, we attempted to reduce much of the overlap in the discussions by reporting specific concerns and recommendations according to the most pertinent group topics.

1. The public schools of the nation should be inclusive and integrated.

This would mean

- reducing all forms of "set-asides" or segregation of students
- decreasing suspensions, expulsions, and dropouts
- merging Chapter 1, learning disability, and related programs
- placing "burden-of-proof" obligations on those who propose separating a student from the mainstream program
- integrating federal and state bureaucratic agencies across all categorical programs, including revisions in monitoring and reporting systems to emphasize teaming and coordination
- integrating professional groups, such as the Council for Exceptional Children (CEC) and The Association for the Severely Handicapped (TASH), and further integrating these with the emerging union of the National Education Association (NEA) and the American Federation of Teachers (AFT)
- setting a common "sunset" date for legislation affecting categorical programs, and organizing efforts to develop coherent, broadly framed revisions of policies and programs in all domains

Narrowly framed and segregated categorical programs, as organized in the past, were unsuccessful. The National Academy of Science special panel (Heller, Holtzman, & Messick, 1982) saw no educational justification for maintaining separate programs for learning disabilities, Chapter 1, and mild mental retardation. It is interesting that recent federal reports in the field of special education show the two largest categories to be learning disability (poorly defined, but now comprising more than half of all "disabled" students) and cross-categorical (U.S. Department of Education, 1992). The abandonment of the categorical approach for mildly disabled children may be occurring very rapidly. Between 1987-1988 and 1989-1990, a 2-year period, the number of teachers employed in cross-categorical programs (23,000) increased 130.5%. That is one of the most remarkable statistics related to school programs of recent years. It seems likely that integration and coherence of programs for students will not fully occur unless and until bureaucratic and professional structures are pulled together. This presents a major challenge to the large bureaucracies and the major professional education associations.

2. *The public schools should be organized into smaller units (minischools, charters, or "houses"), in which groups of students and teachers remain together for several years of study.*

This would entail

- training all teachers (both general education teachers and specialists in various fields, such as second-language learning or special education teachers) for altered roles (such as working in minischools)
- freeing local school teams (teachers, students, and parents) to innovate in significant ways to create revised programs
- making every possible effort to reduce alienation of students from teachers, classmates, and schools
- enabling students and parents to choose the minischools they wish to join
- permitting exceptional students to engage in activities beyond the minischool when necessary to offer appropriate opportunities (e.g., the student athlete on the basketball team, the outstanding violinist who plays in the all-city orchestra, or the

excelling mathematics student who attends an accelerated math program at the local university once a week)
- for the most severely alienated students, providing special opportunities in "street academies" that employ proven principles

Alienation and estrangement of students and teachers are major problems at the margins of inner-city schools. The formation of minischools within a framework of site-based management, extensive choice (by students, teachers, and parents), and major innovations in curriculum and instruction, appear promising. Within these minischools, categorical programs and staff, as we now know them, would be melded into the general programs to work collaboratively. A key feature is the unity of groups of students and teachers over several years. Minischools present opportunities for the implementation of principles emerging from research on resilience—especially relating to continuing contacts with children and youth by caring adults and the encouragement of self-efficacy.

3. The use of labels for students (such as mildly mentally retarded, Chapter 1, learning disabled, and emotionally disturbed) should be discontinued.

This would involve

- shifting labels from students to programs
- making strong efforts to study individuals and to plan individualized programs, but without labels
- shifting diagnostic activities from pathologies to educationally relevant variables, that is, the educational conditions that best promote learning given the individual students' educational strengths and weaknesses
- changing special funding systems, which now frequently encourage a "bounty hunt" mentality, to one that pays off on programmatic units
- extraordinarily concentrating funds and resources in selected schools, such as those that enroll large numbers of low-achieving students from poor families or students facing the second-language learning challenge

- using outcome-oriented variables in choosing students who are offered specialized and intensive forms of education, and in monitoring program effectiveness

Putting labels on programs may, of course, still cause labels to be assigned informally to students, but there should be improvements over present direct child-labeling procedures. One can imagine that programs might bear labels such as the Basic Skills program, Intensive Reading, Braille Reading, the Social Skills program, Reading Recovery, the English as a Second Language program, and so on. There is a tendency to organize programs around presumed dispositional variables, such as migrant status or mental retardation. It would be helpful if diagnostic procedures emphasized variables that educators can manipulate in their attempts to improve learning. An initial step might be to use outcome measures as a first approach in identifying students who need extra help.

4. Research concerning "marginal" students should be enhanced as necessary to provide a growing knowledge base and credible evaluation system for inner-city schools, including attention to students and programs "at the margin."

This would require

- all state and national data collection and dissemination systems to be set up to reflect the general status of education and thus to include literally all students
- the U.S. Department of Education to be given broad authority to grant time-limited waivers of rules and regulations to states and local school districts as one of the necessary conditions for increased innovation in programs and improved student learning outcomes, particularly in school program areas now governed by "categorical" laws, rules, and regulations
- research efforts to include careful and sensitive disaggregation of data to reflect differential effects and conditions for various racial, ethnic, and gender subpopulations
- research to attend to strengths, resilience, and similar "positive" factors, as well as to limitations and deficiencies in inner-city life and learning

- efforts to study the change process, particularly as it relates to changing beliefs and assumptions about the capacity for learning by *all* children, including children who are marginalized in schools

A substantial amount of discussion at the conference centered on the importance of having truly complete data ("all the way to the margins") when attempting to represent all students and programs. A case was also made for disaggregating data for subgroups, such as for race and gender, as an aspect of research. Such disaggregation of data does not imply physical separation of students within the schools, but only separation of data, showing, for example, how various racial, ethnic, and gender groups are advancing in their learning under various conditions.

5. Strong efforts should be made to advance programs for students who show outstanding abilities.

This would entail

- offering beginning programs in important domains of learning in which all students participate and in which extraordinary efforts are made to give students whose background or experience has been disadvantaged an opportunity to show their potentialities for accelerated learning and high competence
- adapting programs for students who emerge from introductory programs with evidence of readiness (shown in learning rate, motivation, commitment to task, etc.) for especially challenging and accelerated instruction

6. Clearly a necessity, maximum implementation of the well-confirmed knowledge base for teaching in inner-city schools should be sought.

This would require

- a strong and continuing staff development program for all teachers and school staff, based on "what works" in instruction, and on the knowledge base on learners and learning

- systematic efforts to place teachers of highest demonstrated competence in inner-city schools
- aggressive teaching—with high expectations for learning—for all students, in a curriculum that includes complex topics such as problem solving and communication in addition to literacy basics
- strong efforts to extend and improve early education programs and development of all promising approaches to the prevention of learning problems

7. Efforts should be made to maximize coordination, within institutions of higher education, of programs in the various "categorical" fields and in general education.

This would involve

- combining elements of programs in general teacher education, special education, and special language learning areas
- relating preparation of teachers, school administrators, school psychologists, and others to newly emerging forms of education (such as minischools)
- educating the public about what is needed and encouraging public dialogue on the needs and purposes of school reforms to ensure equity in educational outcomes for *all* children

8. Efforts should be made to strengthen and meld the work of advocacy groups.

This would mean

- supporting revised and integrated forms of schooling and funding for special programs
- working in support of efforts to coordinate the emerging school-community agencies designed to provide broad patterns of service to children who have special needs and to their families

9. *Federal and state authorities should be challenged to create broad, cross-departmental, and coterminous "empowerment zones" as a basis for comprehensive developments and services.*

This would involve

- building healthy communities
- fostering healthy, well-supported families
- linking school programs and the community to enhance opportunities for learning

There is a tendency for various departments of government to undertake separate and uncoordinated programs intended to help solve the problems of inner cities. We observe "enterprise zones," for example, in which moves are mainly related to business and job opportunities. But rarely are there coordinated efforts in education, human services, transportation, corrections, and other fields in support of enterprise zones. The proposal here is to achieve simultaneous declarations of empowerment zones by all departments of government and to organize broadly coherent efforts for improvements in inner-city life and learning.

10. *Concepts of inclusion and integration should be applied also to the bureaucratic structures of government, professional organizations, and advocacy groups.*

Conclusion

The federal role in education has developed over the past three decades mainly through narrowly framed categorical programs. It appears that most such programs have not worked adequately, and the new strategy is to rework and improve general school programs as the main resource for all students, including those "at the margins."

Current difficulty resides in the highly disjointed nature of government agencies, funding systems, professional associations, university training programs, and advocacy groups. Many rules, regulations, and laws cause continued frustrating separations where coordination would be preferable. It will be challenging to work through these problems of infrastructure. There will be resistance on the part of some who are rewarded by present practices. Paradoxically, some of those who fought hard in the past for rights, opportunities, and the creation of various categories for students may find themselves defending structures that now operate as barriers to needed change. It will take much courage to lead the way to new, coherent, genuinely useful programs at the margins of the schools.

Note

1. For further information on the conference, please contact Margaret C. Wang, Director, National Center on Education in the Inner Cities at Temple University Center for Research in Human Development and Education, 933 Ritter Hall Annex, 13th Street and Cecil B. Moore Avenue, Philadelphia, PA 19122.

References

Heller, K. A., Holtzman, W. H., & Messick, S. (Eds.). (1982). *Placing children in special education: A strategy for equity.* Washington, DC: National Academy Press.

U.S. Department of Education. (1992). *Fourteenth annual report to Congress on the implementation of the Individuals with Disabilities Act.* Washington, DC: Author.

APPENDIX A

LIST OF PARTICIPANTS FOR THE INVITATIONAL CONFERENCE ON MAKING A DIFFERENCE FOR STUDENTS AT RISK, SANTA CRUZ, OCTOBER 1993

Lascelles Anderson
Senior Research Associate,
    National Center on Education in
    the Inner Cities (CEIC)
Temple University Center for
    Research in Human
    Development and Education
Philadelphia, PA

Harriet Arvey
Assistant Superintendent of Pupil
    Services
Houston Independent School
    District
Houston, TX

George Ayers
Executive Director
Council for Exceptional Children
Reston, VA

Mary Barr
Research Assistant, CEIC
Temple University Center for
    Research in Human
    Development and Education
Philadelphia, PA

William Lowe Boyd
Senior Research Associate, CEIC
Temple University Center for
    Research in Human
    Development and Education
Philadelphia, PA

Pauline Brooks
Project Director
Graduate School of Education
University of California, Los
    Angeles
Los Angeles, CA

Barbara Carey
Assistant Superintendent
Multicultural
    Programs/Alternative Education
Miami, FL

Mike Casserly
Executive Director
Council of the Great City Schools
Washington, DC

Donald L. Clark
Director
Bureau of Curriculum and
    Academic Services
Pennsylvania Department of
    Education
Harrisburg, PA

Joseph Conaty
Acting Director
Office of Research
Office of Educational Research and
    Improvement
U.S. Department of Education
Washington, DC

Katherine Conner
Assistant Superintendent
Collaborative Programs and
    Development
School District of Philadelphia
Philadelphia, PA

Michele DeSera
Assistant Bureau Director
Special Education
Pennsylvania Department of
    Education
Harrisburg, PA

Mary E. Driscoll
Professor of Educational
    Administration
New York University
New York, NY

Brian Dumler
Teacher
Dacotah Street Elementary School
Los Angeles, CA

Bonnie Edwards
Graduate Research Assistant, CEIC
Temple University Center for
    Research in Human
    Development and Education
Philadelphia, PA

Edgar Epps
Professor of Urban Education
University of Chicago
Chicago, IL

Deborah Escobedo
Staff Attorney
META
San Francisco, CA

Mary-Beth Fafard
Associate Commissioner of
    Educational Improvement
Massachusetts Department of
    Education
Malden, MA

Doris Flowers
Coordinator of Special Education
Center for Applied Cultural
    Studies and Educational
    Achievement
San Francisco, CA

H. Jerome Freiberg
Senior Research Associate, CEIC
Temple University Center for
    Research in Human
    Development and Education
Philadelphia, PA

Eugene Garcia
Director
Office of Bilingual Education and
    Minority Languages Affairs
U.S. Department of Education
Washington, DC

Michelle Garcia
Graduate Research Assistant, CEIC
Temple University Center for
    Research in Human
    Development and Education
Philadelphia, PA

Antoine Garibaldi
Professor and Vice President for
    Academic Affairs
Xavier University of Louisiana
New Orleans, LA

Patricia Gennari
Director of Elementary Education
Penn Hills School District
Pittsburgh, PA

Charles R. (Dick) Glean
Executive Director of Student
    Services
School District of Philadelphia
Philadelphia, PA

Margaret (Peg) Goertz Professor
Consortium for Policy Research in
    Education
Rutgers University
New Brunswick, NJ

Don Gordon
Research Assistant, CEIC
Temple University Center for
    Research in Human
    Development and Education
Philadelphia, PA

Edmund Gordon
Professor Emeritus
Yale University

Michael Guerra
Executive Director
Secondary School Department
National Catholic Educational
    Association
Washington, DC

Larry Guthrie
Director
Center for Educational Research
    and Evaluation
Burlingame, CA

Kris Gutierrez
Professor
University of California, Los
    Angeles
Culver City, CA

Brenda Harris
Assistant to the Deputy
   Superintendent
Specialized Programs Branch
California State Department of
   Education
Sacramento, CA

Shwu-Yong Huang
Visiting Research Assistant
   Professor
Department of Curriculum and
   Instruction
University of Houston
Houston, TX

Lorna Idol
Editor in Chief
Remedial and Special Education
Austin, TX

Aquiles Iglesias
Associate Director, CEIC
Temple University Center for
   Research in Human
   Development and Education
Philadelphia, PA

Luis Laosa
Senior Research Scientist
Educational Testing Service
Princeton, NJ

Julia Lara
Senior Project Associate
Resource Center and Educational
   Equity
Council of Chief State School
   Officers
Washington, DC

Teresa LeNoir
Principal
Eighth Avenue Elementary School
Houston, TX

Sherrie Madia
Research Assistant, CEIC
Temple University Center for
   Research in Human
   Development and Education
Philadelphia, PA

Richard Maraschiello
Research Associate
School District of Philadelphia
Philadelphia, PA

Ann Masten
Professor of Child Psychology
Institute of Child Development
University of Minnesota
Minneapolis, MN

Patricia Mazzuca
Principal
Elverson Middle School
Philadelphia, PA

Barbara McCombs
Senior Director
Motivation and Human
   Development Group
Mid-Continent Regional
   Educational Laboratory
Aurora, CO

Barry McLaughlin
Associate Director
National Research Center on
    Cultural Diversity and Second
    Language Learning
University of California, Santa
    Cruz
Santa Cruz, CA

Bernadette McNulty
Research Assistant, CEIC
Temple University Center for
    Research in Human
    Development and Education
Philadelphia, PA

James McPartland
Director
National Center on Effective
    Schooling for Disadvantaged
    Students
Johns Hopkins University
Baltimore, MD

Celane McWhorter
Director of Government Relations
The Association for the Severely
    Handicapped
Alexandria, VA

Oliver Moles
Center Monitor
Office of Educational Research and
    Improvement
U.S. Department of Education
Washington, DC

Jane Oates
Center Research Fellow, CEIC
Temple University Center for
    Research in Human
    Development and Education
Philadelphia, PA

John Ogbu
Professor of Anthropology
University of California, Berkeley
Berkeley, CA

Martin Orland
Acting Executive Director
National Education Goals Panel
Washington, DC

Jeffrey Osowski
Director
Special Education Programs
New Jersey Department of
    Education
Trenton, NJ

Diana Oxley
Senior Research Associate, CEIC
Temple University Center for
    Research in Human
    Development and Education
Philadelphia, PA

Valena White Plisko
Director
Elementary and Secondary
    Education Division
U.S. Department of Education
Washington, DC

Jennifer Plumer-Davis
Principal
L. P. Hill Elementary School
Philadelphia, PA

Marleen Pugach
Professor of Curriculum and
    Instruction
University of Wisconsin,
    Milwaukee
Milwaukee, WI

Mary Anne Raywid
Professor
Hofstra University
Hempstead, NY

Joseph Renzulli
Director
National Research Center on the
    Gifted and Talented
University of Connecticut
Storrs, CT

Maynard C. Reynolds
Senior Research Associate, CEIC
Temple University Center for
    Research in Human
    Development and Education
Philadelphia, PA

Leo Rigsby
Associate Director, CEIC
Temple University Center for
    Research in Human
    Development and Education
Philadelphia, PA

Richard Ruiz
Acting Chair of Language,
    Reading and Culture
University of Arizona
Tucson, AZ

Rush L. Russell
Program Officer
Robert Wood Johnson Foundation
Princeton, NJ

Susan K. Sclafani
Associate Superintendent for
    District Administration
Houston Independent School
    District
Houston, TX

Wayman Shiver
Deputy Superintendent of Schools
Birmingham Public Schools
Birmingham, AL

Carolyn Trice
Coordinator, Outreach Program, CEIC
Temple University Center for
    Research in Human
    Development and Education
Philadelphia, PA

Ione Vargus
Fellow
Temple University
Philadelphia, PA

Herbert Walberg
Senior Research Associate, CEIC
Temple University Center for
    Research in Human
    Development and Education
Philadelphia, PA

Margaret C. Wang
Professor and Director, CEIC
Temple University Center for
    Research in Human
    Development and Education
Philadelphia, PA

Hersholt C. Waxman
Associate Professor of Curriculum
    and Instruction
University of Houston
Houston, TX

Nancy Weishew
Research Assistant, CEIC
Temple University Center for
    Research in Human
    Development and Education
Philadelphia, PA

Brenda Lilienthal Welburn
Executive Director
National Association of State
  Boards of Education
Alexandria, VA

Leila Welch
Project Coordinator
Temple University Center for
  Research in Human
  Development and Education
Philadelphia, PA

Belinda Williams
Director
Research for Better Schools
Philadelphia, PA

Kenneth Wong
Associate Professor of Education
University of Chicago
Chicago, IL

William Yancey
Senior Research Associate, CEIC
Temple University Center for
  Research in Human
  Development and Education
Philadelphia, PA

Andrea Zetlin
Senior Research Associate, CEIC
Temple University Center for
  Research in Human
  Development and Education
Philadelphia, PA

Nancy Zollers
Assistant Professor
School of Education
Boston College
Chestnut Hill, MA

APPENDIX B

AGENDA FOR THE INVITATIONAL CONFERENCE ON MAKING A DIFFERENCE FOR STUDENTS AT RISK, SANTA CRUZ, OCTOBER 1993

Thursday, October 14, 1993

7:30-8:30   Breakfast
8:30-9:00   Welcome
            Margaret C. Wang, National Center on Education in the
            Inner Cities (CEIC), Temple University Center for
            Research in Human Development and Education
            Joseph Conaty, Office of Research, Office of Educational
            Research and Improvement (OERI), U.S. Department of
            Education
9:00-9:30   Introduction and Conference Overview
            Margaret C. Wang, CEIC, Temple University Center for
            Research in Human Development and Education
            Maynard Reynolds, CEIC, University of Minnesota
9:30-10:30 "Twice Victims: The Struggle to Educate Children in Urban
            Schools and the Reform of Special Education and Chapter 1"
            Session Chair: Kenneth Wong, CEIC, University of
            Chicago

Overview: Marleen Pugach, University of Wisconsin at Milwaukee

Discussants: Martin Orland, National Education Goals Panel; Jeffrey Osowski, Office of Special Education Programs, New Jersey Department of Education

10:30-10:45 Break

10:45-12:15 "The Plight of High-Ability Students in Urban Schools"

Session Chair: Belinda Williams, Research for Better Schools

Overview: Joseph Renzulli, National Research Center on the Gifted and Talented, University of Connecticut

Discussants: Barbara McCombs, Mid-Continent Regional Educational Laboratory; Brenda Welburn, National Association of State Boards of Education

12:15-1:00 Lunch

1:00-3:30 Group Discussion:

1. Discussion Group on Practice

Chairperson: Mary-Beth Fafard, Office of Educational Improvement, Massachusetts State Department of Education

Reporter: Aquiles Iglesias, CEIC, Temple University Center for Research in Human Development and Education

2. Discussion Group on Research

Chairperson: Barry McLaughlin, National Research Center on Cultural Diversity and Second Language Learning, University of California at Santa Cruz

Reporter: Diana Oxley, CEIC, Temple University Center for Research in Human Development and Education

3. Discussion Group on Policy

Chairperson: Donald Clark, Bureau of Curriculum and Academic Services, Pennsylvania Department of Education

Reporter: Andrea Zetlin, CEIC, California State University at Los Angeles

Note: Discussion groups remain constant throughout the conference.

3:30-3:45 Break

3:45-5:00 "Street Academies and In-School Alternatives to Suspension"

Session Chair: Dick Glean, School District of Philadelphia

Overview: Antoine Garibaldi, Xavier University of Louisiana

Discussants: Harriet Arvey, Houston Independent School District; Edmund Gordon, Yale University

5:00- 6:00   Break
6:00- 7:00   Dinner
7:00- 8:15   "Alternatives and Marginal Students"
             Session Chair: Larry F. Guthrie, Center for Educational
             Research and Evaluation
             Overview: Mary Anne Raywid, Hofstra University
             Discussants: Ann Masten, Institute of Child
             Development, University of Minnesota; Pauline Brooks,
             National Center for Research on Evaluation, Standards
             and Student Testing, University of California at Los Angeles
8:15-?   Informal discussion/debate/playtime

Friday, October 15, 1993

7:30-8:30   Breakfast
8:30-9:30   "Bilingual, Migrant, and Immigrant Education"
             Session Chair: Susan Sclafani, Houston Independent
             School District
             Overview: Eugene Garcia, Office of Bilingual Education
             and Minority Languages Affairs, U.S. Department of
             Education
             Discussants: Richard Ruiz, Department of Languages,
             Reading and Culture, University of Arizona;
             Kris Gutierrez, University of California at Los Angeles
9:30-10:15   "Inner-City Students at the Margins"
             Overview: Margaret C. Wang, CEIC, Temple University
             Center for Research in Human Development and
             Education; Maynard Reynolds, CEIC, University of
             Minnesota; Herbert Walberg, CEIC, University of Illinois
             at Chicago
10:15-10:30 Break
10:30-12:30 Discussion Groups
12:30-1:30   Lunch
1:30-3:30   Recommendations from Discussion Groups
3:30-5:00   Prospects and the Next Step
             Session Chair: Maynard Reynolds, CEIC, University of
             Minnesota
             Discussants: George Ayers, Council for Exceptional
             Children; Eugene Garcia, Office of Bilingual Education
             and Minority Languages Affairs, U.S. Department of
             Education; Valena White Plisko, Elementary and
             Secondary Education Division, U.S. Department of
             Education
5:00   Adjournment

Name Index

Algozzine, B., 32
Allen, B., 126
Allington, R. L., 12, 18, 32, 34
Alvarez, M. D., 74
Alvino, J., 65, 89
Ambert, A. N., 72
Ampadu, M., 144
Armor, D. J., 121, 123
Astuto, T. A., 145
Atkin, J. M., 80
August, D., 162, 169
Ausubel, D., 66

Baenen, N. R., 129
Baldwin, A. Y., 64, 65
Banks, J. A., 63
Bereiter, C., 9
Berger, J., 141
Billson, J., 70
Borges, F., 72

Boyan, N. J., 145
Brown, A. L., 50
Brown, B., 66
Brown, G. H., 72, 74
Bryk, A. S., 74, 133, 134
Bryson, M., 33
Burns, D. E., 84
Butler-Por, N., 126

Campbell, E. Q., 99
Carlson, D. L., 34
Carlson, L. B., 38
Carter, T. P., 169
Carver, S. M., 38, 47, 49
Cattau, D., 37, 44
Chatfield, M. L., 169
Chelemer, C., 33, 34
Chen, B., 80
Chinn, P. C., 37
Chira, S., 142

Subject Index

Achievement:
  among African American
    students, 65-66
  and socioeconomic status (SES),
    66-67
  as influenced by peers, 68-69
Alternative schools, 119-149
  definition of, 123-124
  factors associated with failures
    of, 137-140
  factors associated with successes
    of, 132-137
  features of, 130-131
  history of, 120-123
  movement in favor of, 140-141
  research record of, 127-140
  types of, 124-127

Bilingual education, 48

Title VII (Bilingual Education
    Act), 177-181
  See also Language programs

Categorical programs, 3-10
  coordination of, 194
  curriculum, 34-35
Chapter 1, 5-6, 13, 27-56
  demographics of, 36-39
  funding for, 54-55
  reform of, 46-48, 52-53
  similarity to special education,
    32-39
Collaboration:
  among teachers, 44-46
Cultural diversity:
  impact on education, 156-158
  knowledge base on, 174-176
  magnitude of, 158-163

DATE DUE

MAY 1 5 1995	
JUL 2 4 1997	
FEB 0 6 1999	
JAN 1 5 2008	
APR 0 3 2007	
12/22/22	

BRODART

Cat. No. 23-221